Anonymous

Collection of Psalms and Hymns

Suited to the Various Occasions of Public Worship and Private Devotion

Anonymous

Collection of Psalms and Hymns
Suited to the Various Occasions of Public Worship and Private Devotion

ISBN/EAN: 9783744781756

Printed in Europe, USA, Canada, Australia, Japan

Cover: Foto ©Thomas Meinert / pixelio.de

More available books at **www.hansebooks.com**

COLLECTION OF
PSALMS and HYMNS

SUITED TO THE

VARIOUS OCCASIONS

— OF —

PUBLIC WORSHIP AND PRIVATE
DEVOTION.

COMPILED

BY A COMMITTEE OF MENNONITES.

———o———

ELKHART, INDIANA.
MENNONITE PUBLISHING CO.
1884.

PREFACE.

Singing is an ordinance of divine worship, and when Christians unite with their hearts and voices, "singing with the spirit and with the understanding also," the high praises of God, and thus express to him in psalms and hymns of adoration and praise, their gratitude for the manifold mercies bestowed upon them in Christ Jesus our Lord, or in penitent supplication, with melting strains implore mercy for past offenses, is one of the most delightful, edifying, and heart soothing parts of his worship. Those heavenly strains heighten the believers' holy longing after God and heaven, animate them to press forward in their Christian course "toward the mark for the prize of the high calling of God in Christ Jesus." It makes them feel more fully that in God we live and move and have our being; that all our blessings are bestowed by his paternal kindness, and that our everlasting welfare results from his redeeming love towards us in Christ our Lord.

Thus they are animated and strengthened to march on in their heavenly way, through this barren wilderness, to the wished-for Canaan—the heavenly Jerusalem—there to join the company of those who were redeemed from the earth and are harping upon their harps and singing a new song before the throne.

As the Church of Christ known by the name of MENNONITES, formerly performed their religious exercises in the worship of God almost altogether in the German language, it was thought expedient, as the English language has become so prevalent, to have the word of God preached and the religious exercises in his worship performed in that language also. Hence a Committee was appointed by the Church, to make a selection of Psalms and Hymns, suited to the different occasions in public worship and private devotional exercises. Accordingly the selection was made and the hymns arranged under their different heads, and thus presented to the friends of Zion.

That believers may find this little work a pleasant and edifying companion on their way to the heavenly Zion, is the ardent wish of THE COMMITTEE.

N. B. The names of the tunes at the beginning of each hymn correspond with the music book entitled PHILHARMONIA; and the peculiar meters are numbered as they are in the Metrical Index of said music book.

A COLLECTION OF HYMNS.

PUBLIC WORSHIP.

C. M. [MARLOW.

AWAKE, awake the sacred song,
  To our incarnate Lord;
Let every heart and every tongue
  Adore th'Eternal Word.

That awful Word, that sov'reign Power,
  By whom the worlds were made,
(O happy morn! illustrious hour!)
  Was once in flesh arrayed.

Then shone almighty power and love,
  In all their glorious forms,
When Jesus left his throne above,
  To dwell with sinful worms.

To dwell with misery below,
  The Savior left the skies,
And sunk to wretchedness and woe,
  That worthless man might rise.

5 Adoring angels tune their songs,
    To hail the joyful day;
With rapture then let mortal tongues
    Their grateful worship pay.

2   C. M.   [JEROME.

HOW shall we praise th' Eternal God,
    That infinite Unknown?
Who can ascend his high abode,
    Or venture near his throne?

2 The great Invisible! He dwells
    Concealed in dazzling light;
But his all-searching eye reveals
    The secrets of the night.

3 Those watchful eyes that never sleep,
    Survey the world around;
His wisdom is a boundless deep,
    Where all our thoughts are drowned.

4 Speak we of strength? his arm is strong
    To save or to destroy;
Infinite years his life prolong,
    And endless is his joy.

5 He knows no shadow of a change,
    Nor alters his decrees;
Firm as a rock his truth remains
    To guard his promises.

6 Justice upon a dreadful throne
    Maintains the rights of God;

While mercy sends her pardons down,
  Bought with a Savior's blood.

7 Bought with the blood which freely flow'd
  From our Immanuel's veins;
Which his free love on us bestowed,
  To wash away our stains.

8 Now may that love, Immortal King,
  Speak some forgiving word,
To animate our hearts to sing
  The glories of the Lord.

3   S. M.   [ALBION.

COME, sound His praise abroad,
  And hymns of glory sing!
Jehovah is the sovereign God,
  The universal King.

2 He formed the deeps unknown;
  He gave the seas their bound;
The watery worlds are all his own,
  And all the solid ground.

3 Come, worship at his throne!
  Come, bow before the Lord!
We are his works and not our own;
  He formed us by his word.

4 To-day attend his voice,
  Nor dare provoke his rod;
Come, like the people of his choice,
  And own your gracious God!

5 But if your ears refuse
    The language of his grace,   [Jews,
And hearts grow hard, like stubborn
    That unbelieving race.

6 The Lord in vengeance dressed,
    Will lift his hand and swear—
"You that despised my promised rest,
    Shall have no portion there."

4   C. M.   [BROWN.

COME, let us all unite to praise
    The Savior of mankind!
Our thankful hearts in solemn lays
    Be with our voices joined.

2 But how shall dust his worth declare
    When angels try in vain;
Their faces veil when they appear
    Before the Son of Man?

3 O Lord, we cannot silent be;
    By love we are constrained
To offer our best things to thee,
    Our Savior and our Friend.

4 Though feeble are our best essays,
    Thy love will not despise
Our grateful songs of humble praise,
    Our well-meant sacrifice.

5 Let every tongue thy goodness show,
    And spread abroad thy fame:
Let ev'ry heart with praise o'erflow,
    And bless thy sacred name?

6 Worship and honor, thanks and love
    Be to our Jesus given!
By men below, by hosts above,
    By all in earth and heaven!

5   C. M.   [ARLINGTON.

HOW did my heart rejoice to hear
    My friends devoutly say,
"In Zion let us all appear,
    And keep the solemn day!"

2 I love her gates, I love the road;
    The church, adorned with grace,
Stands like a palace built for God,
    To show his milder face.

3 Up to her courts with joy unknown,
    The holy tribes repair;
The Son of David holds his throne,
    And sits in judgment there.

4 He hears our praises and complaints;
    And while his awful voice
Divides the sinners from the saints,
    We tremble and rejoice.

5 Peace be within this sacred place,
    And joy a constant guest;
With holy gifts and heavenly grace
    Be her attendants blessed!

6 My soul shall pray for Zion still,
    While life or breath remains;
There my best friends, my kindred, dwell,
    There God, my Savior, reigns.

6 C. M. [EVAN.

COME, happy souls, approach your God
    With new melodious songs!
Come, tender to Almighty grace
    The tribute of your tongues!

2 So strange, so boundless was the love
    That pitied dying men,
The Father sent his equal Son
    To give them life again.

3 Thy hands, dear Jesus, were not armed
    With a revenging rod;
No hard commissions to perform,
    The vengeance of a God!

4 But all was mercy, all was mild,
    And wrath forsook the throne
When Christ on the kind errand came,
    And brought salvation down.

5 Here, sinners, you may heal your wounds,
    And wipe your sorrows dry;
Trust in the mighty Savior's name,
    And you shall never die!

6 See, dearest Lord, our willing souls
    Accept thine offered grace;
We bless the great Redeemer's love,
    And give the Father praise.

7 S. M. [SANDUSKY.

MY Savior and my King,
    Thy beauties are divine;

Thy lips with blessings overflow,
And every grace is thine.

2 Now make thy glory known,
Gird on thy dreadful sword,
And rise in majesty to spread,
The conquest of thy word.

3 Strike through thy stubborn foes,
Or make their hearts obey,
While justice, meekness, grace, and truth,
Attend thy glorious way.

4 Thy laws, O God, are right;
Thy throne shall ever stand,
And thy victorious gospel prove
A sceptre in thy hand.

5 [Thy Father and thy God,
Hath without measure shed
His Spirit, like a grateful oil,
T'anoint thy sacred head.]

6 [Behold, at thy right hand
The Gentile Church is seen,
A beauteous bride in rich attire,
And princes guard the queen.]

7 Fair bride, receive His love,
Forget thy father's house;
Forsake thy gods, thy idol gods,
And pay the Lord thy vows!

8 O let thy God and King
Thy sweetest thoughts employ:
Thy children shall his honor sing,
And taste the heavenly joy.

8   C. M.   [DUBLIN.

WITH reverence let the saints appear,
   And bow before the Lord;
His high commands with rev'rence hear,
   And tremble at his word.

2 How terrible thy glories rise!
   How bright thine armies shine!
Where is the power with thee that vies,
   Or truth compared with thine?

3 The northern pole and southern rest
   On thy supporting hand;
Darkness and day, from east to west,
   Move round at thy command.

4 Thy words the raging winds control,
   And rule the boisterous deep:
Thou mak'st the sleeping billows roll,
   The rolling billows sleep.

5 Heaven, earth, and air, and seas are thine,
   And the dark world of hell:
They saw thine arm in vengeance shine
   When Egypt durst rebel.

6 Justice and judgment are thy throne,
   Yet wondrous is thy grace;
While truth and mercy joined in one,
   Invite us near thy face.

9   C. M.   [MEAR.

ONCE more we come before our God,
   Once more his blessing ask;

Oh! may not duty seem a load,
  Nor worship prove a task.

2 Father, thy quick'ning Spirit send
    From heaven in Jesus' name,
  To make our waiting minds attend,
    And put our souls in frame.

3 May we receive the word we hear,
    Each in an honest heart;
  Hoard up the precious treasure there,
    And never with it part.

4 To seek thee all our hearts dispose,
    To each thy blessings suit;
  And let the seed thy servant sows,
    Produce a copious fruit.

5 Bid the refreshing north wind wake!
    Say to the south wind, blow!
  Let every plant the power partake,
    And all the garden grow.

6 Revive the parch'd with heavenly show'rs,
    The cold with warmth divine;
  And as the benefit is ours,
    Be all the glory thine.

10   L. M.   [OLD HUNDRED.

TO God, the great, the ever blessed,
  Let songs of honor be addressed;
His mercy firm forever stands—
Give him the thanks his love demands.

2 Who knows the wonders of thy ways?
Who shall fulfill thy boundless praise?

Blessed are the souls that fear thee still,
And pay their duty to thy will.

3 Remember what thy mercy did
For Jacob's race, thy chosen seed:
And with the same salvation bless
The meanest suppliant of thy grace.

4 O may I see thy tribes rejoice,
And aid their triumphs with my voice;
This is my glory, Lord, to be
Joined to thy saints and near to thee.

11   Metre 5.   [Tremont.

SINNERS, turn, why will ye die?
God, your Maker, asks you why;
God, who did your being give,
Made you with himself to live.
He the fatal cause demands,
Asks the work of his own hands.
Why, ye thankless creatures, why
Will you cross his love and die?

2 Sinners, turn, why will ye die?
God, your Savior, asks you why;
God, who did your souls retrieve,
Died himself that ye might live.
Will you let him die in vain?
Crucify your Lord again?
Why, ye ransomed sinners, why
Will ye slight his grace and die?

3 Sinners, turn, why will ye die?
God, the Spirit, asks you why;

He who all your lives hath strove,
Wooed you to embrace his love.
Will ye not his grace receive?
Will ye still refuse to live?
Why, you long-sought sinners, why
Will you grieve your God and die?

4 Dead already, dead within,
Spiritually dead in sin.
Dead to God while here you breathe;
Pant you after second death?
Will you still in sin remain,
Greedy of eternal pain?
O, ye dying sinners, why,
Why will ye forever die?

12   C. M.   [Marlow.

COME, children, learn to fear the Lord:
And, that your days be long,
Let not a false or spiteful word
Be found upon your tongue!

2 Depart from mischief—practice love:
Pursue the works of peace;
So shall the Lord your ways approve,
And set your souls at ease.

3 His eyes awake to guard the just;
His ears attend their cry;
When broken spirits dwell in dust,
The God of grace is nigh.

4 What, tho' the sorrows here they taste,
Are sharp and tedious, too,

The Lord who saves them all at last,
  Is their supporter now!
5 Evil shall smite the wicked dead,
  But God secures his own;
Prevents the mischief when they slide,
  Or heals the broken bone.

6 When desolation, like a flood,
  O'er the proud sinner rolls,
Saints find a refuge in their God,
  For he redeemed their souls.

13   L. M. [LOVING KINDNESS.

AWAKE, my soul, in joyful lays,
  And sing thy great Redeemer's praise,
He justly claims a song from thee
His loving kindness, oh how free!

2 He saw me ruined in the fall,
Yet loved me notwithstanding all;
He saved me from my lost estate.
His loving kindness, oh how great!

3 Though numerous hosts of mighty foes;
Though earth and hell my way oppose,
He safely leads my soul along
His loving kindness, oh how strong!

4 When trouble, like a gloomy cloud,
Hath gathered thick and thundered loud,
He near my soul has always stood.
His loving kindness, oh how good!

5 Often I feel my sinful heart,
Prone from my Savior to depart;

But though I oft have him forgot,
His loving kindness changes not.

6 Soon shall I pass this gloomy vale,
Soon all my mortal powers must fail:
O! may my last expiring breath,
His loving kindness sing in death

7 Then let me mount and soar away,
To the bright world of endless day;
And sing with rapture and surprise,
His loving kindness in the skies.

14   L. M.   [DEVOTION.

BLESS, O my soul, the living God!
Call home thy tho'ts that rove abroad;
Let all the powers within me join,
In work and worship so divine.

2 Blest, O my soul, the God of grace!
His favor claims the highest praise;
Why sho'd the wonders he hath wrought,
Be lost in silence and forgot?

3 'Tis he, my soul, that sent his Son,
To die for crimes which thou hast done;
He owns the ransom, and forgives
The hourly follies of our lives.

4 The vices of the mind he heals,
And cures the pains that nature feels;
Redeems the soul from hell, and saves
Our wasting lives from threat'ning graves.

5 Our youth decayed his power repairs,
His mercy crowns our growing years,

He fills our store with every good,
And feeds our soul with heavenly food.

6 He sees th' oppressor and th' oppressed,
And often gives the sufferers rest;
But will his justice more display
In the last great rewarding day.

7 [His power he showed by Moses' hands,
And gave to Israel his commands;
But sent his truth and mercy down
To all the nations, by his Son.]

8 Let the whole earth his power confess,
Let the whole earth adore his grace;
The Gentile and the Jew shall join,
In work and worship so divine.

15   C. M. [SOLON—JEROME.

LET every mortal ear attend,
  And every heart rejoice;
The trumpet of the gospel sounds,
  With an inviting voice.

2 Ho! all ye hungry, starving souls,
  That feed upon the wind,
And vainly strive, with earthly toys,
  To fill an empty mind:

3 Eternal wisdom has prepared
  A soul-reviving feast,
And bids your longing appetites
  The rich provision taste.

4 Ho! ye that pant for living streams,
  And pine away and die;

Here you may quench your raging thirst
  With springs that never dry.

5 Rivers of love and mercy here
  In a rich ocean join;
Salvation in abundance flows
  Like floods of milk and wine.

6 [Ye perishing and naked poor,
  Who work with mighty pain,
To weave a garment of your own
  That will not hide your sin.

7 Come naked, and adorn your souls
  In robes prepared by God;
Wrought by the labors of his Son,
  And dyed in his own blood.]

8 Dear God! the treasures of thy love,
  Are everlasting mines,
Deep as our helpless miseries are,
  And boundless as our sins.

9 The happy gates of gospel grace
  Stand open night and day;
Lord, we are come to seek supplies,
  And drive our wants away.

16   Metre 5.   [Welton.

HARK, my soul! it is the Lord;
  'Tis thy Savior, hear his word:
Jesus speaks, he speaks to thee;
  "Say, poor sinner, lov'st thou me?"

2 "I delivered thee when bound,
  And when bleeding healed thy wound:

    Sought thee wandering, set thee right,
    Turned thy darkness into light.

3 Can a mother's tender care
   Cease toward the child she bear?
   Yes, she may forgetful be,
   Yet will I remember thee.

4 "Mine is an unchanging love,
   Higher than the heights above:
   Deeper than the deeps beneath;
   Free and faithful, strong as death.

5 "Thou shalt see my glory soon,
   When the work of grace is done:
   Partner of my throne shall be:
   Say, poor sinner, lov'st thou me?"

6 Lord, it is my chief complaint,
   That my love is weak and faint;
   Yet I love thee, and adore!—
   Oh for grace to love thee more!

17   S. M.   [GERAR.

BEHOLD, the lofty sky,
   Declares its Maker, God;
And all the starry works on high
   Proclaim his power abroad.

2 The darkness and the light
   Still keep their course the same;
While night to day, and day to night,
   Divinely teach his name.

3 In every different land,
   Their general voice is known;

They show the wonders of his hand,
  And orders of his throne

4 Ye Christian lands, rejoice;
  Here he reveals his word;
We are not left to nature's voice
  To bid us know the Lord.

5 His statutes and commands
  Are set before our eyes;
He puts his gospel in our hands,
  Where our salvation lies.

6 His laws are just and pure,
  His truth without deceit;
His promises forever sure,
  And his rewards are great.

7 [Not honey to the taste
  Affords so much delight;
Nor gold that has the furnace passed,
  So much allures the sight.]

8 While of thy works I sing,
  Thy glory to proclaim,
Accept the praise, my God, my King,
  In my Redeemer's name.

18   L. M.   [HEBRON.

WHERE two or three with sweet accord,
  Obedient to their sovereign Lord,
Meet to recount his acts of grace,
And offer solemn prayer and praise.

2 "There," says the Savior, "will I be,
Amid this little company;

To them unveil my smiling face,
And shed my glories round the place."

3 We meet at thy command, dear Lord,
Relying on thy faithful word;
Now send thy Spirit from above—
Now fill our hearts with heavenly love!

19   S. M.   [LAKE EXON.

HOW beauteous are their feet,
  Who stand on Zion's hill!
Who bring salvation on their tongues,
  And words of peace reveal!

2 How charming is their voice!
  How sweet their tidings are!
Zion, behold thy Savior King!
  He reigns and triumphs here.

3 How happy are our ears,
  That hear this joyful sound,
Which kings and prophets waited for,
  And sought but never found!

4 How blessed are our eyes,
  That see this heavenly light!
Prophets and kings desired it long,
  But died without the sight.

5 The watchmen join their voice,
  And tuneful notes employ;
Jerusalem breaks forth in songs
  And deserts learn the joy.

6 The Lord makes bare his arm
  Through all the earth abroad;

Let every nation now behold
  Their Savior and their God.

20 C. M. [CORONATION.

ALL hail, the power of Jesus' name!
  Let angels prostrate fall;
Bring forth the royal diadem
  And crown him Lord of all.

2 Crown him, ye martyrs of our God,
  Who from his altar call;
Extol the stem of Jesse's rod,
  And crown him Lord of all.

3 Ye chosen seed of Israel's race,
  A remnant weak and small,
Hail him who saves you by his grace,
  And crown him Lord of all.

4 Ye Gentile sinners, ne'er forget
  The wormwood and the gall;
Go, spread your trophies at his feet,
  And crown him Lord of all.

5 Babes, men and sires, who know his love,
  Who feel your sin and thrall,
Now join with all the hosts above,
  And crown him Lord of all.

6 Let every kindred, every tribe,
  On this terrestrial ball,
To him all majesty ascribe,
  And crown him Lord of all.

7 O, that with yonder sacred throng,
  We at his feet may fall!

We'll join that everlasting song,
  And crown him Lord of all.

21   C. M. [BALERMA—SOLON.

AWAKE, my heart, arise my tongue,
  Prepare a tuneful voice;
In God, the life of all my joys,
  Aloud will I rejoice.

2 'Tis he adorned my naked soul,
  And made salvation mine;
Upon a poor, polluted worm,
  He makes his graces shine.

3 And, lest the shadow of a spot
  Should on my soul be found,
He took the robe the Savior wrought,
  And cast it all around.

4 How far the heavenly robe exceeds
  What earthly princes wear!
These ornaments, how bright they shine!
  How white the garments are!

5 The spirit wrought by faith and love,
  And hope, and every grace;
But Jesus spent his life to work
  The robe of righteousness.

6 Strangely, my soul, art thou arrayed
  By the great sacred THREE!
In sweetest harmony of praise
  Let all thy powers agree.

22   L. M.   [Hebron—Devotion.

BEFORE Jehovah's awful throne,
  Ye nations, bow with sacred joy;
Know that the Lord is God alone;
  He can create and he destroy.

2 His sovereign power, without our aid,
  Made us of clay and formed us men;
And when like wand'ring sheep we stray'd,
  He brought us to his fold again.

3 We are his people, we his care,
  Our souls, and all our mortal frame;
What lasting honor shall we rear,
  Almighty Maker, to thy name!

                  [songs,
4 We'll crowd thy gates with thankful
  High as the heavens our voices raise:
And earth with her ten thousand tongues,
  Shall fill thy courts with sounding praise.

5 Wide as the world is thy command,
  Vast as eternity thy love;
Firm as a rock thy truth must stand,
  When rolling years shall cease to move.

23   S. M.   [Sandusky.

NOW is th' accepted time,
  Now is the day of grace;
Now, sinners, come without delay,
  And seek the Savior's face.

2 Now is th' accepted time,
  The Savior calls to-day;

  To-morrow it may be too late,
   Then why should you delay?
3 Now is th' accepted time,
   The gospel bids you come;
  And every promise in his word
   Declares there yet is room.
4 Now is th' accepted time,
   O sinners! why delay,
  Come while the gospel trumpet sounds,
   Come in th' accepted day!
5 All yesterday is gone!
   To-morrow's not our own;
  O sinner, come without delay,
   To bow before the throne!
6 O, hear his voice to-day,
   And harden not your heart,
  To-morrow, with a frown, he may
   Pronounce the word—depart!
7 Lord, draw reluctant souls,
   And feast them with thy love;
  Then will the angel swiftly fly
   To bear the news above.

24   C. M.   [SALVATION.

YOUNG people all, attention give,
   And hear what I shall say;
I wish your souls with Christ to live,
   In everlasting day.
Remember, you are hast'ning on
   To death's dark, gloomy shade;
Your joys on earth will soon be gone,
   Your flesh in dust be laid.

2 Death's iron gate you must pass through,
   Ere long, my dear young friends;
With whom, then, do you think to go—
   With saints or fiery fiends?
Pray meditate before too late,
   While in a gospel land;
Behold King Jesus at the gate,
   Most lovingly doth stand.

3 Young men, how can you turn your face
   From such a glorious friend?
Will you pursue your dangerous ways?
   O don't you fear the end?
Will you pursue that dangerous road
   Which leads to death and hell?
Will you refuse all peace with God
   With devils there to dwell?

4 Young women, too, what will you do,
   If out of Christ you die?
From all God's people you must go,
   To weep, lament, and cry;
Where you the least relief can't find,
   To mitigate your pain;
Your good things all be left behind—
   Your souls in death remain.

5 Young people all, I pray then view,
   The fountain opened wide;
The spring of life opened for sin,
   Which flowed from Jesus' side.
There you may drink in endless joy,
   And reign with Christ your King;
In his glad notes your souls employ,
   And hallelujahs sing.

25   C. M.   [ARLINGTON—MEMPHIS.

AM I a soldier of the cross,
  A follower of the Lamb?
And shall I fear to own his cause?
  Or blush to speak his name?

2 Are there no foes for me to face?
  Must I not stem the flood?
Is this vile world a friend to grace,
  To help me on to God?

3 Sure I must fight—if I would reign;
  Increase my courage, Lord!
I'll bear the toil—endure the pain,
  Supported by thy word.

4 Thy saints, in all this glorious war,
  Shall conquer, though they die;
They see the triumph from afar,
  And seize it with their eye.

5 When that illustrious day shall rise,
  And all thine armies shine
In robes of victory through the skies,
  The glory shall be thine.

26   C. M.   [MENDOTA.

LORD, at thy temple we appear,
  As happy Simeon came,
And hope to meet our Savior here;
  O make our joys the same.

2 With what divine and vast delight
  The good old man was filled,
When fondly, in his withered arms,
  He clasped the holy Child!

3 "Now I can leave this world," he cried,
　"Behold thy servant dies;
I've seen thy great salvation, Lord,
　And close my peaceful eyes.

4 "This is the light prepared to shine
　Upon the Gentile lands,
Thine Israel's glory, and their hopes,
　To break their slavish bands."

5 [Jesus! the vision of thy face
　Hath overpowering charms;
Scarce shall I feel death's cold embrace,
　If Christ be in my arms.

6 Then while ye hear my heart-strings [break,
　How sweet my minutes roll!
A mortal paleness on my cheek,
　And glory in my soul.]

27   Meter 11.   [Expostulation.

Come, children of Zion, and help us to sing,
　Loud anthems of praise to our Savior and King,
Whose life once was given our souls to redeem,
And bring us to heaven, to reign there with him.

2 In regions of darkness and sorrow and pains,
We all lay in ruin, in prison and chains;
But Jesus has bought us with his precious blood,
The ransom provided to bring us to God.

3 O come to the Savior and take up the cross—
Seek treasures in heaven, count all else but loss:
His mercy invites us, then let us comply—
O why should we linger when he is so nigh?

4 We'll fear not the dangers that lie in our way—
His arm will protect us by night and by day;

And this we must suffer and patiently bear,
Till Jesus shall take us where suff'rings are o'er.

28   L. M.   [CLARENCE.

JESUS! and shall it ever be,
A mortal man ashamed of thee?
Ashamed of thee whom angels praise,
Whose glories shine through endless days.

2 Ashamed of Jesus? sooner far
Let evening blush to own a star;
He sheds the beams of light divine
O'er this benighted soul of mine.

3 Ashamed of Jesus? just as soon
Let midnight be ashamed of noon.
'Tis midnight with my soul till he,
Bright Morning Star, bids darkness flee.

4 Ashamed of Jesus, that dear Friend,
On whom my hopes of heaven depend?
No, when I blush, be this my shame,
That I no more revere his name.

5 Ashamed of Jesus? yes I may,
When I've no guilt to wash away;
No tears to wipe, no good to crave,
No fears to quell, no soul to save.

6 Till then—nor is my boasting vain—
Till then I boast a Savior slain!
And O, may this my glory be,
That Christ is not ashamed of me!

7 His institutions would I prize,
Take up my cross, the shame despise!

Dare to defend his noble cause,
And yield obedience to his laws.

29   L. M.   [SALEM.

MY hope, my all, my Savior thou,
To thee, lo, now my soul I bow;
I feel the bliss thy wounds impart,
I feel thee, Savior, in my heart.

2 Be thou my strength, be thou my way,
Protect me through my life's short day;
In all my acts my wisdom guide,
And keep me, Savior, near thy side.

3 Correct, reprove, and comfort me,
As I have need, my Savior, be;
And if I would from thee depart,
Then clasp me, Savior, to thy heart.

4 In fierce temptation's darkest hour,
Save me from sin, and Satan's power;
Tear every idol from thy throne,
And reign, my Savior, reign alone.

5 My suffering time shall soon be o'er,
Then shall I sigh and weep no more;
My ransomed soul shall soar away,
To sing thy praise in endless day.

30   L. M.   [OLD HUNDRED.

FROM all that dwell below the skies,
Let the Creator's praise arise;
Let the Redeemer's name be sung,
Through every land, by every tongue.

PUBLIC WORSHIP.

2 Eternal are thy mercies, Lord,
  Eternal truth attends thy word; [shore.
  Thy praise shall sound from shore to
  Till sun shall rise and set no more.

3 Your lofty themes, ye mortals, bring,
  In songs of praise divinely sing;
  The great salvation loud proclaim,
  And shout for joy the Savior's name.

4 In every land begin the song,
  To every land the strains belong;
  In cheerful sound all voices raise,
  And fill the world with loudest praise.

31   C. M. [CONDESCENSION.

COME, thou desire of all thy saints,
  Our humble strains attend,
While with our praises and complaints,
  Low at thy feet we bend!

2 When we thy wondrous glories hear,
    And all thy sufferings trace,
  What sweetly awful scenes appear!
    What rich unbounded grace!

3 How should our songs, like those above,
    With warm devotion rise!
  How should our souls on wings of love,
    Mount upward to the skies!

4 Come, Lord, thy love alone can raise
    In us the heavenly flame!
  Then shall our lips resound thy praise,
    Our hearts adore thy name.

5 Dear Savior, let thy glory shine,
  And fill thy dwellings here,
Till life and love and joy divine,
  And heaven on earth appear.

32 C. M. [Phillips.

AGAIN our earthly cares we leave,
  And to thy courts repair;
Again with joyful feet we come,
  To meet our Savior here.

2 Within these walls let holy peace,
  And love and concord dwell,
Here give the troubled conscience ease—
  The wounded spirit heal.

3 The feeling heart, the melting eye,
  The humble mind bestow:
And shine upon us from on high,
  To make our graces grow.

4 May we in faith receive thy word,
  In faith present our prayers;
And in the presence of our Lord
  Unbosom all our cares.

5 Show us some token of thy love,
  Our fainting hope to raise;
And pour thy blessing from above,
  That we may render praise.

33 C. M. [Balerma—Elkhart.

WITH sacred joy we lift our eyes
  To those bright realms above,

   That glorious temple in the skies,
     Where dwells eternal love.

2 Before the awful throne we bow,
    Of heaven's Almighty King;
  Here we present the solemn vow,
    And hymns of praise we sing.

3 While in thy house of prayer we kneel
    With trust and holy fear;
  Thy mercy and thy truth reveal,
    And lend a gracious ear.

4 With fervor teach our hearts to pray,
    And tune our lips to sing;
  Nor from thy presence cast away
    The sacrifice we bring

34   S. M.   [Golden Hill.

WELCOME sweet day of rest,
    That saw the Lord arise;
Welcome to this reviving breast,
    And these rejoicing eyes.

2 The King himself comes near,
    And feasts his saints today;
  Here we may sit and see him here,
    And love and praise and pray.

3 One day amidst the place
    Where my dear God hath been,
  Is sweeter than ten thousand days
    Of pleasurable sin.

4 My willing soul would stay
    In such a frame as this,

And sit and sing herself away,
  To everlasting bliss.

35   S. M.   [STRAND.

ASSIST thy servant, Lord,
  The gospel to proclaim;
Let power and love attend thy word,
  And every breast inflame.

2 Bid unbelief depart;
  With love his soul inflame;
Take full possession of his heart,
  And glorify thy name.

3 May stubborn sinners bend
  To thy divine control;
Constrain the wandering to attend,
  And make the wounded whole.

4 Extend thy conquering arm,
  With banner wide unfurled,
Until thy glorious grace shall charm,
  And harmonize the world.

36   L. M.   [PORTUGAL

THY presence, gracious God, afford,
  Prepare us to receive thy word;
Now let thy voice engage our ear,
And faith be mixed with what we hear.

2 Distracting thoughts and cares remove,
  And fix our hearts and hopes above;
With food divine may we be fed,
And satisfied with living bread.

3 To us thy sacred word apply,
  With sovereign power and energy;
  And may we in true faith and fear,
  Reduce to practice what we hear.

37 C. M. [Woodland.

O HAPPY is the man who hears
    Religion's warning voice,
  And who celestial wisdom makes
    His early, only choice.

2 For she has treasures greater far
    Than east or west unfold;
  More precious are her bright rewards
    Than gems or stores of gold.

3 Her right hand offers to the just
    Immortal happy days;
  Her left, imperishable wealth,
    And heavenly crowns displays.

4 And as her holy labors rise,
    So her rewards increase;
  Her ways are ways of pleasantness,
    And all her paths are peace.

38 L. M. [Rockingham.

LET me but hear my Savior say,
  "Strength shall be equal to thy day,"
  Then I rejoice in deep distress,
  Leaning on all-sufficient grace.

2 I glory in infirmity,
  That Christ's own power may rest on me;

When I am weak, then I am strong,
Grace is my shield, and Christ my song.

3 I can do all things, or can bear,
All suffering, if my Lord be there;
Sweet pleasures mingle with the pains,
While grace divine my heart sustains.

39   C. M.   [AZMON.

JESUS, thy blessings are not few,
  Nor is thy gospel weak;
Thy grace can melt the stubborn Jew,
  And bow the haughty Greek.

2 Wide as the reach of Satan's rage,
  Does thy salvation flow;
'T is not confined to sex or age,
  The lofty or the low.

3 While grace is offered to the Prince,
  The poor may take their share:
No mortal has a just pretense
  To perish in despair.

4 Come, all ye wretched sinners, come,
  He'll form your souls anew;
His gospel and his heart have room
  For rebels such as you.

40   C. M.   [EVENING TWILIGHT.

I'M not ashamed to own my Lord,
  Or to defend his cause,
Maintain the honor of his word,
  The glory of his cross.

2 Jesus, my God! I know his name—
   His name is all my trust;
Nor will he put my soul to shame,
   Nor let my soul be lost.
3 Firm as his throne his promise stands,
   And he can well secure
What I've committed to his hands
   Till the decisive hour.
4 Then will he own my worthless name
   Before his father's face,
And in the new Jerusalem
   Appoint my soul a place.

41   Metre 7.   [King of Glory.

COME, ye sinners, come to Jesus;
   Think upon your gracious Lord;
He has pitied your condition,
   He has sent his Gospel Word;
     Mercy calls you;
   Mercy flows in Jesus' blood.
2 Dearest Savior, help thy servant
   To proclaim thy wondrous love;
Pour thy grace upon this people,
   That thy truth they may approve;
     Bless, O bless them,
   From thy shining courts above.
3 Now thy gracious word invites them
   To partake the gospel feast;
Let thy spirit sweetly draw them,
   Every soul be Jesus' guest:
     O receive us!
   Let us find thy promised rest.

42. Metre 13. [Pilgrim.

HELP thy servant, gracious Lord,
　Who comes in Jesus' name:
Only thou canst strength afford,
　Thy gospel to proclaim;
Grant his soul a heavenly ray,
　Fill his heart with holy fire,
Help thy servant, Lord, we pray,—
　Regard our soul's desire.

CHORUS.

O, for sanctifying grace!
　O, for love's inspiring power!
Lord, we beg, for Jesus' sake,
　A sweet refreshing shower.

2 Give us to receive thy word,
　With love, and joy, and fear;
Grant thy quick'ning grace, O Lord,
　On all assembled here;
Seal the truth on all to-day;
　All our hearts with heaven inspire;
Help thy servant, Lord, we pray—
　Regard our soul's desire.
　O, for sanctifying grace, &c.

43. C. M. [Jerome.

NOW is the time, th' accepted hour,
　O sinners, come away;
The Savior's knocking at your door,
　Arise without delay!

2 Oh! don't refuse to give him room,
　Lest mercy should withdraw;

  He will in robes of vengeance come,
   To execute his law.

3 Then where, poor mortals, will you be,
  If destitute of grace,
 When you your injured Judge shall see,
  And stand before his face?

4 Oh! could you shun that dreadful sight,
  How would you wish to fly
 To the dark shades of endless night,
  From that all-searching eye?

5 The dead awaked must all appear,
  And you among them stand,
 Before the great impartial bar,
  Arraigned at Christ's left hand.

6 Let not these warnings be in vain,
  But lend a list'ning ear;
 Lest you should meet them all again,
  When wrapped in keen despair.

44   S. M.   [St. Thomas—Aylesbury.

LORD, at thy sacred feet,
  With joy would we appear;
Within thy earthly temple meet,
  To see thy glory here.

2 We come to worship thee,
  For thou art God alone;
 In humble prayer to bend the knee
  Before thy holy throne.

3 Thy word is our delight,
  Thy truth will make us free;

'T is from thyself a heavenly light,
  It leads our souls to thee.

4 Thy goodness we behold,
  While in thy presence, Lord;
Thy wondrous truth and love unfold—
  The treasures of thy word.

5 In all our meetings here,
  Our souls are blessed with good;
Thou wilt to waiting minds be near,
  And give thy children food.

6 So will we render praise
  To thee, the God of love;
With pleasure walk in all thy ways,
  Till we shall meet above.

45   L. M.   [PORTUGAL.

"WE'VE no abiding city here"—
  This may distress the worldly mind,
But should not cost the saint a tear,
  Who hopes a better rest to find.

2 "We've no abiding city here"—
  Sad truth, were this to be my home;
But let this thought our spirits cheer,
  "We seek a city yet to come."

3 "We've no abiding city here"—
  Then let us live as pilgrims do:
Let not the world our rest appear,
  But let us haste from all below.

4 "We've no abiding city here"—
  We seek a city out of sight;

Zion its name—the Lord is there,
　　It shines with everlasting light.

46　　　　Metre 7.　　　[Galena.

ON the mountain top appearing,
　　Lo, the sacred herald stands;
Welcome news to Zion bearing,
　　Zion long in hostile lands;
　　　　Mourning captive,
God himself will loose thy bands.

2 Has thy night been long and mournful,
　　All thy friends unfaithful proved?
Have thy foes been proud and scornful,
　　By thy sighs and tears unmoved?
　　　　Cease thy mourning,
Zion still is well beloved.

3 God, thy God, will now restore thee,
　　He himself appears thy Friend;
All thy foes shall flee before thee,
　　Here thy boasts and triumphs end:
　　　　Great deliverance
Zion's King vouchsafes to send.

4 Peace and joy shall now attend thee,
　　All thy warfare now is past,
God, thy Savior, shall defend thee,
　　Peace and joy are come at last;
　　　　All thy conflicts
End in everlasting rest.

47　　　　C. M.　　　[Dunlap's Creek.

WE sing the glories of thy love,
　　We sound thy dreadful name;

The Christian church unites the songs
  Of Moses and the Lamb.
2 Great God, how wondrous are thy works
    Of vengeance and of grace!
  Thou King of saints, Almighty Lord,
    How just and true thy ways!
3 Who dares refuse to fear thy name,
    Or worship at thy throne?
  Thy judgments speak thy holiness
    Through all the nations known.
4 Great Babylon that rules the earth,
    Drunk with the martyrs' blood,
  Her crimes shall speedily awake
    The fury of our God.
5 The cup of wrath is ready mixed,
    And she must drink the dregs;
  Strong is the Lord, her Sov'reign Judge,
    And shall fulfill the plagues.

48   L. M.   [DEVOTION.

COMFORT, ye ministers of grace,
  Comfort the people of your Lord;
  O lift ye up the fallen race,
    And cheer them by the Gospel Word.
2 Go into every nation, go,
    Speak to their trembling hearts, and cry:
  Glad tidings unto all we show;
    Jerusalem, thy God is nigh!
3 Hark! in the wilderness a cry,
    A voice that loudly calls, Prepare;

Prepare your hearts, for God is nigh,
  And means to make his entrance there.

4 The Lord your God shall quickly come;
  Sinners, repent, the call obey;
  Open your hearts to make him room;
  Ye desert souls, prepare his way.

5 The Lord shall clear his way through all;
  Whate'er obstructs, obstructs in vain;
  The vale shall rise, the mountain fall,
  Crooked be straight, and rugged plain.

6 The glory of the Lord displayed,
  Shall all mankind together view,
  And what his mouth in truth hath said,
  His own almighty hand shall do.

49   L. M.   [ROCKBRIDGE.

COME, let your voices join to raise
  A sacred song of solemn praise;
  God is a Sovereign King; rehearse
  His honor in exalted verse.

2 Come, let our souls address the Lord,
  Who framed our natures with his word;
  He is our Shepherd; we the sheep,
  His mercy choose, his pasture keep.

3 Come, let us hear his voice to-day,
  The counsels of his love obey;
  Now let our hardened hearts renew
  The sins and plagues that Israel knew.

4 Israel, that saw his works of grace,
  Yet tempt their Maker to his face;

  A faithless unbelieving brood,
  That tired the patience of their God.
5 Thus saith the Lord: "How false they
  Forget my power, abuse my love;[prove,
  Since they despise my rest, I swear,
  Their feet shall never enter there."
6 [Look back, my soul, with holy dread,
  And view those ancient rebels dead,
  Attend the offered grace to-day,
  Nor lose the blessings by delay.
7 Seize the kind promise while it waits,
  And march to Zion's heavenly gates;
  Believe, and take the promised rest;
  Obey, and be forever blessed.]

50   L. M.   [GALILEE.

HIGH on his everlasting throne,
  The King of saints his works surveys,
Marks the dear souls he calls his own,
  And smiles on the peculiar race.
2 He rests well pleased their toils to see,
  Beneath his easy yoke they move;
  With all their heart and strength agree
  In the sweet labor of his love.
3 See where the servants of the Lord,
  A busy multitude, appear;
  For Jesus day and night employed,
  His heritage they toil to clear.
4 The love of Christ their heart constrains,
  And strengthens their unwearied hands,

They spend their sweat and blood and pains,
  To cultivate Immanuel's lands.
5 Jesus their toil delighted sees,
  Their industry vouchsafes to crown;
He kindly gives the wished increase,
  And sends the promised blessings down.
6 The sap of life, the Spirits powers,
  He rains incessant from above;
He all his gracious fullness showers,
  To perfect their great work of love.
7 O multiply the sowers' seed,
  And fruit they every hour shall bear;
Throughout the world thy gospel spread,
  Thine everlasting truth declare!
8 We then, in perfect love renewed,
  Shall know the greatness of thy power;
Stand in the temple of our God
  As pillars, and go out no more.

51   L. M.   [SUPPLICATION.

WHEN Jesus did from heav'n descend,
  He came to be the sinner's friend;
Was moved to pity, love, and grace,
To save the human, fallen race.

2 It was the kindness of our God,
A precious gift on us bestowed,
To let us know that Jesus is
Our way, our life, and righteousness.

3 A doctrine of the greatest worth:
The Son of God appeared on earth,

When he assumed our flesh and blood,
And sacrificed himself to God.

4 Was it the angels' great delight
To view that wondrous, glorious Light,
The Son of God in flesh arrayed, [prayed?
For which both kings and prophets

5 How highly thankful then ought we
To him our gracious Savior be!
Who is our life and righteousness,
Our everlasting joy and peace.

52   C. M   [PETERBOROUGH.

COME ye that love the Savior's name,
  And join to make it known;
The sovereign of your hearts proclaim,
  And bow before his throne.

2 Behold your King, your Savior, crowned
  With glories all divine;
And tell the wond'ring nations round,
  How bright those glories shine.

3 Infinite power and boundless grace,
  In him unite their rays;
You, that have e'er beheld his face,
  Can you forbid his praise?

4 When in his earthly courts we view
  The glories of our King,
We long to love as angels do,
  And wish like them to sing.

5 And shall we long and wish in vain?
  Lord, teach our songs to rise;

Thy love can animate the strain,
　And bid it reach the skies.

6 Oh, happy period! glorious day!
　When heaven and earth shall raise.
With all their powers the raptured lay,
　To celebrate thy praise,

53　　L. M.　　[TENDER THOUGHT.

COME, weary souls with sin distrest,
　Come, and accept the promised rest;
The Savior's gracious call obey,
And cast your gloomy fears away.

2 Oppressed with guilt, a painful load,
O come, and spread your woes abroad;
Divine compassion, mighty love,
With all the painful load remove.

3 Here mercy's boundless ocean flows,
To cleanse your guilt and heal your woes;
Pardon and life and endless peace—
How rich the gift, how free the grace!

4 Lord, we accept with thankful heart,
The hope thy gracious words impart;
We come with trembling, yet rejoice,
And bless the kind inviting voice.

5 Dear Savior, let thy powerful love
Confirm our faith, our fears remove!
And sweetly influence every breast,
And guide us to eternal rest.

54   Metre 17.   [Rosefield.

Safely through another week,
  God has brought us on our way;
Let us now a blessing seek,
  Waiting in his courts to-day,
Day of all the week the best,
Emblem of eternal rest.

2 While we seek supplies of grace,
  Through the dear Redeemer's name,
Show thy reconciling face,
  Take away our sin and shame—
From our worldly cares set free,
May we rest this day in thee.

3 Here we've come thy name to praise,
  Let us feel thy presence near;
May thy glory meet our eyes,
  While we in thy house appear.
Here afford us, Lord, a taste,
Of our everlasting feast.

4 May the gospel's joyful sound
  Conquer sinners, comfort saints;
Make the fruits of grace abound,
  Bring relief for all complaints;
Such let all our Sabbaths prove,
Till we join the church above.

55   C. M.   [MEMPHIS.

SALVATION! O the joyful sound,
  'Tis pleasure to our ears;
A Sovereign balm for every wound,
  A cordial for our fears.

2 Buried in sorrow and in sin,
  At hell's dark door we lay;
But we arise by grace Divine,
  To see a heavenly day.

3 Salvation! let the echo fly
  The spacious earth around,
While all the armies of the sky
  Conspire to raise the sound.

56   L. M.   [SALEM.

DISMISS us with thy blessing, Lord—
  Help us to feed upon thy word;
All that has been amiss forgive,
And let thy truth within us live.

2 Though we are guilty, thou art good—
  Wash all our works in Jesus' blood;
Give every fettered soul release,
And bid us all depart in peace.

57   METRE 7.   HAPPY ZION.

LORD, dismiss us with thy blessing—
  Fill our hearts with joy and peace;

Let us each thy love possessing,
  Triumph in redeeming grace;
    O, refresh us!
Traveling through this wilderness.

2 Thanks we give and adoration,
  For the gospel's joyful sound;
May the fruits of thy salvation
  In our hearts and lives abound;
    May thy presence
With us evermore be found.

3 So, whene'er the signal's given,
  Us from earth to call away,
Borne on angels' wings to heaven.
  Glad to leave our cumbrous clay,
    May we, ready,
Rise and reign in endless day.

58   S. M.   [IDUMEA.

ONCE more before we part,
  Oh bless the Savior's name!
Let every tongue and every heart
  Adore and praise the same.

2 Lord, in thy grace we came,
  That blessing still impart;
We met in Jesus' sacred name,
  In Jesus' name we part.

3 Still on thy holy word
  We'll live, and feed, and grow;
And still go on to know the Lord,
  And practice what we know.

4 Now, Lord, before we part,
   Help us to bless thy name:
Let every tongue and every heart,
   Adore and praise the same.

59   S. M.   [SANDUSKY.

THE swift declining day,
   How fast its moments fly!
While evening's broad and gloomy shade
   Gains on the western sky.

2 Ye mortals, mark its pace,
   And use the hours of light,
For know its Maker can command
   An instant, endless night.

3 Give glory to the Lord,
   Who rules the rolling sphere,
Submissive at his footstool bow,
   And seek salvation there.

4 Then shall new lustre break
   Through all the horrid gloom,
And lead you to unchanging light,
   In your celestial home.

60   METRE 4.   [CHARLESTON.

PRINCE of Peace, be ever near us,
   Fix in all our hearts thy home;
With thy blessed presence cheer us,
   Let thy sacred kingdom come.

2 Raise to heaven our expectations,
   Give our favored souls to prove
Glorious and complete salvation,
   In the realms of bliss above.

3 May the grace of Christ, our Savior,
   And the Father's boundless love,
With the Holy Spirit's favor,
   Rest upon us from above.
4 Thus may we abide in union,
   With each other and the Lord;
And possess, in sweet communion,
   Joys which earth cannot afford.

61   Metre 4.   [Merrick.

JESUS, grant us all a blessing,
   Send it down, Lord, from above;
Give us each a heart of prayer,
   Help us to rejoice in love!
Farewell, brethren—farewell, sisters,
   Till we all shall meet above.
2 Jesus, pardon all our follies
   While together we have been;
Make us humble, make us holy,
   Cleanse us all from every sin.
Farewell, brethren—farewell, sisters,
   Till we all shall meet again:
3 May thy blessings, Lord, go with us,
   To each one's respective home,
And the presence of our Jesus
   Rest upon us every one!
Farewell, brethren—farewell, sisters,
   Till we all shall meet at home.

62   L. M.   [Windham.

ALMIGHTY Father! bless the word, [heard;
   Which through thy grace we now have

O may the precious seed take root,
Spring up, and bear abundant fruit.

2 We praise thee for the means of grace,
Thus in thy courts to seek thy face;
Grant, Lord, that we who worship here,
May all at length in heaven appear.

NATIVITY OF CHRIST.

63   C. M.   [AZMON.

ON Judah's plains, as shepherds sat,
  Watching their flocks by night,
The angel of the Lord appeared,
  Clad in celestial light.

2 Awe-struck, the vision they regard,
  Appalled with trembling fear;
When thus a cherub-voice divine
  Breathed sweetly on their ear.

3 Shepherds of Judah, cease your fears
  And calm your troubled mind;
Glad tidings of great joy I bring
  To you and all mankind.

4 "This day Almighty love fulfills
  Its great eternal word;
This day is born in Bethlehem
  A Savior—Christ the Lord.

5 "There you shall find the heavenly Babe,
   In humble weeds arrayed;
 And meanly wrapped in swaddling clothes,
   And in a manger laid."

6 He ceased, and sudden all around,
   Appeared a radiant throng
 Of angels praising God, and thus
   Warbling their choral song.

7 "Glory to God, from whom on high
   All gracious mercies flow!
 Who sends his heaven-descended peace,
   To dwell with man below."

64   C. M.   [POLITZ.

HARK! the glad sound, the Savior comes,
   The Savior promised long;
 Let every heart prepare a throne,
   And every voice a song.

2 On him the Spirit largely poured,
   Exerts his sacred fire;
 Wisdom and might, and zeal and love,
   His holy breast inspire.

3 He comes the pris'ners to release,
   In Satan's bondage held;
 The gates of brass before him burst,
   The iron fetters yield.

4 He comes from thickest films of vice,
   To clear the inward sight;
 And on the eyes obscured by sin,
   To pour celestial light.

NATIVITY OF CHRIST.

5 He comes the broken heart to bind,
  The bleeding soul to cure;
And with the treasures of his grace
  T' enrich the humble poor.

6 Our glad hosannas, Prince of Peace,
  Thy welcome shall proclaim;
And heaven's eternal arches ring
  With thy beloved name.

65 S. M. [ALBION.

REJOICE in Jesus' birth!
  To us a Son is given;
To us a child is born on earth,
  Who made both earth and heaven.

2 He reigns above the sky—
  This universe sustains;
The God supreme, the Lord most high,
  The King Messiah reigns!

3 Th' Almighty God is he,
  Author of heavenly bliss!
The Father of Eternity,
  The glorious Prince of Peace!

4 His government shall grow,
  From strength to strength proceed;
His righteousness the church o'erflow,
  And all the earth o'erspread.

66 METRE 19. [CHURCH'S DESOLATION.

YE nations all, on you I call,
  Come, hear this declaration,

And don't refuse the glorious news
  Of Jesus and salvation.
To royal Jews came first the news
  Of Christ the great Messiah,
As was foretold by prophets old,
  Isaiah, Jeremiah.

2 To Abraham the promise came,
  And to his seed forever,
A light to shine in Isaac's line,
  By Scripture we discover;
Hail, promised morn! the Savior's born,
  The glorious Mediator—
God's blessed Word made flesh and blood,
  Assumed the human nature.

3 His parents poor in earthly store,
  To entertain the Stranger
They found no bed to lay his head,
  But in the ox's manger;
No royal things, as used by king's,
  Were seen by those that found Him,
But in the hay the stranger lay,
  With swaddling bands around him.

4 On the same night a glorious light
  To shepherds there appeared,
Bright angels came in shining flame,
  They saw and greatly feared:
The angels said—"Be not afraid,
  Although we much alarm you,
We do appear good news to bear,
  As now we will inform you.

5 "The city's name is Bethlehem
  In which God hath appointed,

This glorious morn a Savior's born,
　For him God hath anointed;
By this you'll know, if you will go,
　To see this little Stranger,
His lovely charms in Mary's arms,
　Both lying in a manger."

6 When this was said, straightway was made
　A glorious sound from heaven;
Each flaming tongue and anthem sung,
　"To men a Savior's given
In Jesus' name the glorious theme,
　We elevate our voices;
At Jesus' birth be peace on earth
　Meanwhile all heaven rejoices."

7 Then with delight they took their flight
　And winged their way to glory;
The shepherds gazed and were amazed,
　To hear the pleasing story.
To Bethlehem they quickly came,
　The glorious news to carry,
And in the stall they found them all,
　Joseph, the Babe, and Mary.

8 The shepherds then returned again
　To their own habitation,
With joy of heart they did depart.
　Now they have found Salvation.
Glory, they cry, to God on high
　Who sent his Son to save us;
This glorious morn the Savior's born,
　His name it is CHRIST JESUS.

67   Metre 33. [Zion's Glad Morning.

HAIL the blest morn when the great Mediator,
  Down from the regions of glory descends;
Shepherds, go worship the Babe in the manger,
  Lo! for his guard the bright angels attend.

2 Brightest and best of the sons of the morning!
  Dawn on our darkness and lend us thine aid!
Star of the East, the horizon adorning,
  Guide where our infant Redeemer is laid.

3 Cold on his cradle the dew-drops are shining,
  Low lies his head with the beasts of the stall;
Angels adore him in slumber reclining,
  Maker, and Monarch, and Savior of all.

4 Say, shall we yield him, in costly devotion,
  Odors of Edom, and off'rings divine—
Gems of the mountain and pearls of the ocean,
  Myrrh from the forest and gold from the mine?

5 Vainly we offer each ample oblation,
  Vainly with gold would his favor secure;
Richer by far is the heart's adoration—
  Dearer to God are the prayers of the poor.

68   C. M.   [Dunlap's Creek.

WHILE shepherds watched their flocks by night,
  All seated on the ground,
The angel of the Lord came down,
  And glory shone around.

2 "Fear not," said he (for mighty dread
  Had seized their troubled mind),
"Glad tidings of great joy I bring
  To you, and all mankind.

NATIVITY OF CHRIST.

3 "To you in David's town this day,
　　Is born of David's line,
　The Savior who is Christ the Lord,
　　And this shall be the sign:

4 "The heavenly Babe you there shall find,
　　To human view displayed,
　All meanly wrapped in swathing bands,
　　And in a manger laid."

5 Thus spake the seraph and forthwith
　　Appeared a shining throng
　Of angels, praising God on high,
　　And thus addressed their song:

6 "All glory be to God on high,
　　And to the earth be peace;
　Good will, henceforth, from heav'n to men,
　　Begin and never cease."

69　　　　C. M.　　　　[ELKHART.

HARK from on high those blissful strains!
　　Whence can such sweetness be?
　Have angels waked their golden harps,
　　With heaven's own minstrelsy?

2 Or do we hear the cherub voice
　　Of infant bands, who raise,
　Soaring from earth, celestial notes,
　　In their Creator's praise?

3 Thus spake the shepherds, yet with dread,
　　So strange the sounds they heard,
　While o'er their slumb'ring flocks they kept
　　Their wonted nightly guard.

4 And soon they saw a dazzling light
    Beam through the starry way,
  And shining seraphs clustering where
    The infant Jesus lay.

5 They came a Savior's birth to tell,
    And tunes of rapture sing;
  Hence the glad notes that filled the air—
    Each swept his loudest string.

6 But now, in accents soft and kind,
    The chieftain angel said,
  "Heaven's tidings of great joy we bear—
    Shepherds, be not afraid."

7 Then suddenly the angelic choir
    Renewed the rapturous song; [sound,
  While heaven's wide portals caught the
    And echoed it along.

70   Metre 5.   [Eltham.

HARK! the herald angels sing,
  "Glory to the new born King;
Peace on earth, and mercy mild;
God and sinners reconciled;"
Joyful all ye nations rise,
Join the triumphs of the skies;
With th' angelic host proclaim,
"Christ is born in Bethlehem."

2 Christ by highest heaven adored,
  Christ the everlasting Lord;
  Late in time behold him come,
  Offspring of a virgin's womb;

Vailed in flesh the Godhead see,
Hail th'Incarnate deity!
Pleased as man with men t'appear,
Jesus our Immanuel here.
3 Hail the heaven-born Prince of Peace!
Hail the Sun of Righteousness!
Light and life to all he brings,
Ris'n with healing in his wings:
Mild he lays his glory by,
Born that men no more may die;
Born to raise the sons of earth;
Born to give them second birth.
4 Come, DESIRE OF NATIONS, come!
Fix in us thy humble home!
Rise, the woman's conquering seed,
Bruise in us the serpent's head;
Adam's likeness now efface,
Stamp thine image in its place;
Second Adam from above,
Reinstate us in thy love.

71   METRE 4. [DIXON—CHARLESTON.

HARK! what mean those holy voices,
Sweetly sounding through the skies?
Lo! the angelic host rejoices,
Heavenly hallelujahs rise.
2 Hear them tell the wondrous story,
Hear them chant in hymns of joy,
"Glory in the highest—glory!
Glory be to God most high.
3 "Peace on earth—good will from heaven,
Reaching far as man is found,"

"Souls redeemed and sins forgiven"—
　　Loud our golden harps shall sound.

4 Christ is born, the great Anointed;
　　Heaven and earth his praises sing!
Oh receive whom God appointed.
　　For your Prophet, Priest, and King.

5 Haste, ye mortals to adore him;
　　Learn his name, and taste his joy;
Till in heaven ye sing before him,
　　Glory be to God most high!

72 METRE 7. [HAPPY ZION.

ANGELS! from the realms of glory,
　　Wing your flight o'er all the earth;
Ye who sang creation's story,
　　Now proclaim Messiah's birth;
Come and worship—come and worship—
　　Worship Christ, the new-born King.

2 Shepherds! in the field abiding,
　　Watching o'er your flocks by night:
God with man is now residing,
　　Yonder shines the heavenly light:
Come and worship—
　　Worship Christ, the new-born King.

3 Saints! before the altar bending,
　　Watching long in hope and fear,
Suddenly the Lord, descending,
　　In his temple shall appear:
Come and worship—
　　Worship Christ, the new-born King.

4 Sinners! wrung with true repentance,
    Doomed for guilt to endless pains,
Justice now revokes the sentence,
    Mercy calls you, break your chains:
Come and worship—
    Worship Christ, the new-born King.

NEW YEAR.

73.   Metre 32.   [Kendall.

COME, let us anew, our journey pursue,
    Roll round with the year,
And never stand still till the Master appear;
His adorable will let us gladly fulfill,
    And our talents improve,
By the patience of hope, and the labor of love.

2 Our life as a dream, our time as a stream,
    Glides swiftly away,
And the fugitive moment refuses to stay:
The arrow is flown, the moment is gone;
    The millennial year
Rushes on to our view, and eternity's here.

3 O that each in the day of his coming may say,
    "I have fought my way through;
I have finished the work thou didst give me to do!"
O that each from his Lord may receive the glad word,
    "Well and faithfully done!
Enter into my joy, and sit down on my throne."

74   C. M.   [PETERBOROUGH.

NOW, gracious Lord, thine arm reveal,
   And make thy glory known;
Now let us all thy presence feel,
   And soften hearts of stone.

2 From all the guilt and former sin,
   May mercy set us free;
And let the year we now begin,
   Begin and end with thee.

3 Send down thy Spirit from above,
   That saints may love thee more;
And sinners now may learn to love,
   Who never loved before.

4 And when before thee we appear,
   In one eternal home,
May growing numbers worship here,
   And praise thee in our room.

75   C. M.   [POLITZ.

SING to the great Jehovah's praise;
   All praise to him belongs,
Who kindly lengthens out our days,
   Demands our choicest songs;
His providence has brought us through
   Another various year;
We all with vows and anthems new
   Before our God appear.

2 Father, thy mercies past we own,
   Thy still continued care;

To thee presenting through thy Son,
    Whate'er we have or are;
Our lips and lives shall gladly show
    The wonders of thy love,
While on in Jesus' steps we go
    To seek thy face above.
3 Our residue of days or hours,
    Thine, wholly thine, shall be;
And all our consecrated powers,
    A sacrifice to thee;
Till Jesus in the clouds appear,
    To saints on earth forgiven,
And bring the grand sabbatic year,
    The Jubilee of heaven,

76   Metre 9.   [Lenox.

THE Lord of earth and sky,
    The God of ages praise!
Who reigns enthroned on high
    Ancient of endless days!
Who lengthens out our trials here,
And spares us yet another year.
2 Barren and withered trees,
    We cumbered long the ground!
No fruit of holiness
    On our dead souls was found;
Yet doth he us in mercy spare
Another and another year.
3 When Justice bared the sword,
    To cut the fig tree down,
The pity of the Lord
    Cries, "Let it still alone!"

The father mild inclines his ear
And spares us yet another year.

4 Jesus, thy speaking blood
   From God obtained the grace;
Who therefore hath bestowed
   On us a longer space;
Thou didst in our behalf appear,
And lo! we see another year.

5 Then dig about the root,
   Break up their fallow ground,
And let our gracious fruit
   To thy great praise abound!
O let us all thy praise declare.
And fruit unto perfection bear.

77 C. M. [CONDESCENSION.

OUR life is ever on the wing,
   And death is ever nigh;
The moment when our lives begin,
   We all begin to die.

2 Yet, mighty God, our fleeting days
   Thy lasting favors share;
Yet with the bounties of thy grace,
   Thou load'st the rolling year.

3 'T is sov'reign mercy finds us food,
   And we are clothed with love;
While grace stands pointing out the road
   That leads our souls above.

4 His goodness runs an endless round,
   All glory to the Lord!

His mercy never knows a bound,
   And be his name adored!

5 Thus we begin the lasting song,
   And when we close our eyes,
Let future ages praise prolong,
   Till time and nature dies.

78   C. M.   [JEROME.

AND now my soul, another year
   Of this short life is past;
I cannot long continue here,
   And this may be my last.

2 Much of my dubious life is gone,
   Nor will return again;
And swift thy passing moments run,
   The few that yet remain.

3 Awake my soul, with utmost care,
   Thy true condition learn;
What are thy hopes, how sure, how fair,
   And what thy great concern?

4 Now a new scene of time begins,
   Set out afresh for heaven!
Seek pardon for thy former sins,
   In Christ so freely given.

5 Devoutly yield thyself to God,
   And on his grace depend,
With zeal pursue the heavenly road,
   Nor doubt a happy end.

CRUCIFIXION.

79 L. M. [TENDER THOUGHT.

WHEN I survey the wondrous cross
  On which the prince of glory died,
My richest gain I count but loss,
  And pour contempt on all my pride.

2 Forbid it, Lord, that I should boast,
  Save in the death of Christ, my God;
All the vain things that charm me most,
  I sacrifice them to his blood.

3 See from his head, his hands, his feet,
  Sorrow and love flow mingled down;
Did e'er such love and sorrow meet,
  Or thorns compose so rich a crown?

4 [His dying crimson like a robe,
  Spreads o'er his body on the tree;
Then am I dead to all the globe,
  And all the globe is dead to me.]

5 Were the whole realm of nature mine,
  That were a present far too small;
Love so amazing, so divine,
  Demands my soul, my life, my all.

80 L. M. [SALEM.

HE dies, the Friend of sinners dies,
  Lo! Salem's daughters weep around!
A solemn darkness veils the skies!
  A sudden trembling shakes the ground.

2 Come saints, and drop a tear or two
    For him who groaned beneath your load;
He shed a thousand drops for you,
    A thousand drops of richer blood.

3 Here's love and grief beyond degree—
    The Lord of glory dies for men!
But lo! what sudden joys we see!
    Jesus the dead revives again!

4 The rising God forsakes the tomb!
    Up to his Father's courts he flies!
Cherubic legions guard him home,
    And shout him welcome to the skies!

5 Break off your tears, ye saints and tell
    How high your great deliv'rer reigns;
Sing how he spoiled the hosts of hell,
    And led the tyrant, death, in chains.

6 Say, Live forever, glorious King,
    Born to redeem, and strong to save!
Then ask, O death! where is thy sting?
    And where's thy vict'ry, boasting grave?

81   C. M. [BURFORD—DETROIT.

ALAS! and did my Savior bleed,
    And did my Sov'reign die?
Would he devote that sacred head
    For such a worm as I?

2 [Thy body slain, sweet Jesus, thine,
    And bathed in its own blood,
While all exposed to wrath divine,
    The glorious suff'rer stood!]

3 Was it for crimes that I had done
   He groaned upon the tree?
 Amazing pity, grace unknown!
   And love beyond degree!

4 Well might the sun in darkness hide,
   And shut his glories in,
 When God the mighty Maker died
   For man the creature's sin.

5 Thus might I hide my blushing face,
   While his dear cross appears,
 Dissolve my heart in thankfulness,
   And melt my eyes in tears.

6 But drops of grief can ne'er repay
   The debt of love I owe;
 Here, Lord, I give myself away,
   'T is all that I can do.

82   L. M.   [SALEM.

'TWAS on that dark, that doleful night,
   When power of earth and hell arose
 Against the Son of God's delight,
   And friends betrayed him to his foes.

2 Before the mournful scene began,
   He took the bread and blest and brake,
 What love through all his actions ran!
   What wondrous words of grace he spake!

3 "This is my body broke for sin,
   Receive and eat the living food;"
 Then took the cup and blessed the wine;
   "'T is the new cov'nant in my blood."

4 [For us his flesh with nails was torn,
　　He bore the scourge, he felt the thorn;
　And justice poured upon his head
　　Its heavy vengeance in our stead.]

5 For us his vital blood was spilt
　　To buy the pardon of our guilt,
　When for black crimes of biggest size,
　　He gave his soul a sacrifice.

6 "Do this," he cried, "till time shall end,
　　In mem'ry of your dying Friend;
　Meet at my table, and record
　　The love of your departed Lord."

7 [Jesus, thy feast we celebrate,
　　We show thy death, we sing thy name,
　Till thou return, and we shall eat
　　The marriage supper of the Lamb.]

83　　　Metre 4.　　[Shields.

HAIL! thou once despised Jesus,
　　Hail! thou Galilean King!
Thou did'st suffer to release us;
　　Thou did'st free salvation bring.
Hail! thou agonizing Savior,
　　Bearer of our sin and shame!
By thy merits we find favor;
　　Life is given through thy name.

2 Paschal Lamb, by God appointed,
　　All our sins on thee were laid;
　By almighty love anointed,
　　Thou hast full atonement made.

All thy people are forgiven
  Through the virtue of thy blood:
Opened is the gate of heaven;
  Peace is made 'twixt man and God.
3 Jesus hail! enthroned in glory,
  There forever to abide!
All the heavenly hosts adore thee,
  Seated at thy Father's side:
There for sinners thou art pleading;
  There thou dost our place prepare:
Ever for us interceding,
  Till in glory we appear.
4 Worship, honor, pow'r and blessing,
  Thou art worthy to receive:
Loudest praises without ceasing,
  Meet it is for us to give;
Help, ye bright, angelic spirits,
  Bring your sweetest, noblest lays!
Help to sing our Savior's merits;
  Help to chant Immanuel's praise!

84   C. M.   [GRAFTON.

AS on the cross the Savior hung,
  And wept, and bled, and died,
He poured salvation on a wretch
  That languished at his side.
2 His crimes with inward grief and shame,
  The penitent confessed;
Then turned his dying eyes to Christ,
  And thus his prayer addressed:
3 "Jesus, thou Son, and Heir of heaven,
  Thou spotless Lamb of God;

I see thee bathed in sweat and tears,
  And welt'ring in thy blood.

4 "Yet quickly from these scenes of woe,
  In triumph shalt thou rise,
Burst through the gloomy shades of death,
  And shine above the skies.

5 "Amid the glories of that world,
  Dear Savior, think on me,
And in the vict'ries of thy death,
  Let me a sharer be."

6 His prayer the dying Jesus hears,
  And instantly replies:
"To-day thy parting soul shall be
  With me in Paradise."

85   Metre 17.   [Zadoc.

HEARTS of stone, relent, relent,
  Break, by Jesus' cross subdued;
See his body mangled—rent,
  Covered with a gore of blood:
Sinful soul, what hast thou done?
Murdered God's eternal Son.

2 Yes, our sins have done the deed,
  Drove the nails that fixed him there;
Crowned with thorns his sacred head,
  Pierced him with a soldier's spear;
Made his soul a sacrifice—
For a sinful world he dies.

3 Will you let him die in vain,
  Still to death pursue your Lord;

Open tear his wounds again,
 Trample on his precious blood?
No! with all my sins I'll part,
Savior, take my broken heart!

86   Metre 29.   [Behold.

SEE the Lord of glory dying!
 See him gasping, hear him crying!
  See his burdened bosom heave!
Look ye sinners, you that hung him,
Look how deep your sins have stung him,
  Dying sinners, look and live.

2 See the rocks and mountains shaking,
 Earth unto her center quaking—
  Nature's groans awake the dead;
Look on Phœbus struck with wonder,
Whilst the peals of legal thunder
  Smote the dear Redeemer's head.

3 Heaven's bright melodious legions,
 Chanting through the tuneful regions,
  Cease to trill the quivering string;
Songs seraphic all suspended,
'Till the mighty war is ended,
  By the all-victorious King.

4 Hell and all the pow'rs Infernal,
 Vanquished by the King Eternal,
  When he poured his vital flood;
By his groans which shook creation,
Lo! we found a proclamation,
  Peace and pardon by his blood.

5 Shout ye saints, with adoration,
 Fill with praise the wide creation,

Since He's risen from the grave;
Shout with joyful acclamation,
To the Rock of our Salvation,
Who alone has power to save.

87   10, 7, 14, 9.   [CRUCIFIXION.

SAW ye my Savior, saw ye my Savior?
Saw ye my Savior and God? [and me,
Oh! he died on Calvary, to atone for you
And to purchase our pardon with blood.

2 He was extended! He was extended!
   Shamefully nail'd to the cross;
Oh! he bowed his head and died, thus
    my Lord was crucified,
To atone for a world that was lost.

3 Jesus hung bleeding! Jesus hung bleeding,
   Three dreadful hours in pain;
Oh! the sun refused to shine, when the
    Majesty divine,
Was derided, insulted, and slain.

4 Darkness prevailed! Darkness prevailed!
   Darkness prevailed o'er the land,
Oh, the solid rocks were rent, thro' creation's vast extent,
When the Jews crucified the God-Man.

5 When it was finished! when it was
   And the atonement was made, [finish'd,
He was taken by the great, and embalmed
    in spices sweet,
And in a new sepulchre was laid.

6 Hail, mighty Savior! Hail, mighty Savior!
    Prince and the author of peace,
  Oh, he burst the bars of death, and triumphing, left the earth,
He ascended to mansions of bliss.
7 Now interceding, now interceding,
    Pleading that sinners might live;
  Saying, Father, I have died (Oh behold my hands and side!)
To redeem them, I pray thee forgive.
8 I will forgive them, I will forgive them,
    When they repent and believe;
  Let them now return to thee, and be reconciled to me,
And salvation they all shall receive.

88   C. M.   [FIDUCIA.

ANGELS in shining order stand,
  Around the Savior's throne;
They bow with rev'rence at his feet,
  And make his glories known.
Those happy spirits sing his praise,
  To all eternity,
But I can sing redeeming grace,
  For Jesus died for me.
2 The cross of Christ inspires my heart
  To sing redeeming grace;
Awake my soul, and bear a part
  In my Redeemer's praise.
O! what can be compared to Him,
  Who died upon the tree!
This is my dear delightful theme,
  That Jesus died for me.

CRUCIFIXION.

3 When at the table of the Lord
   We humbly take our place,
  The death of Jesus we record,
   With love and thankfulness.
  These emblems bring my Lord to view,
   Upon the bloody tree,
  My soul believes and feels it's true,
   That Jesus died for me.

4 His body broken, nailed, and torn,
   And stained with streams of blood,
  His spotless soul was left forlorn,
   Forsaken of his God.
  'T was then his Father gave the stroke,
   That justice did decree;
  All nature felt the dreadful stroke,
   When Jesus died for me.

5 Eli lama sabachthani,
   My God, my God, he cried,
  Why hast thou thus forsaken me?
   And thus my Savior died.
  But why did God forsake his Son,
   When bleeding on the tree?
  He died for sins, but not his own,
   For Jesus died for me.

6 My guilt was on my surety laid,
   And therefore he must die;
  His soul a sacrifice was made,
   For such a worm as I;
  Was ever love so great as this?
   Was ever grace so free?
  This is my glory, joy, and bliss,
   That Jesus died for me.

7 He took his meritorious blood,
    And rose above the skies,
And in the presence of his God,
    Presents his sacrifice.
His intercession must prevail
    With such a glorious plea:
My cause can never, never fail,
    For Jesus died for me.

8 Angels in shining order sit
    Around my Savior's throne;
They bow with rev'rence at his feet,
    And make his glories known.
Those happy spirits sing his praise,
    To all eternity;
But I can sing redeeming grace,
    For Jesus died for me.

9 O! had I but an angel's voice
    To bear my heart along,
My flowing numbers soon would raise
    To an immortal song.
I'd charm their harps and golden lyres
    In sweetest harmony,
And tell to all the heav'nly choirs,
    That Jesus died for me.

89   Metre 22.   [Mount Calvary.

THE Son of Man they did betray,
    He was condemned and !ed away;
Think, O my soul that mournful day,
    Look on Mount Calvary!
Behold him, Lamb-like, led along,
Surrounded by a wicked throng,
Accused by each lying tongue.

CRUCIFIXION.

And thus the Lamb of God was hung
  Upon the shameful tree.
2 T'was thus the glorious Suff'rer stood,
With hands and feet nailed to the wood;
From every wound a stream of blood
  Came trickling down amain;
His bitter groans all nature struck,
And at his voice the rocks were broke,
And sleeping saints their graves forsook,
The spiteful Jews had round him mock'd,
  And laughed at his pain.
3 Thus hung between the earth and skies,
Behold him tremble as he dies;
O sinners, hear his mournful cries;
  Behold his torturing pain.
The morning sun withdrew his light,
Blushed and refused to own his sight,
All azure clothed in robes of night,
All nature mourned and stood affright,
  When Christ the Lord was slain.
4 Ye men and angels hear the Son,
He cries for help but there is none;
He treads the wine-press all alone.
  His garments stained with blood.
In lamentation hear him cry,
Eli lama sabachthani;
Tho' death may close these languid eyes,
He soon will mount the upper skies,
  The conq'ring Son of God.
5 Both Jews and Romans in a band,
With hearts like steel around him stand,
Saying, if you're come to save the land,
  Now try yourself to free.

CRUCIFIXION.

A soldier pierced him when he died,
And healing streams came from his side,
And thus my Lord was crucified.
Stern justice now is satisfied,
  Sinners, for you and me.

6 Behold him mount a throne of state,
He fills the mediatorial seat,
While millions bowing at his feet,
  In loud hosannas tell.
How he endured exquisite pains,
And lead the monster death in chains:
Ye seraphs, raise your highest strains.
While music fills bright Salem's plains,
  And has conquered death and hell.

7 'Tis done, the dreadful debt is paid,
The great atonement now is made;
Sinners, on me your guilt was laid,
  For you I spilt my blood;
For you my tender soul did move,
For you I left my courts above, [prove,
That you the length and breadth might
The depth and height of perfect love
  In Christ, your smiling God.

8 All glory be to God on high,
Who reigns enthroned above the sky,
Who sent his Son to bleed and die,
  Glory to him be given;
While heaven above his praise resounds,
Won shall sing his grace abounds,
I hope to sing eternal rounds,
In flaming love which knows no bounds,
  When carried up to heaven.

90   Metre 4.   [Possession.

Great High Priest, we view thee stoop-
  With our names upon thy breast, [ing
In the garden, groaning, drooping,
  To the ground with sorrow prest.
Weeping angels stood confounded,
  To behold their Maker thus,
And shall we remain unwounded,
  When we know 't was all for us?

2 On the cross thy body broken,
  Cancels every penal tie;
Tempted souls produce this token
  All demands to satisfy.
All is finished; do not doubt it,
  But believe your dying Lord;
Never reason more about it,
  Only take him at his word.

3 Come, behold your Savior bleeding,
  Streams of mercy from him flow,
Whilst before his Father pleading
  For those men who wrought his woe.
Lo, he cried, Father, forgive them,
  Though they do my life pursue,
I am willing to receive them,
  For they know not what they do.

4 Come, thou everlasting Spirit,
  Bring to every thankful mind,
All the Savior's dying merit,
  All his suffering for mankind.
True recorder of his passion,
  Now thy living fire impart,

CRUCIFIXION.

   Now reveal thy great Salvation,
     Preach his gospel to our heart.

5 Lord, we fain would trust thee solely;
   'T was for us thy blood was spilt;
  Gracious Savior, take us wholly,
   Take and make us what thou wilt.
  Grant us now thy heavenly blessing,
   Let thy love our songs employ;
  Then we'll find, thy peace possessing,
   In thy service all our joy.

91   C. M.   [WALSAL.

BEHOLD the Savior of mankind
   Nailed to the shameful tree;
How vast the love that him inclined
   To bleed and die for thee!

2 Hark how he groans! while nature shakes,
   And earth's strong pillars bend!
The temple's veil in sunder breaks,
   The solid marbles rend!

3 'T is done! the precious ransom's paid!
   "Receive my soul!" he cries:
See where he bows his sacred head!
   He bows his head and dies.

4 But soon he'll break death's envious chain,
   And in full glory shine,
O, Lamb of God! was ever pain,
   Was ever love like thine?

RESURRECTION.

92   C. M.   [SOLON.

THIS is the day the Lord hath made,
  He calls the hours his own:
Let heaven rejoice, let earth be glad,
  And praise surround the throne.

2 To-day he rose and left the dead,
  And Satan's empire fell;
To-day the saints his triumph spread,
  And all his wonders tell.

3 Hosanna to th' anointed King,
  To David's holy Son;
Help us, O Lord; descend and bring
  Salvation from thy throne.

4 Bless'd is the Lord, who comes to men
  With messages of grace;
Who comes in God his Father's name,
  To save our sinful race.

5 Hosanna in the highest strains,
  The church on earth can raise;
The highest heavens in which he reigns,
  Shall give him nobler praise.

93   C. M.   [DUNLAP'S CREEK.

HOSANNA to the Prince of light,
  That clothed himself in clay;
Entered the iron gates of death,
  And tore the bars away.

2 Death is no more the king of dread,
 Since our Immanuel rose;
He took the tyrant's sting away,
 And spoiled our hellish foes.

3 See how the Conq'ror mounts aloft,
 And to his Father flies,
With scars of honor in his flesh,
 And triumph in his eyes.

4 There our exalted Savior reigns,
 And scatters blessings down;
Our Jesus fills the middle seat
 Of the celestial throne.

5 [Raise your devotion, mortal tongues,
 To reach his blest abode;
Sweet be the accents of your songs
 To our incarnate God.]

6 [Bright angels, strike your loudest strings,
 Your sweetest voices raise;
Let heaven and all created things,
 Sound our Immanuel's praise.]

94   C. M.   [BELMONT.

YE humble souls that seek the Lord,
 Chase all your fears away,
And bow with pleasure down to see
 The place where Jesus lay.

2 Thus low the Lord of life was brought;
 Such wonders love can do!
Thus cold in death that bosom lay,
 Which throbbed and bled for you.

3 A moment give aloose to grief—
 Let grateful sorrows rise;
And wash the bloody stains away
 With torrents from your eyes.

4 Then dry your tears and tune your songs,
 The Savior lives again;
Not all the bolts and bars of death,
 The Conq'ror could detain.

5 High o'er th' angelic band he rears
 His once dishonored head;
And thro' unnumbered years he reigns,
 Who dwelt among the dead.

6 With joy like his shall every saint
 His empty tomb survey;
Then rise with his ascending Lord,
 To realms of endless day.

95 METRE 5. [ROLAND.

ANGELS! roll the rock away,
 Death! yield up thy mighty prey;
See! he rises from the tomb,
Glowing with immortal bloom.

2 'T is the Savior! angels, raise
 Fame's eternal trump of praise!
Let the earth's remotest bound
Hear the joy-inspiring sound.

3 Now, ye saints lift up your eyes!
 Now to glory see him rise,
In long triumph up the sky—
Up to waiting worlds on high.

4 Praise him all ye heavenly choirs!
Praise, and sweep your golden lyres!
Shout, O earth, in rapt'rous song,
Let the strains be sweet and strong.

THE WORD OF GOD.

96　　　C. M.　　　[Condescension.

Father of mercies! in thy word
What endless glory shines!
Forever be thy name adored,
For these celestial lines.

2 Here may the wretched sons of want
Exhaustless riches find;
Riches above what earth can grant,
And lasting as the mind.

3 Here the fair tree of knowledge grows,
And yields a free repast:
Sublimer sweets than nature knows
Invite the longing taste.

4 Here the redeemer's welcome voice
Spreads heavenly peace around;
And life and everlasting joys
Attend the blissful sound.

5 O may these heavenly pages be
My ever dear delight;
And still new beauties may I see,
And still increasing light.

6 Divine Instructor, gracious Lord!
    Be thou forever near;
  Teach me to love thy sacred word,
    And view my Savior there!

97   C. M.   [TAMPICO.

HOW shall the young secure their hearts
    And guard their lives from sin?
  Thy word the choicest rules imparts
    To keep the conscience clean.

2 When once it enters to the mind,
    It spreads such light abroad,
  The meanest souls instruction find,
    And raise their thoughts to God.

3 T'is like the sun, a heavenly light,
    That guides us all the day;
  And through the dangers of the night,
    A lamp to lead our way.

4 The men that keep thy law with care,
    And meditate thy word,
  Grow wiser than their teachers are,
    And better know the Lord.

5 Thy precepts make me truly wise;
    I hate the sinner's road;
  I hate my own vain thoughts that rise,
    But love thy law, my God.

6 The starry heavens thy rule obey,
    The earth maintains her place;
  And these, thy servants, night and day,
    Thy skill and power express.

7 [But still thy law and gospel, Lord,
 Have lessons more divine;
Nor earth stands firmer than thy word,
 Nor stars so nobly shine.]

8 Thy word is everlasting truth,
 How pure is every page!
That holy book shall guide our youth,
 And well support our age.

98   S. M. [IDUMEA—LAKE ENON.

LET sinners take their course,
 And choose their road to death;
But in the worship of my God
 I'll spend my daily breath.

2 My thoughts address his throne
 When morning brings the light;
I seek his blessings every noon,
 And pay my vows at night.

3 Thou wilt regard my cries,
 O my eternal God,
While sinners perish in surprise,
 Beneath thine angry rod.

4 Because they dwell at ease,
 And no sad changes feel,
They neither fear nor trust thy name,
 Nor learn to do thy will.

5 But I, with all my cares,
 Will lean upon thee, Lord;
I'll cast my burdens on his arm,
 And rest upon his word.

6 His arm shall well sustain
    The children of his love;
The ground on which their safety stands,
    No earthly power can move.

99   C. M.   [Solon—Balerma.

LET the whole race of creatures lie
    Abased before their God:
Whate'er his sov'reign voice has formed,
    He governs with a rod.

2 [Ten thousand ages ere the skies
    Were into motion brought,
All the long years and worlds to come,
    Stood present to his thought.

3 There's not a sparrow or a worm,
    But's found in his decrees;
He raises monarchs to their thrones,
    And sinks them as he please.]

4 If light attends the course I run,
    'Tis he provides those rays:
And 't is his hand that hides my sun,
    If darkness cloud my days.

5 Yet I would not be much concerned,
    Nor vainly long to see
The volumes of his deep decrees,
    What months are writ for me.

6 When he reveals the book of life,
    O, may I read my name
Among the chosen of his love,
    The foll'wers of the Lamb.

100   C. M.   [Mear.

WHAT glory gilds the sacred page!
  Majestic like the sun;
It gives a light to every age,
  It gives, but borrows none.

2 His hand that gave it, still supplies
  The gracious light and heat;
His truth upon the nations rise:
  They rise, but never set.

3 Let everlasting thanks be thine,
  For such a bright display,
As makes a world of darkness shine
  With beams of heavenly day.

4 My soul rejoices to pursue
  The path of truth and love;
Till glory breaks upon my view
  In brighter worlds above.

FAITH AND REPENTANCE.

101   L. M.   [Devotion.

BLESSED are the humble souls that see
  Their emptiness and poverty:
Treasures of grace to them are given,
And crowns of joy laid up in heaven.

2 Blessed are the men of broken heart,
Who mourn for sin with inward smart;

The blood of Christ divinely flows,
A healing balm for all their woes.

3 Blessed are the meek, who stand afar
From rage and passion, noise and war;
God will secure their happy state,
And plead their cause against the great.

4 Blessed are the souls that thirst for grace,
Hunger and long for righteousness;
They shall be well supplied and fed,
With living streams and living bread.

5 Blessed are the men whose bowels move,
And melt with sympathy and love;
From Christ the Lord shall they obtain
Like sympathy and love again.

6 Blessed are the pure whose hearts are clean
From the defiling power of sin;
With endless pleasures shall they see
A God of spotless purity.

7 Blessed are the men of peaceful life,
Who quench the coals of growing strife;
They shall be called the heirs of bliss,
The sons of God, the God of peace.

8 Blessed are the suff"rers, who partake
Of pain and shame for Jesus' sake;
Their souls shall triumph in the Lord,
Glory and joy are their reward.

102   C. M.   [DUBLIN.

OH! if my soul was formed for woe,
How would I vent my sighs!

FAITH AND REPENTANCE. 93

Repentance should like rivers flow
From beneath my streaming eyes.

2 'T was for my sins my dearest Lord
Hung on the cursed tree,
And groaned away a dying life
For thee, my soul, for thee.

3 Oh! how I hate those lusts of mine,
That crucified my God! [flesh
Those sins that pierced and nailed his
Fast to the fatal wood.

4 Yes, my Redeemer, they shall die,
My heart has so decreed;
Nor will I spare the guilty things
That made my Savior bleed.

5 Whilst with a melting, broken heart,
My murdered Lord I view,
I'll raise revenge against my sins,
And slay the murd'rers too.

103   L. M.   [SUPPLICATION.

O THOU that hearest when sinners cry,
Tho' all my crimes before thee lie,
Behold them not with angry look,
But blot their memory from thy book.

2 Create my nature pure within,
And form my soul averse from sin;
Let thy good spirit ne'er depart,
Nor hide thy presence from my heart.

3 I cannot live without thy light,
Cast out and banished from thy sight:

Thy holy joys, my God, restore,
And guard me that I fall no more.

4 Though I have grieved thy spirit, Lord,
Thy help and comfort still afford,
And let a wretch come near thy throne,
To plead the merits of thy Son.

5 A broken heart, my God, my King,
Is all the sacrifice I bring;
The God of grace will ne'er despise
A broken heart for sacrifice.

6 My soul lies humble in the dust,
And owns the dreadful sentence just;
Look down, O Lord, with pitying eye,
And save the soul condemned to die.

7 Then will I teach the world thy ways;
Sinners shall learn thy sovereign grace;
I'll lead them to my Savior's blood,
And they shall praise a pard'ning God.

8 O may thy love inspire my tongue!
Salvation shall be all my song;
And all my powers shall join to bless
The Lord, my strength and righteousness.

BAPTISM.

104   C. M.   [MENDOTA.

IF glorious angels do rejoice
When sinners turn to God,

BAPTISM. 95

 Let us unite with cheerful voice
  To spread his praise abroad.

2 When Jesus unto Jordan came,
  And was baptized of John,
 A voice from heaven did proclaim,
  "He's my Beloved Son."

3 His ministers he sent about
  To preach the word of grace,
 And to baptize the world throughout,
  Who should his truth embrace.

4 Lord, we have here before our eyes
  Some that have set their hands
 To serve thee and to be baptized,
  As thou didst give command.

5 Glory to God who reigns above,
  For his abounding grace,
 In this the token of his love,
  To us, a guilty race.

6 Let us employ our tongues to sing,
  The praises of the Lord,
 For calling sinners home to him,
  By his all-powerful word.

105   C. M.   [Solon.

COME in, ye blessed of the Lord,
  And join his children here;
Washed in the Savior's cleansing blood,
  For him your Lord appears.

2 Stay not within the wilderness,
  Nor waiting at the door;

For Jesus can your woes redress,
  Were they ten thousand more.

3 Though fearing, trembling, rise and come;
  Yield to the Savior's voice, [room;
For hung'ring, thirsting souls there's
  O make the blissful choice!

4 Room in the Savior's gracious breast,
  That breast which glows with love—
Room in the church, his chosen rest,
  And room in heaven above.

5 Why will you longer ling'ring stay,
  When Jesus says, "There's room?"
Now is the time, th' accepted day;—
  Arise, he bids you come!

106   L. M.   [ROCKBRIDGE.

'TWAS the commission of our Lord—
  "Go teach the nations and baptize."
The nations have received the word,
  Since he ascended to the skies.

2 He sits upon th' eternal hills,
  With grace and pardon in his hands,
And sends his covenant with the seals,
  To bless the distant Christian lands.

3 "Repent and be baptized," he saith,
  "For the remission of your sins;"
And thus our sense assists our faith,
  And shows us what the gospel means.

4 Our souls he washes in his blood,
  As water makes the body clean;

And the good Spirit from our God
  Descends like purifying rain.

5 Thus we engage ourselves to thee,
  And seal our cov'nant with the Lord;
O may the great eternal Three
  In heav'n our solemn vows record.

107 Metre 195.

THE name of the Lord is a fountain of life,
  Its waters are sweeter than honey;
No taste of the gall of terrestial strife,
  Come buy without price, without money.

2 The name of the Lord is a full flowing stream
  From Zion's immovable mountain,
Its currents with virtue unspeakably teem,—
  Come, come to the life-giving fountain!

3 The Name of the Lord is a river of grace,
  Whose waters as soon as they're tasted,
New energy give to the sons of a race,
  With passion enfeebled and wasted.

4 Then come to its banks, all ye tribes of mankind
  And drink of the stream of salvation,
Its course is no longer to Judah confined,
  It flows through the guiltiest nation.

5 Come drink living waters, though Jesus is gone
  His Name still conveys absolution;
Come, drink where the stream of remission flows down,
  Through a rite of his own institution.

108   C. M.   [JEROME.

WHEN Jesus Christ, the Virgin's Son,
   Of David's royal race,
His brilliant course of works begun,
   And preached the reign of grace—

2 He call'd on Abram's seed in vain,
   His mission to believe:
To own his right to rule and reign,
   His Name as Prince receive.

3 This Name the scribes refused to wear,
   And spurned the Nazarene,
Would not the fame of Jesus share,
   Or in his train be seen.

4 What lofty names could Jesus bring,
   His princely birth to show?
Could Galilee produce a king?
   Or good from Naz'reth flow?

5 They taunted thus the birth obscure,
   Of chaste Maria's Son,
And scorned his favor to secure,
   His Name by putting on.

6 But found at length without disguise,
   This Name they must receive,
No other known beneath the skies,
   Could life eternal give.

7 And skillful men of later days,
   Have splendid systems built,
To shun its use by various ways,
   Of cleansing souls from guilt.

8 But they, too, like the Jews of old,
    Would they salvation win,
  Must come and be with Christ enroll'd,
    And wash away their sin.

9 Then let us all to Christ repair,—
    To Christ, the Virgin's Son,
  His name our badge of glory wear,
    And put his armor on.

109   C. M.   [Mear.

THE Lord's disciples when they spread
    O'er Judah's sacred plains,
  Relieved the sick, restored the dead,
    And cast out plagues and pains.

2 They poured no drugs through Palestine,
    No medicines they had;
  They only used the Name divine,
    Its power alone displayed.

3 And strange the virtues of that Name,
    From which diseases fled,
  The devils trembled where it came,
    And spirits foul obeyed.

4 And still, O Lord, thy name conveys,
    To Adam's ruined race,
  If used in thy appointed ways,
    A sure and real grace.

5 No useless mark, no naked sign,
    It so renews the soul,
  As long ago in Palestine
    It made the sinner whole.

110   Metre 12.   [Deliverance.

WHEN sinners awake and perceive
  What desperate creatures they are,
How shall they obtain a relief
  From misery, guilt, and despair?
In vain is our search and our cry,
  Till we in submission and zeal
The word of our Savior apply,
  "To do his adorable will."

2 God will not be pleased with our prayer
  If we disobey his command,
But if we obedient are,
  Will bring us unto his right hand,
Sincerely believe in his word,
  Put on his adorable name,
Salvation in Jesus our Lord,
  The penitent then shall obtain.

3 Thus Peter to inquiring Jews,
  Convinced in their hearts as they were;
Their interest in Jesus should lose,
  Eternal damnation must bear.
He said that they all should repent,
  Be baptized in Jesus' name;
Then shall his good Spirit be sent,
  They all shall be blest with the same.

4 "This promise is even to you—
  And all that are yet afar off,
For Jesus' command we pursue,
  Though infidel mockers may scoff,
The Lord will yet bring many nigh,
  His house and his mansion to fill,

To share in his ample supply,
  Who meekly submit to his will."

111   L. M.   Tender Thought.

AS the apostles sat at meat,
  Before our Savior did ascend,
He did them with his presence greet,
  And gave to them his last command.

2 Upbraided them with unbelief,
  And hardness of each stubborn heart;
His counsels we all must receive,
  Else we with Christ can have no part.

3 "Go preach my gospel," Jesus saith,
  "And bring them all unto the host,
Baptize believers in the name
  Of Father, Son, and Holy Ghost.

4 "He that believes and is baptized,
  Shall dwell in realms of joy above,—
Who don't believe the word of Christ
  Shall never taste redeeming love."

PRAYER AND SUPPLICATION.

112   C. M.   [Azmon.

COME, Holy Spirit, heavenly Dove,
  With all thy quick'ning powers;
Kindle a flame of sacred love
  In these cold hearts of ours.

2 Look how we grovel here below,
    Fond of these trifling toys;
  Our souls can neither fly nor go,
    To reach eternal joys.

3 In vain we tune our formal songs,
    In vain we strive to rise;
  Hosannas languish on our tongues,
    And our devotion dies.

4 Dear Lord! and shall we ever live
    At this poor dying rate?
  Our love so faint, so cold to thee,
    And thine to us so great?

5 Come, Holy Spirit, heavenly Dove,
    With all thy quick'ning powers;
  Come, shed abroad a Savior's love,
    And that shall kindle ours.

113   L. M.   [COLUMBIA.

O THOU, to whose all-searching sight,
  The darkness shineth as the light,
Search, prove my heart, it pants for thee,
O burst these bonds, and set it free.

2 Wash out its stains, refine its dross,
  Nail my affections to the cross;
  Hallow each thought, let all within
  Be clean, as thou, my Lord, art clean.

3 If in this darksome wild I stray,
  Be thou my light, be thou my way;
  No foes, no violence I fear,
  No fraud, while thou, my God, art near.

4 When rising floods my soul o'erflow,
  When sinks my heart in waves of woe,
  Jesus, thy timely aid impart,
  And raise my head, and cheer my heart.

5 Savior, where'er thy steps I see,
  Dauntless, untired, I follow thee;
  O let thy hand support me still,
  And lead me to thy holy hill.

6 If dark and thorny be the way,
  My strength proportion to my day;
  Till toil and grief and pain shall cease,
  Where all is calm and joy and peace.

114. C. M. [PRAYER.

FATHER, I stretch my hands to thee,
  No other help I know;
If thou withdraw thyself from me,
  Ah, whither shall I go?

2 What did thine only Son endure,
  Before I drew my breath?
  What pain, what labor to secure
  My soul from endless death!

3 O Jesus, could I this believe,
  I now should feel thy power;
  Now my poor soul thou would'st retrieve,
  Nor let me wait one hour.

4 Author of faith, to thee I lift
  My weary, longing eyes;
  O let me now receive that gift,
  My soul without it dies!

5 Surely thou canst not let me die;
   O speak, and I shall live;
And here I will unwearied lie,
   Till thou thy Spirit give.

6 The worst of sinners would rejoice,
   Could they but see thy face;
O let me hear thy quick'ning voice,
   And taste thy pard'ning grace.

115 C. M. [ELIZABETHTOWN.

O FOR a closer walk with God,
   A calm and heavenly frame;
A light to shine upon the road,
   That leads me to the Lamb.

2 Where is the blessedness I knew,
   When first I saw the Lord?
Where is the soul refreshing view
   Of Jesus and his word?

3 What peaceful hours I once enjoyed!
   How sweet their mem'ry still!
But they have left an aching void,
   The world can never fill.

4 Return, O holy Dove, return,
   Sweet Messenger of rest;
I hate the sins that made thee mourn,
   And drove thee from my breast.

5 The dearest idol I have known,
   Whate'er that idol be,
Help me to tear it from thy throne,
   And worship only thee.

6 So shall my walk be close with God,
   Calm and serene my frame ;
So purer light shall mark the road
   That leads me to the Lamb.

116   L. M.   [Supplication.

SHOW pity, Lord, O Lord, forgive ;
   Let a repenting rebel live ;
Are not thy mercies large and free ?
May not a sinner trust in thee ?

2 My crimes are great, but can't surpass
   The power and glory of thy grace ;
Great God, thy nature hath no bound.
So let thy pard'ning love be found.

3 O wash my soul from every sin,
   And make my guilty conscience clean ;
Here on my heart the burden lies,
And past offenses pain my eyes.

4 My lips with shame my sins confess,
   Against thy law, against thy grace ;
Lord, should thy judgments grow severe,
I am condemned, but thou art clear.

5 Should sudden vengeance seize my breath,
   I must pronounce thee just in death ;
And if my soul were sent to hell,
Thy righteous law approves it well.

6 Yet save a trembling sinner, Lord,
   Whose hope still hov'ring round thy word,
Would light on some sweet promise there,
Some sure support against despair.

117   C. M.   [BROWN.

I'LL bless the Lord from day to day;
  How good are all his ways!
Ye humble souls that used to pray,
  Come help my lips to praise.

2 Sing to the honor of his name,
  How a poor suff'rer cried;
Nor was his hope exposed to shame,
  Nor was his suit denied.

3 When threat'ning sorrows round me stood,
  And endless fears arose
Like the loud billows of a flood,
  Redoubling all my woes:

4 I told the Lord my sore distress,
  With heavy groans and tears;
He gave my sharpest torments ease,
  And silenced all my fears.

5 O sinners, come, and taste his love;
  Come, learn his pleasant ways;
And let your own experience prove
  The sweetness of his grace.

6 He bids his angels pitch their tents
  Round where his children dwell;
What ills their heav'nly care prevents
  No earthly tongue can tell.

7 O love the Lord, ye saints of his;
  His eye regards the just;
How richly bless'd their portion is
  Who make the Lord their trust!

8 Young lions, pinched with hunger, roar,
   And famish in the wood;
But God supplies his holy poor
   With every needful good.

118   C. M.   [SALVATION.

COME, humble sinner, in whose breast
   A thousand thoughts revolve;
Come, with your guilt and fears opprest,
   And make this last resolve:

2 "I'll go to Jesus, though my sins
   Have like a mountain rose;
I know his courts, I'll enter in,
   Whatever may oppose.

3 "Prostrate I'll lie before his throne,
   And there my guilt confess;
I'll tell him I'm a wretch undone
   Without his sov'reign grace.

4 "I'll to the gracious King approach,
   Whose sceptre pardon gives;
Perhaps he will command my touch,
   And then the suppliant lives.

5 "Perhaps he will admit my plea,
   Perhaps will hear my prayer;
But if I perish, I will pray,
   And perish only there.

6 "I can but perish if I go;
   I am resolved to try;
For if I stay away, I know
   I must forever die.

7 "But if I die with mercy sought,
     When I the King have tried,
   This were to die (delightful thought!)
     As sinners never died."

119   C. M.   [Evan.

BESTOW, dear Lord, upon our youth,
  The gift of saving grace;
And let the seed of sacred truth
  Fall in a fruitful place.

2 Grace is a plant where'er it grows,
  Of pure and heav'nly root;
But fairest in the youngest, shows,
  And yields the sweetest fruit.

3 Ye careless ones, O hear betimes
  The voice of sov'reign love;
Your youth is stained with many crimes,
  But mercy reigns above.

4 True, you are young, but there's a stone
  Within the youngest breast,
Or half the crimes which you have done
  Would rob you of your rest.

5 For you the public prayer is made,
  O join the public prayer!
For you the secret tear is shed,
  O shed yourself a tear!

6 We pray that you may early prove
  The Spirit's power to teach;
You cannot be too young to love
  That Jesus, whom we preach.

120   L. M.   [Bourbon.

GREAT God, indulge my humble claim;
   Thou art my hope, my joy, my rest;
The glories that compose thy name
   Stand all engaged to make me blest.

2 Thou great and good, thou just and wise;
   Thou art my Father and my God;
And I am thine by sacred ties,
   Thy Son, thy servant bought with blood.

3 With heart and eyes, and lifted hands,
   For thee I long, to thee I look,
As travelers in thirsty lands,
   Pant for the cooling water-brook.

4 With early feet I love t' appear
   Among thy saints, and seek thy face;
Oft have I seen thy glory there,
   And felt the pow'r of sov'reign grace.

5 No fruits nor wines, that tempt or taste,
   No pleasures that to sense belong,
Could make me so divinely blest,
   Or raise so high my cheerful song.

6 My life itself, without thy love,
   No taste or pleasure could afford:
'T would but a tiresome burden prove,
   If I were banished from the Lord.

7 Amidst the wakeful hours of night,
   When busy cares afflict my head,
One thought of thee gives new delight,
   And adds refreshment to my bed.

8 I'll lift my hands, I'll raise my voice,
   While I have breath to pray or praise;
This work shall make my heart rejoice,
   And bless the remnant of my days.

121   Metre 8.   [Saunders.

JESUS, thy boundless love to me
   No tho't can reach, no tongue declare;
O knit my thankful heart to thee,
   And reign without a rival there!
Thine, wholly thine, alone I am;
Be thou alone my constant flame.

2 O grant that nothing in my soul
   May dwell but thy pure love alone!
O may thy love possess me whole,
   My joy, my treasure, and my crown,
Strange flames far from my heart remove;
My every act, word, thought, be love.

3 O Love, how cheering is thy ray!
   All pain before thy presence flies;
Care, anguish, sorrow, melt away,
   Where'er thy healing beams arise;
O Jesus, nothing may I see,
Nothing desire or seek but thee!

4 Unwearied may I thus pursue,
   Dauntless to the high prize aspire;
Hourly within my soul renew
   This holy flame, this heav'nly fire;
And day and night be all my care
   To guard the sacred treasures there.

122   Metre 8.   [Rakem.

MY Savior, thou thy love to me
  In shame, in wrath, in pain hast show'd;
For me on the accursed tree,
  Thou pouredst forth thy guiltless blood;
Thine image on my heart impress,
Nor aught shall the loved stamp efface.

2 More hard than marble is my heart,
  And foul with sins of deepest stain:
But thou the mighty Savior art,
  Nor flowed thy cleansing blood in vain;
Ah, soften, melt this rock, and may
Thy blood wash all these stains away.

3 O that I, as a little child,
  May follow thee, and never rest,
Till sweetly thou hast breathed thy mild
  And lowly mind into my breast;
Nor ever may we parted be,
Till I one spirit be with thee.

4 Still let thy love point out my way;
  How wondro's things thy love has wro't;
Still lead me, lest I go astray;
  Direct my work, inspire my thought;
And if I fall, soon may I hear
Thy voice, and know that love is near.

5 In suff'ring be thy love my peace,
  In weakness be thy love my power;
And when the storm of life shall cease,
  Jesus, in that important hour,
In death as life be thou my guide,
And save me, who for me hast died.

123   C. M.   [JEROME.

WHILE thee I seek, protecting pow'r!
    Be my vain wishes still'd;
And may this consecrated hour
    With better hopes be filled.

2 Thy love the pow'r of tho't bestowed,
    To thee my thoughts would soar;
Thy mercy o'er my life has flow'd;
    That mercy I adore.

3 In each event of life how clear
    Thy ruling hand I see!
Each blessing to my soul most dear,
    Because conferred by thee.

4 In every joy that crowns my days,
    In every pain I bear,
My heart shall find delight in praise,
    Or seek relief in prayer.

5 When gladness wings my favor'd hour,
    Thy love my thoughts shall fill:
Resigned when storms of sorrow lower,
    My soul shall seek thy will.

6 My lifted eyes without a tear,
    The gath'ring storm shall see;
My steadfast heart shall know no fear;
    That heart will rest on thee.

124   METRE 5.   [WELTON.

LORD, I cannot let thee go
    Till a blessing thou bestow;
Do not turn away thy face,
Mine's an urgent, pressing case.

2 Dost thou ask me who I am?
  Ah! my Lord, thou knowest my name;
  Yet the question gives a plea
  To support my suit with thee.

3 Thou didst once a wretch behold,
  In rebellion blindly bold,
  Scorn thy grace, thy power defy;
  That poor rebel, Lord, was I.

4 Once a sinner, near despair,
  Sought thy mercy-seat by prayer;
  Mercy heard, and set him free;
  Lord, that mercy came to me.

5 Many days have passed since then,
  Many changes I have seen,
  Yet have been upheld till now;
  Who could hold me up but thou?

6 Thou hast helped in every need;
  This emboldens me to plead;
  After so much mercy past,
  Canst thou let me sink at last?

7 No—I must maintain my hold,
  'Tis thy goodness makes me bold,
  I can no denial take,
  When I plead for Jesus' sake.

125   Metre 5.   [Martin.

JESUS! lover of my soul,
  Let me to thy bosom fly,
While the raging billows roll,—
  While the tempest still is high!

Hide me, O my Savior, hide,
    Till the storm of life be past;
  Safe into the haven guide—
    O, receive my soul at last!
2 Other refuge have I none—
    Hangs my helpless soul on thee;
  Leave, ah leave me not alone,
    Still support and comfort me;
  All my TRUST on thee is stayed,
    All my HELP from thee I bring;
  Cover my defenseless head
    With the shadow of thy wing.
3 Thou, O Christ, art all I want,
    All in all in thee I find!
  Raise the fallen, cheer the faint,
    Heal the sick, and lead the blind.
  Just and holy is thy name,
    I am all unrighteousness;
  Vile and full of sin I am,
    Thou art full of truth and grace.
4 Plenteous grace with thee is found,
    Grace to pardon all my sins—
  Let the healing stream abound,
    Make and keep me pure within;
  Thou of life the fountain art,
    Freely let me take of thee;
  Spring thou up within my heart,
    Rise to all eternity.

126 L. M. [GALILEE.

JESUS, my Savior, let me be
  More perfectly conformed to thee;

Implant each grace, each sin dethrone,
And form my temper like thine own.

2 My foe, when hungry, let me feed,
Share in his grief, supply his need:
The haughty frown may I not fear,
But with a lowly meekness bear.

3 Let the envenomed heart and tongue,
The hand outstretched to do me wrong,
Excite no feelings in my breast,
But such as Jesus once expressed.

4 To others let me always give
What I from others would receive;
Good deeds for evil ones return,
Nor when provoked, with anger burn.

5 This will proclaim how bright and fair
The precepts of the gospel are:
And God himself, the God of love,
His own resemblance will approve.

127   METRE 8. [MOORESTOWN.

GO watch and pray; thou canst not tell
How near the hour of death may be;
Thou canst not know how soon the bell
May toll its doleful notes for thee;
Death's countless snares beset thy way,
Frail child of dust, go watch and pray.

2 Fond youth, while free from blighting care,
And while thy vig'rous pulse beats high,
Do hope's glad visions, bright and fair,
Dilate thy young and sparkling eye?

Soon these must change, must pass away;
Frail child of dust, go watch and pray.

3 Thou aged man, life's wintry storm
    Hath seared thy past and vernal bloom;
With trembling limbs and wasting form,
    Now thou art bending o'er the tomb;
And can vain hope lead thee astray?
Go, weary pilgrim, watch and pray.

4 Ambition, stop thy panting breath,
    Pride, humbly sink thy lifted eye;
Behold the caverns dark with death,
    Which now before you open lie;
The heavenly warning now obey,
Ye sons of pride, go watch and pray.

128   Metre 5.   [Vermont.

LORD, we come before thee now,
    At thy feet we humbly bow;
Oh! do not our suit disdain,
Shall we seek thee, Lord, in vain?

2 Lord, on thee our souls depend,
In compassion now descend;
Fill our hearts with thy rich grace,
Tune our lips to sing thy praise.

3 In thine own appointed way,
Now we seek thee, here we stay:
Lord, we know not how to go,
Till a blessing thou bestow.

4 Send some message from thy word,
That may peace and joy afford;

Let thy Spirit now impart,
Full salvation to each heart.

5 Comfort those who weep and mourn,
Let the time of joy return;
Those that are cast down lift up,
Make them strong in faith and hope.

6 Grant that all may seek and find
Thee a gracious God and kind;
Heal the sick, the captive free,
Let us all rejoice in Thee.

129   S. M.   [AYLESBURY.

MY soul, be on thy guard,
  Ten thousand foes arise,
And hosts of sins are pressing hard,
  To draw thee from the skies.

2 O watch and fight and pray,
  The battle ne'er give o'er;
Renew it boldly every day,
  And help divine implore.

3 Ne'er think the vict'ry won,
  Nor once at ease sit down;
Thy arduous work will not be done,
  Till thou hast got thy crown.

4 Fight on, my soul, till death
  Shall bring thee to thy God;
He'll take thee at thy parting breath,
  Up to his blest abode.

130   C. M.   [Evan.

APPROACH, my soul, the mercy seat,
  Where Jesus answers prayer;
There humbly fall before his feet,
  For none can perish there.

2 Thy promise is my only plea,
  With this I venture nigh;
Thou callest burdened souls to thee,
  And such, O Lord, am I.

3 Bowed down beneath a load of sin
  By Satan sorely prest;
By war without, and fears within,
  I come to thee for rest.

4 Be thou my shield and hiding place;
  That, sheltered near thy side,
I may my fierce accuser face,
  And tell him, Thou hast died.

5 O wondrous love to bleed and die,
  To bear the cross and shame,
That guilty sinners, such as I,
  Might plead thy gracious name.

6 " Poor tempest-tossed soul, be still,
  My promised grace receive;"
'T is Jesus speaks—I must—I will,
  I can—I do believe.

131   L. M.   [Windham.

HOW long, O Lord, shall I complain,
  Like one who seeks his God in vain?

Canst thou thy face forever hide,
And I still pray and be denied?

2 Shall I forever be forgot,
As one whom thou regardest not?
Shall still my soul thy absence mourn?
And still despair of thy return?

3 How long shall my poor troubled breast
Be with these anxious tho'ts oppressed?
And Satan, my malicious foe,
Rejoice to see me sunk so low?

4 Hear, Lord, and grant me quick relief,
Before my death concludes my grief;
If thou withold'st thy heavenly light,
I sleep in everlasting night.

5 How will the powers of darkness boast,
If but one praying soul be lost!
But I have trusted in his grace,
And shall again behold thy face.

6 Whate'er my fears or foes suggest,
Thou art my hope, my joy, my rest;
My heart shall feel thy love, and raise
My cheerful voice to songs of praise.

132   S. M.   [Marlborough.

WITH humble heart and tongue,
   My God, to thee I pray;
Oh make me learn, while I am young,
   How I may cleanse my way.

2 Make an unguarded youth
   The object of thy care;

Help me to choose the way of truth,
  And fly from every snare.

3 My heart to folly prone,
  Renew by power divine;
Unite it to thyself alone,
  And make me wholly thine.

4 Oh let thy word of grace
  My warmest thoughts employ;
Be this, through all my foll'wing days,
  My treasure and my joy.

5 To what thy laws impart,
  Be my whole soul inclined;
Oh let them dwell within my heart,
  And sanctify my mind.

6 May thy young servant learn,
  By these to cleanse his way;
And may I here the path discern,
  That leads to endless day.

133   C. M.   [Vanwert.

PRAYER is the soul's sincere desire,
  Unuttered or expressed
The motion of a hidden fire
  That trembles in the breast.

2 Prayer is the burden of a sigh,
  The falling of a tear;
The upward glancing of an eye,
  When none but God is near.

3 Prayer is the simplest form of speech
  That infant lips can try;

Prayer, the sublimest strains that reach,
　　The majesty on high.

4 Prayer is the Christian's vital breath,
　　The Christian's native air,
His watchword at the gate of death—
　　He enters heaven with prayer.

5 Prayer is the contrite sinner's voice
　　Returning from his ways,
While angels in their songs rejoice,
　　And say, "Behold, he prays!"

134　　　L. M.　　[UXBRIDGE.

WHAT various hindrances we meet,
　　In coming to the mercy seat!
Yet who that knows the worth of prayer,
But wishes to be often there.

2 Prayer makes the darkest clouds with-
Pray'r climbs the ladder Jacob saw; [draw;
Gives exercise to faith and love—
Brings every blessing from above.

3 Restraining prayer, we cease to fight;
Pray'r keeps the Christian's armor bright;
And Satan trembles when he sees,
The weakest saint upon his knees.

4 Have you no words?—ah, think again;
Words flow apace when you complain,
And fill your fellow creature's ear
With the sad tale of all your care.

5 Were half the breath thus vainly spent,
To heaven in supplication sent—

Your cheerful song would oftener be
"Hear what the Lord hath done for me!"

135   Metre 5.   [Welton.

HOLY Jesus, lovely Lamb,
Thine and only thine I am;
Take my body, spirit, soul,
Only thou possess the whole.

2 Thou my dearest object be,
Let me ever cleave to thee;
Let me choose the better part,
Let me give thee all my heart.

3 Whom have I on earth below?
Only thee I wish to know;
Whom have I in heaven but thee?
Thou art all in all to me.

4 All my treasure is above,
My best portion is thy love;
Who the worth of love can tell?
Infinite unsearchable!

5 Nothing else may I require;
Let me thee alone desire;
Pleased with what thy love provides,
Weaned from all the world besides.

136   Metre 16.   [Mendon.

LAMB of God, for sinners slain,
To thee I humbly pray;
Heal me of my grief and pain,
O take my sins away,

From this bondage, Lord, release,
  No longer let me be oppressed;
Jesus, Master, seal my peace,
  And take me to thy breast.
2 Wilt thou cast a sinner out
  Who humbly comes to thee?
No, my God, I cannot doubt;
  Thy mercy is for me.
Let me then obtain the grace,
  And be of Paradise possessed;
Jesus, Master, seal my peace,
  And take me to thy breast.
3 Worldly good I do not want,
  Be that to others given;
Only for thy love I pant,
  My all on earth or heaven;
This the crown I fain would seize,
  The good wherewith I would be blest;
Jesus, Master, seal my peace,
  And take me to thy breast.
4 This delight I fain would prove,
  And then resign my breath,
Join the happy few whose love
  Was mightier than death,
Let it not my Lord displease,
  That I would die to be thy guest!
Jesus, Master, seal my peace,
  And take me to thy breast.

137   Metre 12.   [Portland.

HOW shall a lost sinner in pain,
  Recover his forfeited peace?

When brought into bondage again,
  What hope of a second release?
Will mercy itself be so kind,
  To spare such a rebel as me?
And O, can I possibly find
  Such plenteous redemption in thee?

2 O Jesus, of thee I inquire,
  If still thou art able to save,
The brand to pluck out of the fire,
  And ransom my soul from the grave!
The help of thy Spirit restore,
  And show me the life-giving blood,
And pardon a sinner once more,
  And bring me again unto God.

3 O Jesus, in pity draw near,
  Come quickly to help a lost soul,
To comfort a mourner, appear,
  And make a poor Lazarus whole;
The balm of thy mercy apply,
  Thou seest the sore anguish I feel!
Save, Lord, or I perish, I die,
  O save, or I sink into hell!

4 I sink if thou longer delay
  Thy pardoning mercy to show;
Come quickly, and kindly display,
  The power of thy passion below.
By all thou hast done for my sake,
  One drop of thy blood I implore;
Now, let it touch me and make
  The sinner a sinner no more.

138 C. M. [CONDESCENSION.

JESUS, thou art the sinner's friend,
  As such I look to thee;
Now in the bowels of thy love,
  O Lord, remember me!

2 Remember thy pure word of grace,
  Remember Calvary!
Remember all thy dying groans,
  And then remember me.

3 Thou wondrous Advocate with God,
  I yield myself to thee;
While thou art sitting on thy throne,
  O Lord, remember me!

4 I own I'm guilty, own I'm vile,
  But thy salvation's free;
Then in thine all-abounding grace,
  O Lord, remember me!

5 Howe'er forsaken or distressed
  Howe'er oppressed I be;
Howe'er afflicted here on earth,
  Do thou remember me!

6 And when I close my eyes in death,
  And creature helps all flee,
Then, O my great Redeemer God,
  I pray, remember me!

139 C. M. [DUNLAP'S CREEK.

LORD, teach thy servants how to pray,
  With rev'rence and with fear;
Though dust and ashes, yet we may,
  We must to thee draw near.

2 We come, then, God of grace, to thee!
  Give broken, contrite hearts;
Give what thine eye delights to see,
  Truth in the inward parts.

3 Give deep humility—the sense
  Of godly sorrow give;
A strong desiring confidence
  To see thy face and live.

4 Give faith in that one Sacrifice,
  Which can for sin atone;
To cast our hopes, to fix our eyes
  On Christ—on Christ alone.

5 Give patience still to wait and weep,
  Though mercy long delay—
Courage our fainting souls to keep,
  And trust thee, though thou slay.

6 Give these—and then thy will be done!
  Thus strengthened with all might,
We, through thy Spirit and thy Son,
  Shall pray, and pray aright.

140 METRE 10. [STOCKBRIDGE.

COME Lord from above, the mountains remove;
O'erturn all that hinders the course of thy love,
My bosom inspire, enkindle the fire,
And wrap my whole soul in the flames of desire.

2 I languish and pine for the comfort divine,
O when shall I say, My Beloved is mine?
I've chosen the good part, my portion thou art,
O love, let me find thee, O God, in my heart!

3 For this my heart sighs, nothing else can suffice,
How, Lord, can I purchase the pearl of great price?

It cannot be bought; thou knowest I've naught,
Not an action, a word, or a truly good thought.

4 But I hear a voice say, without money you may
Receive it, whoever hath nothing to pay :
Who on Jesus relies, without money or price,
The pearl of forgiveness and holiness buys.

5 The blessing is free, so, Lord, let it be ;
I yield that thy love should be given to me ;
I freely receive what thou freely dost give,
And consent to thy love, in thine Eden to live.

6 The gift I embrace, the Giver I praise,
And ascribe my salvation to Jesus' grace ;
It came from above, the foretaste I prove,
And I soon shall receive all thy fullness of love.

141   C. M.   [GRAFTON.

MY God, consider my distress,
  Let mercy plead my cause ;
Though I have sinned against thy grace,
  I ne'er forget thy laws.

2 Forbid, forbid the sharp reproach,
  Which I so justly fear ;
Uphold my life, uphold my hope,
  Nor let my shame appear.

3 Be thou a surety, Lord, for me,
  Nor let the proud oppress ;
But make thy waiting servant see
  The shinings of thy face.

4 My eyes with expectation fail ;
  My heart within me cries ;

"When will the Lord his truth fulfill,
  And bid my comforts rise?

5 Look down upon my sorrows, Lord,
  And show thy grace the same;
Thy tender mercies still afford
  To those that love thy name.

142   C. M.   [WALSEL.

WITH my whole heart I've sought thy face,
  O let me never stray,
From thy commands, O God of grace,
  Nor tread the sinner's way.

2 Thy word I've hid within my heart,
  To keep my conscience clean,
And be an everlasting guard
  From every rising sin.

3 I'm a companion of the saints,
  Who fear and love the Lord;
My sorrows rise, my nature faints,
  When men transgress thy word.

4 While sinners do thy gospel wrong,
  My spirit stands in awe;
My soul abhors a lying tongue,
  But loves thy righteous law.

5 My heart with sacred rev'rence hears
  The threat'nings of thy word;
My flesh, with holy trembling, fears
  The Judgments of the Lord.

6 My God, I long, I hope, I wait,
  For thy salvation still;

While thy whole law is my delight,
And I obey thy will.

143   L. M.   [PORTUGAL.

JESUS, the spring of joys divine,
Whence all our hopes and comforts flow;
Jesus, no other name but thine
Can save us from eternal woe.

2 In vain would boasting reason find
The way to happiness and God;
Her weak directions leave the mind
Bewildered in a dubious road.

3 Nor other name will heaven approve;
Thou art the true, the living Way,
Ordained by everlasting love,
To the bright realms of endless day.

4 Here let our constant feet abide,
Nor from the heavenly path depart;
O let thy Spirit, gracious Guide!
Direct our steps and cheer our heart.

5 Safe lead us through this world of night,
And bring us to the blissful plains,—
The regions of unclouded light,
Where perfect joy forever reigns.

144   L. M.   [BOURBON.

JESUS, my Savior, brother, friend,
On whom I cast my every care,
On whom for all things I depend,
Inspire, and then accept my prayer.

2 If I have tasted of thy grace,
   Thy grace that sure salvation brings;
If with me now thy Spirit stays,
   And hovering, hides me in his wings:

3 Still let him with my weakness stay,
   Nor for a moment's space depart;
Evil and danger turn away,
   And keep till he renew my heart.

4 When to the right or left I stray,
   His voice behind me may I hear,
"Return, and walk in Christ the way,
   Fly back to Christ, for sin is near."

5 His sacred unction from above,
   Be still my comforter and guide,
Till thou my wayward thoughts remove,
   And in my humbled heart reside.

6 Jesus, I fain would walk in thee,
   From nature's every path retreat;
Thou art my way, my leader be,
   And set upon the rock my feet.

7 Uphold me, Savior, or I fall;
   O reach me out thy gracious hand!
Only on thee for help I call,
   Only by faith in thee I stand.

145   L. M.   HEALING BALM.

COME, gracious spirit, heavenly Dove,
   With light and comfort from above,
Be thou our guardian, thou our guide,
O'er every thought and step preside.

SUPPLICATION.

2 Conduct us safe, conduct us far
From every sin and hurtful snare;
Lead to thy word that rules must give,
And teach us lessons how to live.

3 The light of truth to us display,
But make us know and choose thy way;
Plant holy fear in every heart,
That we from God may ne'er depart.

4 Lead us to holiness, the road
That we must take to dwell with God;
Lead us to Christ the living way,
Nor let us from his pastures stray.

5 Lead us to God, our final rest,
In his enjoyment to be blessed;
Lead us to heaven, the seat of bliss,
Where pleasure in perfection is.

INVITATION.

146 Metre 5. [Welton.

JESUS' precious name excels
Jordan's streams and Salem's wells;
Thirsty sinners, come and draw,
Quench the flames of Sinai's law.

2 Fearful sinners, come and try;
Draw and drink a sweet supply;
Christ is ever full and free;
Sinner, come, where'er you be.

3 See the waters springing up,
  To revive your languid hope;
  Fill your vessels as it rolls,
  And refresh your weary souls.

4 Lo! the Spirit now invites;
  Lo! the cheerful bride unites;
  Jesus calls, be not afraid,
  Lo! for you the well was made.

5 Haste thou to the Lamb of God,
  Seek salvation in his blood;
  In it there is boundless store
  For ten thousand thousand more.

6 Let us still our vessels bring,
  To the soul-refreshing spring;
  Constant let our praises rise,
  Till we drink above the skies.

147   C. M.   [ORTONVILLE.

AMAZING sight, the Savior stands
  And knocks at every door!
Ten thousand blessings in his hands,
  To satisfy the poor.

2 "Behold," he saith, "I bleed and die,
    To bring you to my rest;—
  Hear, sinners, while I'm passing by,
    And be forever blest.

3 Will you despise my bleeding love,
    And choose the way to hell?
  Or in the glorious realms above,
    With me forever dwell?

4 "Not to condemn your wretched race,
    Have I in judgment come;
  But to display unbounded grace,
    And bring lost sinners home.

5 "Will you go down to endless night,
    And bear eternal pain?
  Or in the glorious realms of light,
    With me forever reign?

6 "Say—will you hear my gracious voice,
    And have your sins forgiven?
  Or will you make that wretched choice,
    And bar yourselves from heaven?"

148   L. M.   [BOURBON.

TO-DAY, if ye will hear his voice,
Now is the time to make your choice;
Say, will you to Mount Zion go?
Say, will you have this Christ or no?

2 Ye wandering souls who find no rest,
  Say, will you be forever blest?
  Will you be saved from sin and hell?
  Will you with Christ in glory dwell?

3 Come, now, dear youth, for ruin bound,
  Obey the gospel's joyful sound;
  Come, go with us, and you shall prove
  The joy of Christ's redeeming love.

4 Once more we ask you in his name—
  For yet his love remains the same,
  Say, will you to Mount Zion go?
  Say, will you have this Christ or no?

5 Leave all your sports and glit'ring toys;
   Come share with us eternal joys;
   Or must we leave you bound to hell?
   Then, dear young friends, a long farewell.

149 Metre 60. [Healing Fountain.

SEE the fountain opened wide,
   That from pollution frees us,
Flowing from the wounded side,
   Of our Immanuel Jesus!

CHORUS.

Ho! every one that thirsts,
   Come ye to the waters;
Freely drink and quench your thirst,
   With Zion's sons and daughters.

2 Sinner's, hear the Savior's call,
   Consider what you're doing;
Jesus Christ can cleanse you all,
   Will you not come unto him?
   Ho! every one that thirsts, &c.

3 Dying sinners, come and try;
   These waters will relieve you;
Without money come and buy,
   For Christ will freely give you.
   Ho! every one that thirsts, &c.

4 He who drinks shall never die;
   These waters fail him never;
Sinners, come, and now apply,
   And drink and live forever.
   Ho! every one that thirsts, &c.

5 Weeping Mary, full of grief,
    Came begging for these waters;
Jesus gave her full relief,
    With Zion's sons and daughters.
    Ho! every one that thirsts, &c.

6 See the woman at the well,
    Conversing with the Savior;
Soon she found that he could tell
    The whole of her behavior.
    Ho! every one that thirsts, &c.

7 When she asked, and thus obtained
    A drink, her heart was flaming;
Thus the gift divine she gained,
    And ran to town proclaiming.
    Ho! every one that thirsts, &c.

8 The thief had only time to think,
    And tell the doleful story:
Jesus gave him leave to drink—
    He drank and fled to glory.
    Ho! every one that thirsts, &c.

9 Christians, you can fully tell
    The virtue of these waters;
You were once the heirs of hell,
    But now are sons and daughters.
    Ho! every one that thirsts, &c.

150   Metre 10.   [Stockbridge.

O ALL that pass by, to Jesus draw near;
He utters a cry, ye sinners, give ear! [hands,
From hell to retrieve you he spreads out his
Now, now to receive you he graciously stands.

2 If any man thirst and happy would be,
　The vilest and worst may come unto me;
　May drink of my Spirit, excepted is none,
　Lay claim to my merit, and take for his own.

3 Whoever receives the life-giving word,
　In Jesus believes, in his God and his Lord;
　In him a pure River of Life shall arise;
　Shall in the believer spring up to the skies.

4 My God and my Lord! thy call I obey,
　My soul on thy word of promise I stay;
　The kind invitation I gladly embrace,
　Athirst for salvation, salvation by grace.

5 O hasten the hour, send down from above
　The Spirit of power, of health, and of love;
　Of filial fear, of knowledge and grace;
　Of wisdom and prayer, of joy and of praise.

6 The Spirit of faith, of faith in thy blood,
　Which saves us from wrath and brings us to God;
　Removes the huge mountain of indwelling sin,
　And opens a fountain that washes us clean.

151   Metre 11.   [Huger.

WHY sleep we, my brethren? come let us arise,
O why should we slumber in sight of the prize?
Salvation is nearer, our days are far spent,
O let us be active; awake and repent.

2 Oh how can we slumber! The Master is come;
　And calling on sinners to seek them a home;
　The Spirit and Bride now in concert unite,
　The weary they welcome, the careless invite.

3 O how can we slumber! our foes are awake;
To ruin poor souls every effort they make;
T'accomplish their object no means are untried.
The careless they comfort, the wakeful misguide.

4 O how can we slumber when so much was done
To purchase salvation by Jesus the Son!
Now mercy is proffered, and justice displayed;
Now God can be honored and sinners be saved.

5 O how can we slumber, when death is so near,
And sinners are sinking to endless despair!
Now prayers may avail and gain the high prize,
Before they in torment shall lift up their eyes.

6 O how can ye slumber, ye sinners look round,
Before the last trumpet your hearts shall con-
O fly to the Savior, he calls thee to-day; [found!
While mercy is waiting, O make no delay.

152   Metre 10.   [Lyons.

YE thirsty of God to Jesus give ear,
  And take, through his blood, a power to draw near;
His kind invitation, ye sinners, embrace,
Accepting salvation, salvation by grace.

2 Sent down from above, who governs the skies,
In vehement love, to sinners, he cries,
"Drink into my Spirit who happy wo'ld be
And all things inherit by coming to me."

3 O Savior of all, thy word we believe,
And come at thy call, thy grace to receive;
The blessing is given wherever thou art:
The earnest of heaven is love in the heart.

4 To us at thy feet the Comforter give;
  Who gasp to admit thy Spirit and live;
  The weakest believers acknowledge for thine,
  And fill us with rivers of water divine.

153   METRE 33.   STAR IN THE EAST.

RESTLESS thy Spirit, poor wandering sinner,
  Restless and roving—O come to thy home!
Come to the arms—the bosom of mercy;
  Jesus the Savior invites thee to come.

2 Darkness surrounds thee, and tempests are rising
  Fearful and dang'rous the path thou hast trod:
  Mercy shines forth in the rainbow of promise,
  Welcomes the wanderer home to his God.

3 Peace to the storm in thy soul shall be spoken,
  Guilt from thy bosom be banished away;
  Heaven's sweet breezes, o'er death's rolling bil-
  Waft thee at last to the regions of day. [lows,

4 But if regardless of God's gracious warnings,
  Far from his favor your soul must remove;
  O may you live to his honor and glory,
  Loving his precepts, and die in his love.

154   L. M.   [ROCKINGHAM.

HARK! the Redeemer, from on high,
  Sweetly invites his favorites nigh;
From caves of darkness and of doubt;
He gently speaks and calls us out.

2 "My dove, who hidest in the rock,
   Thine heart almost with sorrow broke;
   Lift up thy face, forget thy fear,
   And let thy voice delight mine ear.

3 "Thy voice to me sounds ever sweet;
   My graces in thy count'nance meet;
   Though the vain world thy face despise,
   'Tis bright and comely in mine eyes."

4 Dear Lord, our thankful heart receives
   The hope that thy invitation gives;
   To thee our joyful lips shall raise
   The voice of prayer and of praise.

5 I am my Love's and he is mine,
   Our hearts, our hopes, our passions join
   Nor let a motion nor a word,
   Nor thought arise to grieve my Lord.

6 My soul to pastures fair he leads,
   Among the lilies where he feeds;
   Among the saints (whose robes are white,
   Washed in his blood,) is his delight.

7 Till the day breaks and shadows flee,
   Till the sweet dawning light I see,
   Thine eyes to me-ward often turn,
   Nor let my soul in darkness mourn.

8 Be like a hart on mountains green,
   Leap o'er the hills of fear and sin;
   Nor guilt, nor unbelief, divide
   My Love, my Savior, from my side.

INVITATION.

155   Metre 9.   [Lenox.

COME, every pious heart,
  That loves the Savior's name,
Your noblest powers exert,
  To celebrate his fame;
Tell all above and all below,
The debt of love to him you owe.

2 Such was his zeal for God,
  And such his love for you,
He nobly undertook
  What Gabriel could not do;
His every deed of love and grace
All words exceed and thoughts surpass.

3 He left his starry crown,
  And laid his robes aside;
On wings of love came down;
  And wept and bled and died;
What he endured, O who can tell,
To save our souls from death and hell!

4 From the dark grave he rose,
  The mansions of the dead;
And thence his mighty foes
  In glorious triumph led;
Up through the sky the Conq'ror rode.
And reigns on high the Savior God.

5 From thence he'll quickly come,
  His chariot will not stay;
And bear our spirits home
  To realms of endless day;
There shall we see his lovely face,
And ever be in his embrace.

6 Jesus, we ne'er can pay,
   The debt we owe thy love,
Yet tell us how we may
   Our gratitude approve;
Our hearts our all to thee we give;
The gift, though small, thou wilt receive.

156   C. M.   [MEAR.

OH, what amazing words of grace
   Are in the gospel found!
Suited to every sinner's case
   Who knows the joyful sound.

2 Poor, sinful, thirsty, fainting souls,
   Are freely welcome here;
Salvation, like a river, rolls,
   Abundant, free, and clear.

3 Come, then, with all your wants and
   Your every burden bring! [wounds;
Here love, unchanging love, abounds,—
   A deep, celestial spring!

4 Whoever will—O gracious word!—
   Shall of this stream partake:
Come, thirsty souls, and bless the Lord,
   And drink, for Jesus' sake!

5 Millions of sinners, vile as you,
   Have here found life and peace;
Come, then, and prove its virtues too,
   And drink, adore, and bless!

157   C. M.   [BALERMA.

THE Savior calls—let every ear
   Attend the heavenly sound;

Ye doubting souls, dismiss your fear,
  Hope smiles reviving round.

2 For every thirsty, longing heart,
  Here streams of bounty flow;
And life, and health, and bliss impart,
  To banish mortal woe.

3 Here springs of sacred pleasure rise,
  To ease your every pain;
(Immortal fountain! full supplies!)
  Nor shall we thirst in vain.

4 Ye sinners, come, 't is mercy's voice,
  The gracious call obey;
Mercy invites to heav'nly joys—
  And can you yet delay?

5 Dear Savior, draw reluctant hearts—
  To thee let sinners fly,
And take the bliss thy love imparts,
  And drink, and never die.

158 L. M. [HEBRON.

WHILE life prolongs its precious light,
  Mercy is found, and peace is given;
But soon, ah soon! approaching night
  Shall blot out every hope of heaven.

2 While God invites, how blest the day!
  How sweet the gospel's joyful sound!
"Come, sinners, haste, O haste away,
  While yet a pard'ning God is found.

3 "Soon borne on time's most rapid wing,
  Shall death command you to the grave;

    Before his bar your spirits bring,
        And none be found to hear or save.
4 "In that lone land of deep despair,
        No Sabbath's heavenly light shall rise,
    No God regard your bitter prayer,
        No Savior call you to the skies."
5 No wonders to the dead are shown,
        (The wonders of redeeming love;)
    No voice his glorious truth makes known,
        Nor sings the bliss of climes above.
6 Silence and solitude and gloom,
        In these forgetful realms appear,
    Deep sorrows fill the dismal tomb,
        And hope shall never enter there.

159   C. M.   [Dunlap's Creek.

SINNERS, the voice of God regard;
        'Tis mercy speaks to-day;
He calls you by his sov'reign word,
        From sin's destructive way.

2 Like the rough sea that cannot rest,
        You live devoid of peace,
    A thousand stings within your breast
        Deprive your souls of ease.

3 Your way is dark and leads to hell;
        Why will you persevere?
    Can you in endless torments dwell,
        Shut up in black despair?

4 Why will you in the crooked ways
        Of sin and folly go?

In pain you travel all your days
　　　To reap eternal woe!

5 But he that turns to God shall live,
　　　Through his abounding grace;
　　His mercy will the guilt forgive
　　　Of those that seek his face.

6 Bow to the sceptre of his word,
　　　Renouncing every sin;
　　Submit to him your sov'reign Lord,
　　　And learn his will divine.

7 His love exceeds your highest thoughts;
　　　He pardons like a God;
　　He will forgive your num'rous faults,
　　　Through a Redeemer's blood.

160   L. M.   [DEVOTION.

THE voice of my Beloved sounds,
　Over the rocks and rising grounds;
O'er hills of guilt and seas of grief,
He leaps, he flies to my relief.

2 Now through the vale of flesh, I see;
With eyes of love he looks at me;
Now in the gospel's clearest glass,
He shows the beauties of his face.

3 Gently he draws my heart along,
Both with his beauties and his tongue;
"Rise," saith my Lord, "make haste away,
No mortal joys are worth thy stay."

4 "The Jewish wintry state is gone,
The mists are fled, the spring comes on,

The sacred turtle-dove we hear
  Proclaim the new, the joyful year.
5 "Th' immortal Vine of heavenly root,
  Blossoms, and buds, and gives her fruit."
  Lo! we are come to taste the wine;
  Our souls rejoice and bless the Vine.
6 And when we hear our Jesus say,
  "Rise up, my Love, and haste away;
  Our hearts would fain outfly the wind,
  And leave all earthly love behind.

161   Metre 40.   [Boundless Mercy.

DROOPING souls, no longer grieve,
  Heaven is propitious;
If in Christ you do believe,
  You will find him precious;
Jesus now is passing by,
  Calls the mourners to him,
Brings salvation from on high—
  Now look up and view him.

2 From his hands, his feet, his side,
  Runs the healing lotion;
See the consolating tide,
  Boundless as the ocean;
See the healing waters move
  For the sick and dying;
Now resolve to gain his love,
  Or to perish trying.

3 Grace's store is ever free
  Drooping souls to gladden;
Jesus calls "Come unto me,
  Ye weary, heavy laden;

Though your sins like mountains high,
  Rise and reach to heaven;
Soon as you on me rely,
  All shall be forgiven."
4 Now methinks I hear one say,
  I will go and prove him;
If he takes my sins away,
  Surely I shall love him.
Yes! I see the Father smile,
  Now I lose my burden;
All is grace—for I am vile,
  Yet he seals my pardon.
5 Streaming mercy, how it flows!
  Now I know, I feel it;
Tongue can not the half disclose,
  Yet I long to tell it:
Jesus' blood has healed my wound;
  O the wond'rous blessing!
I, through mercy, now have found
  All in him possessing.

162   L. M.   Tender Thought.

COME hither, all ye weary souls,
  Ye heavy laden sinners, come,
I'll give you rest from all your toils,
  And bring you to my heavenly home.
2 "They shall find rest that learn of me;
  I'm of a meek and lowly mind;
But passion rages like the sea,
  And pride is restless as the wind."
3 Blest is the man whose shoulders take
  My yoke and bear it with delight;

INVITATION. 147

   My yoke is easy to his neck,
     My grace shall make the burden light.
4 Jesus, we come at thy command;
     With faith and hope and humble zeal:
   Resign our spirits to thy hand,
     To mould and guide us at thy will.

163   Metre 56. [Royal Proclamation.

HEAR the royal proclamation,
   The glad tidings of Salvation,
Publishing to every creature,
To the ruined sons of nature.
        CHORUS.
Jesus reigns, he reigns victorious,
   Over heaven and earth most glorious,
      Jesus reigns.
2 See the royal banner flying,
   Hear the heralds loudly crying,
  "Rebel sinners, royal favor,
  Now is offered by the Savior."
      Jesus reigns, &c.
3 Turn unto the Lord most holy,
   Shun the path of vice and folly;
   Turn, or you are lost forever;
   Oh! now turn to God the Savior.
      Jesus reigns, &c.
4 Here is wine and milk and honey.
   Come and purchase without money;
   Mercy flowing like a fountain
   Streaming from the holy mountain,
      Jesus reigns, &c.

5 For his love, let rocks and mountains,
  Purling streams, and crystal fountains,
  Roaring thunders, lightning blazes,
  Shout the great Messiah's praises.
        Jesus reigns, &c.

164   Metre 7.   [Happy Zion.

COME ye sinners, poor and needy,
  Weak and wounded, sick and sore;
Jesus ready stands to save you,
  Full of pity, love, and power:
    He is able,
  He is willing: doubt no more.

2 Now, ye needy, come and welcome,
    God's free bounty glorify;
  True belief and true repentance,
    Every grace that brings you nigh,
      Without money,
    Come to Jesus Christ and buy.

3 Let not conscience make you linger;
    Nor of fitness fondly dream;
  All the fitness he requireth
    Is to feel your need of him;
      This he gives you,
    'T is the Spirit's glimm'ring beam.

4 Come, ye weary, heavy laden,
    Bruised and mangled by the fall,
  If you tarry till you're better,
    You will never come at all;
      Not the righteous,
    Sinners Jesus came to call.

5 Agonizing in the garden,
    Lo! your Maker prostrate lies!
On the bloody tree behold him,
    Hear him cry before he dies,
        "It is finished!"
Sinners, will not this suffice?

6 Lo! th' incarnate God ascending,
    Pleads the merit of his blood;
Venture on him, venture freely;
    Let no other trust intrude:
        None but Jesus,
Can do helpless sinners good.

7 Saints and angels join in concert,
    Sing the praises of the Lamb;
While the blissful seats of heaven
    Sweetly echo with his name:
        Hallelujah!
Sinners here may do the same.

165   C. M.   [MEAR.

YE wretched, hungry, starving poor,
    Behold a royal feast!
Where mercy spreads her bounteous store,
    For every humble guest.

2 There Jesus stands with open arms;
    He calls—he bids you come;
Though guilt restrains, and fear alarms,
    Behold, there yet is room.

3 Oh come, and with his children taste
    The blessings of his love;
While hope expects the sweet repast
    Of nobler joys above.

4 There, with united heart and voice,
    Before th' Eternal throne,
Ten thousand thousand souls rejoice,
    In songs on earth unknown.

5 And yet ten thousand thousand more
    Are welcome still to come:
Ye longing souls, the grace adore,
    And enter while there's room.

166   S. M.   [AYLESBURY.

YE sinners fear the Lord,
    While yet 't is called to-day;
Soon will the awful voice of death
    Command your souls away.

2 Soon will the harvest close;
    The summer soon be o'er;
And soon your injured, angry God,
    Will hear your prayers no more.

3 Then while 't is called to-day,
    O hear the gospel sound;
Come, sinner, haste—O haste away,
    While pardon may be found!

COMFORT IN TRIBULATION.

167   C. M.   [AZMON.

IF Paul in Cæsar's court must stand,
    He need not fear the sea;

Secured from harm on every hand
  By the divine decree.

2 Although the ship wherein he sailed,
  By dreadful storms was tossed;
The promise over all prevailed,
  And not a life was lost.

3 Jesus, the God whom Paul adored,
  Who saves in time of need,
Was then confessed by all on board,
  A present help indeed.

4 Though neither sun nor stars were seen,
  Paul knew the Lord was near;
And faith preserved his soul serene,
  When others shook with fear.

5 Believers thus are tossed about
  On life's tempestuous main,
But grace assures beyond a doubt,
  They shall their port attain.

6 They must, they shall appear one day,
  Before their Savior's throne;
The storms they meet with by the way
  But makes his power known.

7 Their passage lies across the brink
  Of many a threat'ning wave;
The world expects to see them sink,
  But Jesus lives to save.

8 Lord, though we are but feeble worms,
  Yet since thy word is past,
We'll venture through a thousand storms,
  To see thy face at last.

168   C. M.   [Solon.

OPPRESSED with fear, oppressed with grief,
  To God I breathed my cry;
His mercy brought divine relief,
  And wiped my tearful eye.

2 His mercy chased the shades of death,
  And snatched me from the grave;
O may his praise employ that breath
  Which mercy deigns to save!

3 Come, O ye saints! your voices raise
  To God in grateful songs;
And let the memory of his grace
  Inspire your hearts and tongues.

4 Her deepest gloom when sorrow spreads,
  And light and hope depart,
His smiles celestial morning sheds,
  And joy revives the heart.

5 Then let thy utmost glory be
  To raise thy honors high;
Nor let my gratitude to thee
  In guilty silence die.

6 To thee, my gracious God, I raise
  My thankful heart and tongue,
O be thy goodness and thy praise
  My everlasting song!

169   Metre 8.   [Moorestown.

WOULD Jesus have the sinner die?
  Why hang he then on yonder tree?

What means that strange expiring cry?
  (Sinner, he prays for you and me;)
"Forgive them, Father, O forgive,
They know not that by me they live!"

2 Jesus descended from above,
  Our loss of Eden to retrieve;
Great God of universal love,
  If all the world through thee may live,
In us a quickening Spirit be,
And witness, thou hast died for me.

3 Thou loving, all-atoning Lamb,
  Thee, by thy painful agony,
Thy bloody sweat, thy grief and shame,
  Thy cross and passion on the tree,
Thy precious death and life—I pray
Take all, take all my sins away.

4 O let me kiss thy bleeding feet,
  And bathe and wash them with my tears,
The story of thy love repeat
  In every drooping sinner's ears;
That all may hear the quick'ning sound,
Since I, even I, have mercy found.

5 O let thy love my heart constrain,
  Thy love for every sinner free,
That every fallen son of man,
  May taste the grace that found out me;
That all mankind with me may prove,
Thy sov'reign, everlasting love.

INFINITE MERCY.

170   Metre 5.   [Norwick.

DEPTH of mercy! can there be
Mercy still reserved for me?
Can my God his wrath forbear?
Me, the chief of sinners, spare?

2 I have long withstood his grace;
Long provoked him to his face;
Would not hearken to his calls;
Grieved him by a thousand falls.

3 Kindled his relentings are;
Me he now delights to spare:
Cries, "How can I give thee up?"
Lets the lifted thunder drop.

4 There for me the Savior stands;
Shows his wounds and spreads his hands!
God is love! I know, I feel!
Jesus weeps, and loves me still.

5 Jesus answers from above,
Is not all thy nature love?
Wilt not thou the wrong forget?
Suffer me to kiss thy feet?

6 Now incline me to repent;
Let me now my fall lament;
Now my foul revolt deplore,
Weep, believe, and sin no more.

171   Metre 11.   [Huger.

How firm a foundation ye saints of the Lord!
Is laid for your faith in his excellent word,
What more can he say than to you he hath said,
Who unto the Savior for refuge have fled?

2 " Fear not, I am with thee, O be not dismayed,
For I am thy God and will still give thee aid;
I'll strengthen thee, help thee, and cause thee to stand,
Upheld by my righteous, omnipotent hand.

3 " When through the deep waters I call thee to go,
The rivers of sorrow shall not overflow;
For I will be with thee thy troubles to bless,
And sanctify to thee thy deepest distress.

4 "When through fiery trials thy pathway shall lie,
My grace all-sufficient shall be thy supply;
The flames shall not hurt thee—I only design
Thy dross to consume and thy gold to refine.

5 " E'en down to old age all my people shall prove,
My sov'reign, eternal, unchangeable love;
And then when grey hairs shall their temples adorn,
Like Lambs, they shall still in my bosom be borne.

6 " The soul that on Jesus hath leaned for repose,
I will not, I will not desert to his foes;
That soul, tho' all hell should endeavor to shake,
I'll never, no never, no never forsake."

172   C. M.   [Condescension.

How condescending and how kind
Was God's eternal Son!

Our misery reached his heavenly mind,
   And pity brought him down.

2 When justice by our sins provoked,
   Drew forth its dreadful sword,
He gave his soul up to the stroke,
   Without a murm'ring word.

3 He sunk beneath our heavy woes,
   To raise us to his throne;
There's ne'er a gift his hand bestows,
   But costs his heart a groan.

4 This was compassion like a God,
   That, when the Savior knew
The price of pardon was his blood,
   His pity ne'er withdrew.

5 Now, though he reigns exalted high,
   His love is still as great;
Well he remembers Calvary,
   Nor let his saints forget.

6 Here we behold his bowels roll
   As kind as when he died,
And see the sorrows of his soul
   Bleed through his wounded side.

7 Here we receive repeated seals
   Of Jesus' dying love;
Hard is the wretch that never feels
   One soft affection move.

8 Here let our hearts begin to melt,
   While we his death record,

And with our joy for pardoned guilt,
Mourn that we pierced the Lord.

173   Metre 6.   [Probation.

MY God! thy boundless love we praise;
How bright on high its glories blaze—
  How sweetly bloom below!
It streams from thy eternal throne;
Through heaven its joys forever run,
  And o'er the earth they flow.

2 'T is love that guilds the vernal ray,
Adorns the flow'ry robe of May;
  Perfumes the breathing gale;
'T is love that loads the plenteous plain
With blushing fruits and golden grain,
  And smiles o'er every vale.

3 But in thy gospel it appears
In sweeter, fairer characters,
  And charms the ravished breast;
There love immortal leaves the skies,
To wipe the drooping mourner's eyes,
  And give the weary rest.

4 There smiles a kind, propitious God,
There flows a dying Savior's blood,
  The pledge of sins forgiven?
There faith, bright cherub, points the way
To regions of eternal day,
  And opens all her heaven.

 5 Then in redeeming love rejoice,
  My soul! and hear a Savior's voice
   That calls thee to the skies;
  Above life's empty scenes aspire,
  Its sordid cares and mean desire,—
   And seize th' eternal prize.

174   S. M.   [ALBION.

MY soul, with joy attend,
  While Jesus silence breaks;
No angel's harps such music yields,
  As what my Shepherd speaks.
2 "I know my sheep," he cries,
  "My soul approves them well;
Vain is the treach'rous world's disguise,
  And vain the rage of hell.
3 "I freely feed them now
  With tokens of my love;
But richer pastures I prepare,
  And sweeter streams above.
4 "Unnumbered years of bliss
  I to my sheep will give;
And while my throne unshaken stands,
  Shall all my chosen live.
5 "This tried Almighty hand
  Is raised for their defense;
Where is the power shall reach them there?
  Or what shall force them thence?
6 Enough, my gracious Lord,
  Let faith triumphant cry:
My heart can on this promise live,
  Can on this promise die.

THE LOVE OF GOD.

175   L. M.   [DEVOTION.

OF all the joys we mortals know,
  Jesus, thy love exceeds the rest;
Love, the best blessing here below,
  The highest rapture of the blest.

2 While we are held in thine embrace,
  There's not a thought attempts to rove;
Each smile that's seen upon thy face,
  Fixes and charms and fires our love.

3 When of thine absence we complain,
  And long and weep and humbly pray,
There's a strange pleasure in the pain;
  The tears are sweet that mourn thy stay.

4 When round thy courts by day we rove,
  Or ask the watchman of the night,
For some kind tidings from above.
  Thy very name creates delight.

5 Jesus, our God, descend and come;
  Our eyes would dwell upon thy face;
'T is heaven to see our Lord at home,
  And feel the presence of his grace.

176   L. M.   [BACA.

SO let our lives and lips express
  The holy gospel we profess;
So let our works and virtue's shine,
To prove the doctrine all divine.

2 Thus shall we best proclaim abroad
   The honor of our Savior God;
   When the salvation reigns within,
   And grace subdues the power of sin.

3 Our flesh and sense must be denied;
   Passion and envy, lust and pride;
   While justice, temp'rance, truth and love
   Our inward piety approve.

4 Religion bears our spirits up,
   While we expect that blessed hope,
   The bright appearance of the Lord,
   And faith stands leaning on his word.

177   L. M.   [GALILEE.

WHO is this fair one in distress,
   That travels through the wilderness,
And pressed with sorrows and with sins,
On our beloved Lord she leans?

2 This is the spouse of Christ our God,
   Bought with the treasure of his blood;
   And her request and her complaint
   Is but the voice of every saint.

3 "O let my name engraven stand,
   Both on thy heart and on thy hand,
   Seal me upon thy arm, and wear
   The pledge of love forever there.

4 "Stronger than death thy love is known,
   Which floods of wrath could never drown;
   And hell and earth in vain combine
   To quench a fire so much divine.

5 " But I am jealous of my heart,
  Lest it from thee should once depart;
  Then let thy name be well impressed,
  As a fair signet on my breast.

6 " Till thou hast brought me to thy home,
  Where fears and doubts can never come,
  Thy count'nance let me often see,
  And often thou shalt hear from me.

7 " Come, my Beloved, haste away,
  Cut short the hours of thy delay:
  Fly like a youthful hart or roe
  Over the hills where spices grow."

178   Metre 10.   [Unity.

O TELL me no more of this world's vain store,
  The time for such trifles with me now is o'er;
A country I've found where true joys abound,
  To dwell I'm determined on that happy ground.

2 The souls that believe, in Jesus shall live,
And me in that number will Jesus receive;
My soul, don't delay—he calls thee away,
Rise, follow thy Savior, and bless the glad day.

3 No mortal doth know what he can bestow,
What light, strength, and comfort, go after him
  —go:
Lo! onward I move to a city above:
None guesses how wondrous my journey will
  prove.

4 Great spoils I shall win from death, hell and sin,
'Midst outward afflictions shall feel Christ within;
And when I'm to die, receive me, I cry,
For Jesus hath loved me, I cannot tell why.

5 But this I do find, we two are so joined,
He'll not live in glory and leave me behind;
So this is the race I'm running through grace,
Henceforth, till admitted to see my Lord's face.

6 And now I'm in care, my neighbors may share
These blessings—to seek them will none of you dare?
In bondage, O why! in death will you lie,
When one here assures you free grace is so nigh?

179 Metre 10. [Stockbridge.

BEGONE unbelief! my Savior is near,
And for my relief will surely appear;
By prayer let me wrestle, and he will perform;
With Christ in the vessel, I smile at the storm.

2 Though dark be my way, since he is my guide,
'T is mine to obey, 'tis his to provide:
Though cisterns be broken, and creatures all fail,
The word he has spoken shall surely prevail.

3 His love in time past forbids me to think,
He'll leave me at last in trouble to sink;
Each sweet Ebenezer I have in review,
Confirms his good pleasure to help me quite thro'.

4 Why should I complain of want and distress,
Temptation or pain?—he told me no less;
The heirs of Salvation—I know from his word,
Thro' much tribulation must follow their Lord.

5 Since all that I meet shall work for my good,
The bitter is sweet, the medicine food;
Tho' painful at present, 'twill cease before long,
And then, O how pleasant—the conqueror's song!

180   Metre 4.   [Charleston.

GOD is love; his mercy brightens
   All the path in which we move;
Bliss he forms, and woe he lightens;
   God is light, and God is love.

2 Chance and change are busy ever;
   Worlds decay, and ages move;
But his mercy waneth never:
   God is light, and God is love.

3 E'en the hour that darkest seemeth
   Will his changeless goodness prove;
From the mist his brightness streameth;
   God is light, and God is love.

4 He with earthly cares entwineth,
   Hope and comfort from above;
Everywhere his glory shineth:
   God is light, and God is love.

181   Metre 21.   [Eden of Love.

HOW sweet to reflect on those joys that await
      me,
In yon blissful region, the haven of rest,
Where glorified spirits with welcome shall greet
      me,
And lead me to mansions prepared for the blest;
Encircled in light, and with glory enshrouded,
My happiness perfect, my mind's sky unclouded,
I'll bathe in the ocean of pleasure unbounded;
And range with delight through the Eden of Love.

2 While angelic legions, with harps tuned celestial
Harmoniously join in the concert of praise,
The saints, as they flock from the regions terrestrial,
In loud Hallelujahs their voices will raise :
The Songs of the Lamb shall re-echo through heaven,
My soul will respond, To Immanuel be given
All glory, all honor, all might and dominion,
Who brought us through grace to the Eden of Love.

3 Then hail, blessed state! Hail, ye songsters of glory!
Ye harpers of bliss, soon I'll meet you above,
And join your full choir in rehearsing the story,
"Salvation from sorrow through Jesus' love."
Though prisoned in earth, yet by anticipation,
Already my soul feels a sweet prelibation,
Of joys that await me, when freed from probation:
My heart's now in heaven, the Eden of Love.

182   Metre 11.   [Hinton.

THY mercy, my God, is the theme of my song,
  The joy of my heart and the boast of my tongue ;
Thy free grace alone from the first to the last,
Hath won my affections, and bound my soul fast.

2 Without thy sweet mercy I could not live here;
Sin soon would reduce me to utter despair ;
But through thy free goodness my spirit revive,
And he that first made me still keeps me alive.

3 Thy mercy is more than a match for my heart,
Which wonders to feel its own hardness depart;
Dissolved by the sunshine, I fall to the ground,
And weep to the praise of the mercy I found.

4 The door of thy mercy stands open all day
To the poor and the needy who knock by the way;
No sinner shall ever be empty sent back.
Who comes seeking mercy for Jesus' sake.

5 Thy mercy in Jesus exempts me from hell;
Its glories I'll sing and its wonders I'll tell:
T was Jesus, my friend. when he hung on the tree
Who opened the channel of mercy for me.

6 Great Father of mercies! thy goodness I own,
And the covenant love of thy crucified Son;
All praise to the Spirit. whose whisper divine
Seals mercy, and pardon, and righteousness mine!

MORNING HYMNS.

183   L. M.   [HEBRON—DEVOTION.

SWEET is the work, my God, my King,
  To praise thy name, give thanks and sing;
To show thy love by morning light,
And talk of all thy truths at night.

2 Sweet is the day of sacred rest;
No mortal cares shall seize my breast;
O may my heart in tune be found,
Like David's harp, of solemn sound.

3 My heart shall triumph in my Lord,
And bless his works, and bless his word:
Thy works of grace, how bright they shine!
How deep thy counsels! How divine!

4 Fools never raise their thoughts so high;
Like brutes they live, like brutes they die;
Like grass they flourish, till thy breath
Blasts them in everlasting death.

5 But I shall share a glorious part
When grace hath well refined my heart;
And fresh supplies of joy are shed,
Like holy oil, to cheer my head.

6 Sin (my worst enemy before),
Shall vex my eyes and ears no more;
My inward foes shall all be slain,
Nor Satan break my peace again.

7 Then shall I see, and hear, and know
All I desired or wished below;
And every power find sweet employ
In that eternal world of joy.

184   C. M.   [CONSOLATION.

ONCE more, my soul, the rising day
  Salutes thy waking eyes;
Once more, my voice, thy tribute pay
  To him that rules the skies.

2 Night unto night his name repeats,
  The day renews the sound,
Wide as the heaven on which he sits
  To turn the seasons round.

3 'T is he supports my mortal frame:
   My tongue shall speak his praise;
My sins would rouse his wrath to flame,
   And yet his wrath delays.

4 On a poor worm thy power might tread,
   And I could ne'er withstand;
Thy justice might have crushed me dead,
   But mercy held thy hand.

5 A thousand wretched souls are fled
   Since the last setting sun,
And yet thou lengthenest out my thread,
   And yet my moments run.

6 Dear God, let all my hours be thine,
   Whilst I enjoy the light;
Then shall my sun in smiles decline,
   And bring a pleasant night.

185   Metre 55.   [Holy Rest.

AGAIN the day returns of holy rest,
   Which when He made the world Jehovah blest;
When like his own he bid our labors cease,
And all be piety, and all be peace.

2 Let us devote this consecrated day,
To learn his will, and all we learn obey;
So shall we hear when fervently we raise
Our supplication, and our songs of praise.

3 Father of heav'n! in whom our hopes
    confide,
   Whose power defends us, and whose precepts guide;

In life our Guardian, and in death our
    Friend;
Glory supreme be thine till time shall end.

186   C. M.   [MEAR.

LORD, in the morning thou shalt hear
    My voice ascending high;
To thee will I direct my prayer,
    To thee lift up mine eye.

2 Up to the hills where Christ is gone,
    To plead for all his saints,
Presenting at his Father's throne,
    Our songs and our complaints.

3 Thou art a God, before whose sight
    The wicked shall not stand;
Sinners shall ne'er be thy delight,
    Nor dwell at thy right hand.

4 But to thy house will I resort,
    To taste thy mercies there;
I will frequent thy holy court,
    And worship in thy fear.

5 O may thy Spirit guide my feet,
    In ways of righteousness,
Make every path of duty straight,
    And plain before my face.

6 My watchful enemies combine
    To tempt my feet astray;
They flatter with a base design
    To make my soul their prey.

7 Lord, crush the serpent in the dust,
    And all his plots destroy;

While those that in thy mercy trust
  For ever shout for joy.

8 The men that love and fear thy name,
  Shall see their hopes fulfilled;
The mighty God will compass them
  With favor, as a shield.

187   Metre 5.   [Cookham.

NOW the shades of night are gone;
  Now the morning light is come;
Lord, may I be thine to-day—
Drive the shades of sin away.

2 Fill my soul with heavenly light,
Banish doubt, and cleanse my sight;
In thy service, Lord, to-day,
Help me labor, help me pray.

3 Keep my haughty passions bound—
Save me from my foes around;
Going out and coming in,
Keep me safe from every sin.

4 When my work of life is past,
Oh! receive me then at last!
Night of sin will be no more,
When I reach the heavenly shore.

188   C. M.   [Liberty Hall.

MY lovely Jesus, while on earth
  Arose before 't was day,
And to a solitary place
  Departed, there to pray.

2 I'll do as did my blessed Lord—
　　His footsteps I will trace;
　I love to meet him in the grove,
　　And view his smiling face.

3 Early I'll rise and sing and pray,
　　While I the light enjoy;
　May this blessed work from day to day,
　　My heart and tongue employ.

189　　　　C. M.　　　　[DUBLIN.

GREAT God, preserved by thine arm,
　　I passed the shades of night;
Serene—and safe from every harm,
　　And see returning light.

2 Oh! let the same Almighty care
　　My wakeful hours defend;
　From every danger, every snare,
　　My heedless steps defend.

3 Smile on my minutes as they roll,
　　And guide my future days:
　And let thy goodness fill my soul
　　With gratitude and praise.

190　　　　C. M.　　　　[AUGUSTA.

WHEN we with welcome slumber
　　Had closed our weary eyes,[pres'd,
A power unseen secured our rest,
　　And made us joyful rise.

2 Numbers this night have doubtless met,
　　Their long eternal doom; .

And lost the joy of morning light,
   In death's tremendous gloom.
3 But life to us its light prolongs,
   Let warmest thanks arise;
Great God, accept our morning songs,
   Our willing sacrifice.

191   C. M.   [MEAR.

GOD of my life, my morning song
   To thee I cheerful raise:
Thy act of love 'tis good to sing,
   And pleasant 'tis to praise.
2 Preserved by thy Almighty arm,
   I passed the shades of night,
Serene—and safe from every harm,
   To see the morning light.
3 While numbers spent the night in sighs
   And restless pains and woes,
In gentle sleep I closed mine eyes,
   And rose from sweet repose.
4 When sleep, death's image, o'er me spread,
   And I unconscious lay,
Thy watchful care was round my bed,
   To guard my feeble clay.
5 O let the same Almighty care
   Through all this day attend;
From every danger, every snare;
   My heedless steps defend.
6 Smile on my minutes as they roll,
   And guide my future days;
And let thy goodness fill my soul
   With gratitude and praise.

EVENING HYMNS.

192   S. M.   [SHIRLAND.

THE day is past and gone,
  The evening shades appear,
O may we all remember well
  The night of death draws near!

2 We lay our garments by,
  Upon our beds to rest;
So death will soon disrobe us all,
  Of what we here possess.

3 Lord, keep us safe this night,
  Secure from all our fears;
May angels guard us while we sleep,
  Till morning light appears.

4 And if we early rise,
  And view th' unwearied sun,
May we set out to win the prize,
  And after glory run!

5 And when our days are past,
  And we from time remove,
O may we in thy bosom rest,
  The bosom of thy love!

193   L. M.   [ROCKBRIDGE.

GLORY to thee, my God, this night,
  For all the blessings of the light;
Keep me, O keep me, King of kings
Beneath thine own Almighty wings.

2 Forgive me, Lord, for thy dear Son,
The ill that I this day have done;
That with the world, myself, and thee,
I, ere I sleep, at peace may be.

3 Teach me to live, that I may dread
The grave as little as my bed;
Teach me to die, so that I may
Rise glorious at the awful day.

4 O let my soul on thee repose,
And may sweet sleep mine eye-lids close;
Sleep that shall me more vig'rous make,
To serve my God when I awake.

5 If in the night I sleepless lie,
My soul with heavenly thought supply;
Let no ill dreams disturb my rest,
No powers of darkness me molest.

194   C. M.   [LIBERTY HALL.

LORD, thou wilt hear me when I pray;
  I am for ever thine:
I fear before thee all the day,
  Nor would I dare to sin.

2 And while I rest my weary head,
  From care and business free,
'T is sweet conversing on my bed
  With my own heart and thee.

3 I pay this evening sacrifice;
  And when my work is done,
Great God, my faith, my hope relies
  Upon thy grace alone.

4 Thus with my thoughts composed to
    I'll give mine eyes to sleep;   [peace,
  Thy hand in safety keeps my days
    And will my slumbers keep.

195   C. M.   [Youthful Piety.

DREAD Sov'reign, let my ev'ning song
    Like holy incense, rise;
Assist the off'rings of my tongue,
    To reach the lofty skies.

2 Through all the dangers of the day
    Thy hand was still my guard;
And still to drive my wants away,
    Thy mercy stood prepared.

3 Perpetual blessings from above
    Encompass me around;
But O, how few returns of love,
    Hath my Creator found!

4 What have I done for him who died
    To save my wretched soul?
How are my follies multiplied,
    Fast as my minutes roll?

5 Lord, with this guilty heart of mine,
    To thy dear cross I flee,
And to thy grace my soul resign,
    ·To be renewed by thee.

6 Sprinkled afresh with pard'ning blood,
    I lay me down to rest,
As in th' embraces of my God,
    Or in my Savior's breast.

196 C. M. [DIVINITY.

INDULGENT Father, by whose care,
   I've passed another day,
Let me this night thy mercy share,
   And teach me how to pray.

2 Show me my sins, and how to mourn
   My guilt before thy face;
Direct me, Lord, to Christ alone,
   And save me by thy grace.

3 Let each returning night declare
   The tokens of thy love;
And every hour thy grace prepare
   My soul for joys above.

4 And when on earth I close mine eyes,
   To sleep in death's embrace,
Let me to heaven and glory rise,
   T' enjoy thy smiling face.

197 C. M. [AWFUL MAJESTY.

ALL praise to him who dwells in bliss,
   Who made both day and night;
Whose throne is darkness in th' abyss,
   Of uncreated light.

2 Each thought and deed, his piercing eyes
   With strictest search survey;
The deepest shades no more disguise,
   Than the full blaze of day.

3 Whom thou dost guard, O King of kings,
   No evil shall molest;

Under the shadow of thy wings
  Shall they securely rest.

4 Thy angels shall around their beds
    Their constant stations keep: [heads,
  Thy faith and truth shall shield their
    For thou dost never sleep.

5 May we with calm and sweet repose,
    And heavenly thoughts refreshed,
  Our eyelids with the morn unclose,
    And bless Thee, ever blest.

198   Metre 12.   [New Jerusalem.

INSPIRER and Hearer of prayer,
  Before whom a sinner may bend;
My all to thy covenant care,
  I sleeping or waking commend.

2 If thou art my Shield and my Sun,
    The night is no darkness to me;
  And fast as my moments roll on,
    They bring me but nearer to thee.

3 From evil secure, and its dread,
    I rest, if my Savior be nigh;
  And songs, his kind presence indeed,
    Shall in the night season supply.

4 He smiles, and my comforts abound;
    His grace as the dew shall descend;
  And walls of Salvation surround
    The soul he delights to defend.

199   Metre 5.   [Brian.

SOFTLY now the light of day
Fades upon my sight away;
Free from care—from labor free,
Lord, I would commune with thee.

2 Soon for me the light of day
Shall for ever pass away;
Then from sin and sorrow free,
Take me, Lord, to dwell with thee.

200   C. M.   Evening Twilight.

I LOVE to steal awhile away,
From every cumb'ring care;
And spend the hours of setting day,
In humble, grateful prayer.

2 I love in solitude to shed
The penitential tear,
And all his promises to plead,
Where none but God can hear.

3 I love to think on mercies past,
And future good implore;
And all my cares and sorrows cast
On Him whom I adore.

4 I love by faith to take a view
Of brighter scenes in heaven;
The prospect doth my strength renew
While here by tempests driven.

5 Thus when life's toilsome day is o'er,
May its departing ray,
Be calm as this impressive hour,
And lead to endless day.

FRAILTY OF MAN.

201   C. M.   [DUBLIN.

LORD, what is man, poor feeble man,
   Born of the earth at first?
His life a shadow, light and vain,
   Still hast'ning to the dust.

2 Of what is feeble, dying man,
   Or all his sinful race,
That God should make it his concern
   To visit him with grace!

3 That God who darts his lightnings down,
   Who shakes the worlds above!
What terrors wait his awful frown!
   How wondrous is his love!

202   C. M.   [MEAR.

OUR God, our help in ages past,
   Our hope for years to come;
Our shelter from the stormy blast,
   And our eternal home!

2 Beneath the shadow of thy throne
   Thy saints have dwelt secure;
Sufficient is thy arm alone,
   And my defense is sure.

3 Before the hills in order stood,
   Or earth received her frame,
From everlasting thou art God,
   To endless years the same.

4 Thy word commands our flesh to dust,
   " Return, ye sons of men;"
  All nations rose from earth at first,
   And turn to earth again.

5 A thousand ages in thy sight
   Are like an evening gone:
  Short as the watch that ends the night
   Before the rising dawn.

6 The busy tribes of flesh and blood,
   With all their lives and cares,
  Are carried downwards by the flood,
   And lost in following years.

7 Time, like an ever-rolling stream,
   Bears all its sons away;
  They fly, forgotten as a dream
   Dies at the opening day.

8 Like flowery fields the nations stand,
   Pleased with the morning light;
  The flowers beneath the mower's hand
   Lie withered ere 't is night.

9 Our God, our help in ages past,
   Our hope for years to come,
  Be thou our guard while troubles last,
   And our eternal home.

203   C. M.   [CONDESCENSION.

TEACH me the measure of my days,
   Thou maker of my frame;
  I would survey life's narrow space,
   And learn how frail I am.

2 A span is all that we can boast,
    An inch or two of time;
Man is but vanity and dust,
    In all his flower and prime.

3 See the vain race of mortals move,
    Like shadows o'er the plain;
They rage and strive, desire and love,
    But all their noise is vain.

4 Some walk in honor's gaudy show,
    Some dig for golden ore;
They toil for heirs they know not who,
    And straight are seen no more.

5 What should I wish or wait for then,
    From creatures, earth and dust,
They make our expectations vain,
    And disappoint our trust.

6 Now I forbid my carnal hope,
    My fond desires recall;
I give my mortal interest up,
    And make my God my all.

204   S. M.   [IDUMEA.

LORD, what a feeble piece,
    Is this our mortal frame!
Our life! how poor a trifle 't is,
    That scarce deserves the name!

Alas, this brittle clay
    That built our bodies first!
And every month and every day,
    'T is mould'ring back to dust.

3 Our moments fly apace,
   Our feeble powers decay;
 Swift as a flood our hasty days
   Are sweeping us away.

4 Yet if our days must fly,
   We'll keep their end in sight;
 We'll spend them all in wisdom's ways,
   And let them speed their flight.

5 They'll waft us sooner o'er
   This life's tempestuous sea:
 Soon we shall reach the peaceful shore
   Of bless'd eternity.

FUNERAL.

205 S. M. [AYLESBURY.

AND must this body die?
   This mortal frame decay?
 And must these active limbs of mine
   Lie mould'ring in the clay?

2 Corruption, earth and worms,
   Shall but refine this flesh,
 Till my triumphant spirit comes,
   To put it on afresh.

3 God, my Redeemer, lives,
   And often from the skies
 Looks down, and watches all my dust,
   Till he shall bid it rise.

4 Arrayed in glorious grace
 Shall these vile bodies shine;
And every shape and every face
 Look heavenly and divine.

5 These lively hopes we owe
 To Jesus' dying love;
We would adore his grace below,
 And sing his power above.

6 Dear Lord, accept the praise
 Of these our humble songs,
Till tunes of nobler sounds we raise,
 With our immortal tongues.

206   C. M.   [GRAFTON.

HARK! from the tombs a doleful sound!
 Mine ears attend the cry!
Ye living men, come view the ground
 Where you must shortly lie.

2 "Princes, this clay must be your bed,
 In spite of all your towers:
The tall, the wise, the rev'rend head
 Must lie as low as ours."

3 Great God! is this our certain doom?
 And are we still secure?
Still walking downward to the tomb,
 And yet prepared no more?

4 Grant us the power of quick'ning grace,
 To fit our souls to fly;
Then, when we drop this dying flesh,
 We'll rise above the sky.

207   C. M.   [BOURFORD.

LORD, if thine eyes survey our faults,
  And justice grows severe,
Thy dreadful wrath exceeds our thoughts,
  And burns beyond our fear.

2 Thine anger turns our frame to dust:
  By one offense to thee,
Adam, and all his sons, have lost
  Their immortality.

3 Life, like a vain amusement, flies,
  A fable or a song;
By swift degrees our nature dies,
  Nor can our joys be long.

4 'Tis but a few whose days amount
  To threescore years and ten;
And all beyond that short account
  Is sorrow, toil, and pain.

5 Our vitals, with laborious strife,
  Bear up the crazy load,
And drag these poor remains of life
  Along the tiresome road.

6 Almighty God, reveal thy love,
  And not thy wrath alone;
O let our sweet experience prove
  The mercies of thy throne.

7 Our souls would learn the heavenly art,
  T" improve the hours we have,
That we may act the wiser part,
  And live beyond the grave.

208   C. M.   [DUBLIN.

WHY do we mourn departing friends,
  Or shake at death's alarms?
'T is but the voice that Jesus sends,
  To call them to his arms.

2 Are we not tending upward too,
  As fast as time can move?
Nor should we wish the hours more slow,
  To keep us from our love.

3 Why should we tremble to convey
  Their bodies to the tomb?
There the dear flesh of Jesus lay,
  And left a long perfume.

4 The graves of all his saints he blest,
  And softened every bed;
Where should the dying members rest,
  But with their dying Head?

5 Thence he arose, ascending high,
  And showed our feet the way;
Up to the Lord our flesh shall fly
  At the great rising day.

6 Then let the last, loud trumpet sound,
  And bid our kindred rise;
Awake, ye nations under ground,
  Ye saints, ascend the skies.

209   C. M.   [AZMON.

THY life I read, my dearest Lord,
  With transport all divine;

Thine image trace in every word,—
  Thy love in every line.

2 Methinks I see a thousand charms
  Spread o'er thy lovely face,
While infants in thy tender arms,
  Receive the smiling grace.

3 "I take these little lambs," said he,
  And lay them in my breast;
Protection they shall find in me,
  In me be ever blest.

4 "Death may the bands of life unloose,
  But can't dissolve my love;
Millions of infant souls compose
  The family above.

5 "Their feeble frames my power shall
  And mould with heavenly skill; [raise,
I'll give them tongues to sing my praise,
  And hands to do my will."

6 His words the happy parents hear,
  And shout with joys divine:
Dear Savior, all we have and are,
  Shall be forever thine.

210   C. M.   [Salvation.

ATTEND, young friends, while I relate
  The dangers you are in;
The evils that around you wait,
  While subject unto sin.
Although you flourish like the rose,
  While in its branches green;

Your sparkling eyes in death must close,
  No more will they be seen.
2 In silent shades you must lie down,
  Long in your graves to dwell;
Your friends will then stand weeping 'round,
  And bid a long farewell.
How small this world will then appear
  At the tremendous hour,
When you Jehovah's voice shall hear,
  And feel his mighty power.
3 In vain you'll mourn, your days are past.
  Alas! those days are gone;
Your golden hours are spent at last,
  And never to return.
O come this moment, and begin,
  While life's sweet moments last,
Turn to the Lord, forsake all sin,
  And he'll forgive what's past.

211   C. M.   [GRAFTON.

DEATH! 't is a melancholy day,
  To those that have no God,
When the poor soul is forced away,
  To seek her last abode.
2 In vain to heaven she lifts her eyes;
  But guilt, a heavy chain,
Still drags her downward from the skies,
  To darkness, fire, and pain.
3 Awake and mourn, ye heirs of hell,
  Let stubborn sinners fear;
You must be driven from earth, and dwell,
  A long forever there.

4 See how the pit gapes wide for you,
    And flashes in your face;
  And thou, my soul, look downward too,
    And sing recovering grace.
5 He is a God of sovereign love,
    Who promised heaven to me,
  And taught my thoughts to soar above,
    Where happy spirits be.
6 Prepare me, Lord, for thy right hand;
    Then come the joyful day;
  Come, death, and some celestial band,
    To bear my soul away.

212   C. M.   [RESIGNATION.

AND let this feeble body fail,
    And let it faint or die;
  My soul shall quit the mournful vale,
    And soar to worlds on high:
  Shall join the disembodied saints,
    And find its long-sought rest,
  That only bliss for which it pants,
    In the Redeemer's breast.
2 In hope of that immortal crown
    I now the cross sustain;
  And gladly wander up and down
    And smile at toil and pain:
  I'll suffer on my threescore years,
    Till my Deliv'rer come,
  And wipe away his servant's tears,
    And take his exile home.
3 O what hath Jesus bought for me!
    Before my ravished eyes,

Rivers of life divine I see,
    And trees of Paradise!
I see a world of spirits bright,
    Who taste the pleasures there!
They all are robed in spotless white,
    And conq'ring palms they bear.

4 O what are all my suff'rings here,
    If, Lord, thou count me meet,
With that enraptured host t' appear,
    And worship at thy feet!
Give joy or grief, give ease or pain,
    Take life or friends away;
But let me find them all again,
    In that eternal day.

213   Metre 12.   [Deliverance.

HOW blest is our brother, bereft,
    Of all that can burden his mind;
How easy the soul that has left
    This wearisome body behind.
Of evil incapable thou,
    Whose relics with envy I see;
No longer in misery now,
    No longer a sinner like me.

2 This earth is affected no more
    With sickness, or shaken with pain;
The war in the members is o'er,
    And never shall vex him again:
No anger, henceforward, or shame,
    Shall redden this innocent clay;
Extinct is the animal flame,
    And passion is vanished away.

3 This languishing head is at rest;
    It's thinking and aching are o'er,
This quiet, immovable breast,
    Is heaved by affliction no more;
This heart is no longer the seat
    Of trouble and torturing pain;
It ceases to flutter and beat—
    It never shall flutter again.

4 The lids he so seldom could close,
    By sorrow forbidden to sleep,
Sealed up in eternal repose,
    Have strangely forgotten to weep;—
These fountains can yield no supplies;
    These hollows from water are free;
The tears are all wiped from these eyes,
    And evil they never shall see.

214   L. M.   [HEBRON.

WHY should we start and fear to die?
    What tim'rous worms we mortals are!
Death is the gate to endless joy,
    And yet we dread to enter there.

2 The pains, the groans, the dying strife
    Fright our approaching souls away;
Still we shrink back again to life,
    Fond of our prison and our clay.

3 Oh! if my Lord would come and meet,
    My soul should stretch her wings in haste,
Fly fearless through death's iron gate,
    Nor feel the terrors as they pass'd.

4 Jesus can make a dying bed
    Feel soft as downy pillows are,

While on his breast I lean my head,
And breathe my life out sweetly there.

215   C. M.   [DUBLIN.

THEE we adore, Eternal Name!
And humbly own to thee,
How feeble is our mortal frame,
What dying worms are we!

2 Our wasting lives grow shorter still,
As months and days increase;
And every beating pulse we tell,
Leaves but the number less.

3 The year rolls round, and steals away
The breath that first it gave;
Whate'er we do, where'er we be,
We're trav'ling to the grave.

4 Dangers stand thick thro' all the ground,
To push us to the tomb;
And fierce diseases wait around,
To hurry mortals home.

5 Good God! on what a slender thread
Hangs everlasting things!
Th' eternal state of all the dead
Upon life's feeble strings!

6 Infinite joy, or endless woe;
Attends on every breath;
And yet how unconcerned we go
Upon the brink of death.

7 Waken, O Lord, our drowsy sense
To walk this dang'rous road:

And if our souls are hurried hence,
May they be found with God.

216 L. M. [SALEM.

REMEMBER, Lord, our mortal state,
How frail our life, how short the date!
Where is the man that draws his breath,
Safe from disease, secure from death!

2 Lord, while we see whole nations die,
Our flesh and strength repine and cry,
"Must death forever rage and reign?
Or hast thou made mankind in vain?

3 "Where is thy promise to the just?
Are not thy servants turned to dust?"
But faith forbids these mournful sighs,
And sees the sleeping dust arise.

4 That glorious hour that dreadful day,
Wipes the reproach of saints away,
And clears the honor of thy word;
Awake our souls, and bless the Lord.

217 L. M. [WINDHAM.

THROUGH every age, eternal God,
Thou art our rest, our safe abode;
High was thy throne ere heaven was made
Or earth, thy humble footstool, laid.

2 Long hadst thou reigned ere time began,
Or dust was fashioned into man:
And long thy kingdom shall endure
When earth and time shall be no more.

3 But man, weak man, is born to die,
  Made up of guilt and vanity;
  Thy dreadful sentence, Lord, was just,
  "Return, ye sinners, to your dust."

4 A thousand years of ours amount
  Scarce to a day in thine account;
  Like yesterday's departing light,
  Or the last watch of ending night.

5 Death, like an overflowing stream,
  Sweeps us away; our life's a dream;
  An empty tale; a morning flower,
  Cut down and withered in an hour.

6 Our age to seventy years is set;
  How short the time, how frail the state!
  And if to eighty we arrive,
  We rather sigh and groan than live.

7 But oh, how oft thy wrath appears,
  And cuts off our expected years!
  Thy wrath awakes our humble dread!
  We fear the Power that strikes us dead.

8 Teach us, O Lord, how frail is man;
  And kindly lengthen out the span,
  Till a wise care of piety
  Fits us to die and dwell with thee.

218   C. M.   [MENDOTA.

LORD, must I die? O let me die
  Trusting in thee alone!
My living testimony given!
  Then leave my dying one!

2 If I must die—O let me die,
   In peace with all mankind;
And change these fleeting joys below
   For pleasures all refined.

3 If I must die—as die I must—
   Let some kind seraph come,
And bear me on his friendly wing
   To my celestial home!

4 Of Canaan's land from Pisgah's top,
   May I but have a view;
Though Jordan should o'erflow its banks,
   I'll boldly venture through.

219   C. M.   [DUBLIN

WHEN blooming youth is snatched
   By death's resistless hand, [away
Our hearts the mournful tribute pay,
   Which pity must demand.

2 While pity prompts the rising sigh,
   Oh, may this truth imprest
With awful power—"I too must die!"
   Sink deep in every breast.

3 Let this vain world engage no more;
   Behold the gaping tomb;
It bids us seize the present hour:
   To-morrow death may come.

4 The voice of this alarming scene
   May every heart obey;
Nor be the heavenly warning vain,
   Which calls to watch and pray.

5 O let us fly, to Jesus, fly,
    Whose powerful arm can save;
Then shall our hopes ascend on high,
    And triumph o'er the grave.

6 Great God! thy sov'reign grace impart,
    With cleansing, healing power;
This only can prepare the heart
    For death's surprising hour.

JUDGMENT.

220   C. M.   [DUNLAP'S CREEK.

SING to the Lord, ye heavenly hosts,
    And thou, O earth adore;
Let death and hell, through all their
    Stand trembling at his power. [coasts,

2 His sounding chariot shakes the sky,
    He makes the clouds his throne;
There all his stores of lightning lie
    Till vengeance darts them down.

3 His nostrils breathe out fiery streams,
    And from his awful tongue,
A sovereign voice divides the flames,
    And thunders roar along.

4 Think, O my soul, the dreadful day,
    When this incensed God
Shall rend the skies and burn the seas,
    And fling his wrath abroad.

JUDGMENT.   195

5 What shall the wretch, the sinner do?
    He once defied the Lord?
But he shall dread the Thund'rer now,
    And sink beneath his word.

6 Tempests of angry fire shall roll,
    To blast the rebel worm,
And beat upon his naked soul
    In one eternal storm.

221   Metre 4.   [Melody.

SINNERS, take the friendly warning—
    Soon that awful day shall break,
And the trumpet with its dawning,
    All the slumb'ring millions wake.

2 See assembled every nation!
    Lofty cities, temples, towers,
Wrapped in dreadful conflagration,
    Earth and sea the flame devours.

3 Ye who to the world dissemble,
    While you practice deeds of night,
Sinners, now behold and tremble,
    All your crimes are brought to light.

4 Lost in ease or carnal pleasure,
    Sporting on the burning brink;
Now you say you have no leisure,
    You can find no time to think.

5 Ye who now conviction stifling,
    Waste your time, the loss deplore;
Hear the angel—cease your trifling—
    "Time," he cries, "shall be no more."

6 Pause and hear the voice of reason;
  Catch the moments as they fly;
You who lose the present season.
  You must all find time to die.

222 C. M. [DUNLAP'S CREEK.

AND must I be to judgment brought,
  And answer in that day,
For every vain and idle thought,
  And every word I say?

2 Yes, every secret of my heart
    Shall shortly be made known,
  And I receive my just desert
    For all that I have done.

3 How careful then ought I to live;
    With what religious fear,
  Who such a strict account must give
    For my behavior here!

4 Thou awful Judge of quick and dead,
    The watchful pow'r bestow;
  So shall I to my ways take heed,
    To all I speak or do.

5 If now thou standest at the door,
    O let me feel thee near!
  And make my peace with God, before
    I at thy bar appear.

223 METRE 7. [MERRICK.

DAY of judgment! day of wonders!
  Hark! the trumpet's awful sound,

JUDGMENT. 197

Louder than a thousand thunders,
  Shake the vast creation round;
    How the summons
Will the sinners heart confound!

2 See the Judge our nature wearing,
  Clothed in majesty divine!
You who long for his appearing,
  Then shall say, "This God is mine!"
    Gracious Savior,
Own me in that day for thine!

3 At his call the dead awaken,
  Rise to life from earth and sea;
All the pow'rs of nature shaken,
  By his looks prepare to flee;
    Careless sinner,
What will then become of thee?

4 Horrors past imagination,
  Will surprise your trembling hearts,
When you hear your condemnation,
  "Hence, accursed wretch depart!
    Thou with Satan
And his angels, have thy part!"

5 But to those who have confessed,
  Loved and served the Lord below,
He will say, "Come near, ye blessed,
  See the kingdom I bestow!
    You forever
Shall my love and glory know,"

6 Under sorrows and reproaches,
  May this thought our courage raise;

Swiftly God's great day approaches,
  Sighs will then be changed to praise!
    May we triumph,
When the world is in a blaze!

224   Metre 7.   [Happy Zion.

LO! he comes in clouds descending,
  Once for favored sinners slain!
Thousand thousand saints attending,
  Swell the triumph of his train!
    Hallelujah!
Jesus now shall ever reign!

2 Every eye shall now behold him
  Robed in dreadful majesty;
Those who set at naught and sold him,
  Pierced and nailed him to the tree,
    Deeply wailing,
Shall the great Messiah see!

3 Every island, sea, and mountain,
  Heaven and earth shall flee away;
All who hate him, must confounded,
  Hear the trump proclaim the day
    Come, to judgment!
Come to judgment, come away!

4 Now redemption long expected,
  See in solemn pomp appear!
All his saints by man rejected,
  Now shall meet him in the air!
    Hallelujah!
See the day of God appear!

5 Answer thine own Bride and Spirit!
  Hasten, Lord, the general doom!

JUDGMENT. 199

    The new heaven and earth t' inherit,
      Take thy pining exiles home:
        All creation
      Travails, groans, and bids thee come!
6 Yea, Amen! let all adore thee,
      High on thine exalted throne!
    Savior, take the power and glory:
      Claim the kingdom for thine own!
        O come quickly!
    Hallelujah! come, Lord, come!

225   METRE 7.   [MERRICK.

LO! he cometh! countless trumpets
    Blow to raise the sleeping dead:
'Mid ten thousand saints and angels,
    See their great exalted Head:
      Hallelujah
Welcome, welcome, Son of God!
2 Now his merit, by the harpers,
    Through th' eternal deep resounds;
Now resplendent shine his nail prints,
    Every eye shall see his wounds:
      They who pierced him
Shall at his appearance wail.
3 Full of joyful expectation,
    Saints, behold the Judge appear;
Truth and justice go before him,
    Now the joyful sentence hear,
      Hallelujah!
Welcome, welcome, Judge Divine!
4 "Come, ye blessed of my Father,
    Enter into life and joy!

Banish all your fears and sorrows:
 Endless praise be your employ!
  Hallelujah!
Welcome, welcome to the skies!

5 Now at once they rise to glory,
 Jesus brings them to the King;
There, with all the hosts of heaven,
 They eternal anthems sing;
  Hallelujah!
Boundless glory to the Lamb!

VANITY OF EARTHLY THINGS.

226   C. M.   [MEMPHIS.

WHY doth the man of riches grow
 To insolence and pride,
To see his wealth and honors flow
 With every rising tide?

2 Why doth he treat the poor with scorn,
 Made of the self-same clay;
And boasts, as though his flesh were born
 Of better dust than they?

3 Not all his treasures can procure
 His soul a short reprieve,
Redeem from death one guilty hour,
 Or make his brother live.

4 Eternal life can ne'er be sold,
 The ransom is too high;

Justice will ne'er be bribed with gold,
  That man may never die.

5 He sees the brutish and the wise,
  The tim'rous and the brave,
Quit their possessions, close their eyes,
  And hasten to the grave;

6 Yet 't is his inward thought and pride,
  "My house shall ever stand;
And that my name may long abide,
  I'll give it to my land."

7 Vain are his thoughts, his hopes are lost,
  How soon his mem'ry dies!
His name is buried in the dust
  Where his own body lies.

8 This is the folly of their way;
  And yet their sons, as vain,
Approve the words their fathers say,
  And act their works again.

9 Men, void of wisdom and of grace,
  Though honor raise them high,
Live like the beasts, a thoughtless race,
  And like the beasts they die.

10 Laid in the grave, like silly sheep,
  Death triumphs o'er them there,
Till the last trumpet breaks their sleep,
  And wakes them in despair.

227   C. M.   [SOLON.

HOW vain are all things here below,
  How false, and yet how fair!

Each pleasure has its poison too,
  And every sweet a snare.

2 The brightest things below the sky
   Give but a flatt'ring light;
  We should suspect some danger nigh
   Where we possess delight.

3 Our dearest joys and nearest friends,
   The partners of our blood,
  How they divide our wav'ring minds,
   And leave but half for God!

4 The fondness of a creature's love,
   How strong it strikes the sense!
  Thither the warm affections move,
   Nor can we call them thence.

5 Dear Savior! let thy beauties be
   My soul's eternal food;
  And grace command my heart away
   From all created good.

HEAVENLY JOY.

228   C. M.   [BROWN.

THERE is a house not made with hands,
   Eternal, and on high;
  And here my Spirit waiting stands,
   Till God shall bid it fly.

2 Shortly this prison of my clay
    Must be dissolved and fall;
Then, O my soul, with joy obey
    Thy heavenly Father's call.

3 'T is he, by his Almighty grace,
    That forms thee fit for heaven;
And as an earnest of the place,
    Has his own Spirit given.

4 We walk by faith of joys to come;
    Faith lives upon his word;
But while the body is our home,
    We're absent from the Lord.

5 'T is pleasant to believe thy grace;
    But we had rather see;
We would be absent from the flesh,
    And present, Lord, with thee.

229   S. M.   [SPRAGUE.

COME, we that love the Lord,
    And let our joys be known:
Join in a song with sweet accord,
    And thus surround the throne.

2 The sorrows of the mind,
    Be banished from the place!
Religion never was designed
    To make our pleasures less.

3 Let those refuse to sing
    Who never knew our God;
But fav'rites of the heavenly King
    May speak their joys abroad.

4 The God that rules on high,
   And thunders when he please,
Who rides upon the stormy sky,
   And manages the seas:
5 This awful God is ours,
   Our Father and our love,
He shall send down his heavenly powers
   To carry us above.
6 There shall we see his face,
   And never, never sin:
There from the rivers of his grace,
   Drink endless pleasures in.
7 Yes, and before we rise
   To that immortal state,
The thoughts of such amazing bliss
   Should constant joys create.
8 The men of grace have found
   Glory begun below,
Celestial fruit on earthly ground,
   From faith and hope may grow.
9 The hill of Zion yields
   A thousand sacred sweets,
Before we reach the heavenly fields,
   Or walk the golden streets.
10 Then let our songs abound,
   And every tear be dry;
We're marching thro' Immanuel's ground
   To fairer worlds on high.

230   C. M.   [ATWATER.

ON Jordan's stormy banks I stand,
   And cast a wishful eye

To Canaan's fair and happy land,
  Where my possessions lie.

2 Oh the transporting, rapt'rous scene,
  That rises to my sight:
Sweet fields arrayed in living green,
  And rivers of delight!

3 There gen'rous fruits that never fail,
  On trees immortal grow:
There rock, and hill, and brook, and vale,
  With milk and honey flow.

4 All o'er those wide extended plains
  Shines one eternal day:
There God the Son forever reigns,
  And scatters night away.

5 No chilling winds, nor pois'nous breath
  Can reach that healthful shore:
Sickness and sorrow, pain and death,
  Are felt and feared no more.

6 When shall I reach that happy place,
  And be forever blest?
When shall I see my Father's face,
  And in his bosom rest?

7 Filled with delight, my raptured soul
  Can here no longer stay;
Though Jordan's waves around me roll,
  Fearless I'd launch away.

231   C. M.   [SALVATION.

EARTH has engrossed my love too long!
  'T is time I lift mine eyes.

HEAVENLY JOY.

Upward, dear Father, to thy throne,
   And to my native skies.

2 There the blest Man, my Savior sits,
   The God! how bright he shines!
  And scatters infinite delight
   On all the happy minds.

3 Seraphs with elevated strains,
   Circle the throne around,
  And move and charm the starry plains
   With an immortal sound.

4 Jesus, the Lord, their harps employs:
   Jesus, my love, they sing;
  Jesus the life of both our joys,
   Sounds sweet from every string.

5 Hark! how beyond the narrow bounds
   Of time and space they run,
  And echo in majestic sounds
   The Godhead of the Son.

6 And now they sink the lofty tune,
   And gentler notes they play;
  And bring the Father's Equal down
   To dwell in humble clay.

7 O sacred beauties of the Man!
   (The God resides within;)
  His flesh all pure, without a stain,
   His soul without a sin.

8 But when to Calvary they turn,
   Silent their harps abide;
  Suspended songs, a moment, mourn
   The God that loved and died.

9 Then all at once to living strains
   They summon every chord;
Tell how he triumphed o'er his pains,
   And chant the rising Lord.

10 Now let me mount and join their song,
   And be an angel, too;
My heart, my hand, my ear, my tongue—
   Here's joyful work for you.

11 I would begin the music here,
   And so my soul should rise;
O for some heavenly notes, to bear
   My passions to the skies!

12 Where ye that love my Savior, sit,
   There I would fain have place,
Among your thrones, or at your feet
   So I might see his face.

232   C. M.   [Woodland.

From thee, my God, my joys shall rise,
   And run eternal rounds,
Beyond the limits of the skies,
   And all created bounds.

2 The holy triumphs of my soul
   Shall death itself outbrave;
Leave dull mortality behind,
   And fly beyond the grave.

3 There, where my blessed Jesus reigns,
   In heaven's unmeasured space,
I'll spend a long eternity
   In pleasure and in praise.

4 Millions of years my wond'ring eyes
   Shall o'er thy beauties rove,
And endless ages I'll adore
   The glories of thy love.

5 Sweet Jesus! every smile of thine
   Shall fresh endearments bring;
And thousand tastes of new delight
   From all thy graces spring.

7 Haste, my Beloved, bear my soul
   Up to thy blest abode;
Fly, for my spirit longs to see
   My Savior and my God.

233   L. M.   [DEVOTION.

O FOR a sweet, inspiring ray.
   To animate our feeble strains,
From the bright realms of endless day,
   The blissful realms where Jesus reigns.

2 There low before his glorious throne,
   Adoring saints and angels fall;
And, with delightful worship, own, .[all.
   His smile, their bliss, their heav'n, their

3 Immortal glories crown his head,
   While tuneful hallelujahs rise;
And love and joy and triumph spread
   Through all th' assemblies of the skies.

4 He smiles, and seraphs tune their songs
   To boundless rapture while they gaze;
Ten thousand thousand joyful tongues
   Resound his everlasting praise.

5 There all the favorites of the Lamb
    Shall join at last the heavenly choir;
Oh, may the joy-inspiring theme
    Awake our faith and warm desire.

6 Dear Savior, let thy Spirit seal
    Our int'rest in that blissful place,
Till death remove this mortal veil,
    And we behold thy lovely face.

234   Metre 20.   [Howard.

OH! how happy are they,
    Who their Savior obey,
And have laid up their treasures above!
    Oh! what tongue can express
    The sweet comfort and peace
Of a soul in its earliest love?

2 'T was a heaven below,
    My Redeemer to know;
And the angels could do nothing more,
    Than to fall at his feet,
    And the story repeat,
And the Lover of sinners adore.

3 Jesus, all the day long,
    Was my joy and my song:
Oh! that more his salvation might see!
    He hath loved me I cried;
    He hath suffered and died,
To redeem such a rebel as me!

4 Now my remnant of days
    Would I spend in his praise,
Who hath died, me from death to redeem;

HEAVENLY JOY.

Whether many or few.
All my days are his due—
May they all be devoted to him.

5 What a mercy is this!
What a heaven of bliss!
How unspeakably happy am I!
Gathered into the fold,
With believers enrolled—
With believers to live and to die.

6 Lo! the day's drawing nigh.
When my soul, thou shalt fly
To the place thy salvation began—
Where the Three and the One,
Father, Spirit, and Son,
Laid the scheme of redemption for man.

235   C. M.   [JEROME.

JERUSALEM! my happy home,
  Name ever dear to me!
When shall my labors have an end,
  In joy and peace and thee!

2 When shall these eyes thy heav'n-built
  And pearly gates behold?   [walls
Thy bulwarks with salvation strong,
  And streets of shining gold?

3 O when, thou city of my God,
  Shall I thy courts ascend,
Where congregations ne'er break up,
  And Sabbath has no end?

4 There happier bowers, than Eden's, bloom,
  Nor sin nor sorrow know:

Blest seats! through rude and stormy
   I onward press to you.   [scenes,

5 Why should I shrink at pain or woe,
   Or feel, at death, dismay?
I've Canaan's goodly land in view,
   And realms of endless day.

6 Apostles, martyrs, prophets, there,
   Around my Savior stand;
And soon my friends in Christ below
   Will join the glorious band.

7 Jerusalem, my happy home!
   My soul still pants for thee;
Then shall my labors have an end,
   When I thy joys shall see.

236   METRE 12.   [GREENFIELDS.

AWAY with our sorrow and fear,
   We soon shall recover our home:
The city of saints shall appear;
   The day of eternity come.
From earth we shall quickly remove,
   And mount to our native abode;
The house of our Father above—
   The palace of angels and God.

2 Our mourning is all at an end,
   When, raised by the life-giving Word,
We see the new city descend,
   Adorned as a bride for her Lord:
The city, so holy and clean,
   No sorrow can breathe in the air;
No gloom of affliction or sin;
   No shadow of evil is there.

HEAVENLY JOY.

3 By faith we already behold
   That lovely Jerusalem here;
Her walls are of jasper and gold,
   As crystals, her buildings are clear;
Immovably founded in grace,
   She stands as she ever hath stood,
And brightly her Builder displays,
   And flames with the glory of God.

4 No need of the sun in that day,
   Which never is followed by night,
Where beauties of Jesus display
   A pure and a permanent light.
The Lamb is their light and their Sun,
   And lo! by reflection they shine;
With Jesus ineffably one,
   And bright in effulgence divine.

5 The saints in his presence receive
   Their great and eternal reward;
In Jesus, in heaven they live;
   They reign in the smile of their Lord.
The flame of angelical love
   Is kindled at his holy face;
And all the enjoyment above
   Consists in the rapturous gaze.

237   Metre 11.   [Frederick.

I WOULD not live alway; I ask not to stay
  Where storm after storm rises dark o'er the way;
The few cloudy mornings that dawn on us here,
Enough for life's woes, full enough for its cheer.

2 I would not live alway, thus fettered by sin,
Temptation without and corruption within;

Where rapture of pardon is mingled with fears,
The cup of thanksgiving with penitent tears.

3 I would not live alway ; no—welcome the tomb—
Since Jesus hath lain there I'll enter its gloom ;
There sweet be my rest till he bid me arise,
To hail him in triumph descending the skies.

4 Who, who would live alway, away from his God,
Away from yon heaven, that blissful abode,
Where rivers of pleasure flow o'er the bright
        plains,
And noontide of glory eternally reigns.

5 There saints of all ages in harmony meet,
Their Savior and brethren transported to greet ;
While anthems of rapture unceasingly roll,
The smile of the Lord is the feast of the soul.

238   Metre 7.   [Happy Zion.

SEE, from Zion's sacred mountain,
  Streams of living waters flow ;
God has opened there a fountain ;
  This supplies the plains below ;
    They are blessed,
  Who its sov'reign virtues know.

2 Through ten thousand channels flowing,
  Streams of mercy find their way ;
Life and health and joy bestowing,
  Making all around look gay,
    O, ye nations!
Hail the long expected day.

3 Gladdened by the flowing treasure,
   All enriching as it goes:
Lo, the desert smiles with pleasure,
   Buds and blossoms as the rose;
     Every object
Sings for joy where'er it flows.

4 Trees of life the banks adorning,
   Yield their fruit to all around;
Those who eat are saved from mourning;
   Pleasures come and hopes abound;
     Fair their portion!
Endless life with glory crowned.

239   C. M. [DUNLAP'S CREEK.

"THESE glorious minds, how bright they shine!
   Whence all their white array?
How came they to the happy seats
   Of everlasting day?"

2 From torturing pains to endless joys,
   On fiery wheels they rode,
And strangely washed their raiment
   In Jesus' dying blood.   [white

3 Now they approach a spotless God,
   And bow before his throne;
Their warbling harps and sacred songs,
   Adore the Holy One.

4 The unveiled glories of his face
   Among his saints reside,
While the rich treasure of his grace
   Sees all their wants supplied.

5 Tormenting thirst shall leave their souls,
    And hunger flee as fast;
The fruit of life's immortal tree
    Shall be their sweet repast.

6 The Lamb shall lead his heavenly flock
    Where living fountains rise;
And love divine shall wipe away
    The sorrows of their eyes.

240   C. M.   [JEROME.

LO, what a glorious sight appears
    To our believing eyes!
The earth and seas are passed away,
    And the old rolling skies.

2 From the third heaven where God re-
    That holy, happy place,   [sides,
The New Jerusalem comes down,
    Adorned with shining grace.

3 Attending angels shout for joy,
    And the bright armies sing,
"Mortals, behold the sacred seat
    Of your descending King.

4 "The God of glory down to men
    Removes his blest abode:
Men, the dear objects of his grace,
    And he, the loving God.

5 "His own soft hand shall wipe the tears
    From every weeping eye;
And pains and groans and griefs and fears
    And death itself shall die."

6 How long, dear Savior, O how long
  Shall this bright hour delay?
Fly swiftly round, ye wheels of time,
  And bring the welcome day.

BREATHING AFTER GOD AND HOLINESS.

241   Metre 15.   [Beloved.

O THOU, in whose presence my soul takes delight,
  On whom in affliction I call,
My comfort by day, and my song in the night,
  My hope, my salvation, my all.

2 Where dost thou at noontide resort with thy sheep,
  To feed on the pastures of love?
For why in the valley of death should I weep?
  Alone in the wilderness rove!

3 O! why should I wander an alien from thee,
  And cry in the desert for bread?
My foes will rejoice when my sorrows they see,
  And smile at the tears I have shed.

4 Ye daughters of Zion, declare, have you seen
  The star that on Israel shone?
Say, if in your tents my Beloved has been,
  And where with his flock he has gone?

5 This is my Beloved; his form is divine;
  His vestments shed odors around:
The locks on his head are as grapes on the vine
  When autumn with plenty is crowned.

6 The roses of Sharon, the lilies that grow
  In vales, on the banks of the stream.
His cheeks in the beauty of excellence glow,
  His eyes all invitingly beam.

7 His voice as the sound of a dulcimer sweet,
  Is heard through the shadows of death;
The cedars of Lebanon bow at his feet,
  The air is perfumed with his breath;

8 His lips as a fountain of righteousness, flow,
  That waters the garden of grace.   [know,
From which their salvation the Gentiles shall
  And bask in the smiles of his face.

9 Love sits in his eyelids, and scatters delight
  Through all the bright mansions on high;
Their faces the cherubim veil in his sight,
  And tremble with fullness of joy.

10 He looks, and ten thousand of angels rejoice,
  And myriads wait for his word;
He speaks, and eternity, filled with his voice,
  Re-echoes the praise of her Lord.

11 His vestment of righteousness who shall describe?
  Its purity words would defile:
The heavens from his presence fresh beauties imbibe,
  And earth is made rich by his smile.

12 Such is my Beloved, in excellence bright,
  When pleased, he looks down from above.

(Like the morn when it breathes from the cham-
    bers of light,)
And comforts his people with love.

242   S. M.   [SPRAGUE.

ALMIGHTY Maker, God!
　How wondrous is thy name!
Thy glories now diffused abroad
　Through the creation's frame!

2 Nature in every dress,
　　Her humble homage pays;
　And finds a thousand ways t' express
　　Thine undissembled praise.

3 My soul would rise and sing
　　To her Creator, too;
　Fain would my tongue adore my King,
　　And pay the worship due.

4 But pride, that busy sin,
　　Spoils all that I perform,
　Cursed pride, that creeps securely in,
　　And swells a haughty worm.

5 Create my soul anew,
　　Else all my worship's vain;
　This wretched heart will ne'er be true,
　　Until 't is formed again.

6 Let joy and worship spend
　　The remnant of my days;
　And to my God my soul ascend,
　　In sweet perfumes of praise.

243   C. M.   [FAREWELL.

WHEN I can read my title clear,
    To mansions in the skies,
I'll bid farewell to every fear,
    And wipe my weeping eyes.

2 Should earth against my soul engage,
    And hellish darts be hurled.
Then I can smile at Satan's rage,
    And face a frowning world.

3 Let cares, like a wild deluge, come,
    And storms of sorrow fall;
May I but safely reach my home,
    My God, my heaven, my all.

4 There shall I bathe my weary soul
    In seas of heavenly rest,
And not a wave of trouble roll
    Across my peaceful breast.

244   METRE 4.   [NETTLETON.

COME, thou Fount of every blessing,
    Tune my heart to sing thy grace;
Streams of mercy never ceasing,
    Call for songs of loudest praise:
Teach me some melodious sonnet,
    Sung by flaming tongues above;
Praise the mount—I'm fixed upon it—
    Mount of thy redeeming love.

2 Here I'll raise mine Ebenezer,
    Hither by thy help I'm come;
And I hope by thy good pleasure,
    Safely to arrive at home.

Jesus sought me when a stranger,
  Wand'ring from the fold of God;
He to rescue me from danger,
  Interposed his precious blood.

3 O! to grace how great a debtor,
  Daily I'm constrained to be;
Let thy goodness like a fetter,
  Bind my wand'ring heart to thee;
Prone to wander, Lord, I feel it;
  Prone to leave the God I love—
Here's my heart, O take and seal it:
  Seal it for thy courts above.

245   L. M.   [TENDER THOUGHT.

ARISE, my tend'rest thoughts, arise;
  To torrents melt my streaming eyes;
And thou, my heart, with anguish feel
Those evils which thou canst not heal.

2 See human nature sunk in shame;
See scandals poured on Jesus' name;
The Father wounded through the Son;
The world abused, the soul undone.

3 See the short course of vain delight,
Closing in everlasting night—
In flames that no abatement know,
Though briny tears forever flow.

4 My God, I feel the mournful scene;
My bowels yearn o'er dying men;
And fain my pity would reclaim,
And snatch the firebrands from the flame.

5 But feeble my compassion proves,
  And can but weep where most it loves;
  Thy own all-saving arm employ,
  And turn those drops of grief to joy.

246   Metre 5.   [Brian.

TELL me, Savior, from above,
  Dearest object of my love,
Where thy little flock abide,
Sheltered near thy bleeding side!

2 Tell me, Shepherd, all divine,
  Where I may my soul recline;
  Where for refuge I shall fly,
  While the burning sun is high!

3 Wilt thou let me run astray,
  Mourning, grieving all the day?
  Wilt thou bear to see me rove,
  Seeking base and mortal love?

4 Never had I sought thy name,
  Never felt the inward flame,
  Had not love first touched my heart
  With the painful pleasing smart.

5 Didst thou leave thy glorious throne,
  Put a mortal raiment on,
  On the tree a victim die,
  For a wretch so vile as I?

247   C. M.   [Devizes.

MY Savior, my Almighty Friend,
  When I begin thy praise,

Where will the growing numbers end,
    The numbers of thy grace?

2 Thou art my everlasting trust,
    Thy goodness I adore;
And since I knew thy graces first,
    I speak thy glories more.

3 My feet shall travel all the length
    Of the celestial road,
And march with courage in thy strength,
    To see my Father, God.

4 When I am filled with sore distress
    For some surprising sin,
I'll plead thy perfect righteousness,
    And mention none but thine.

5 How will my lips rejoice to tell
    The victories of my king?
My soul, redeemed from sin and hell,
    Shall thy salvation sing.

6 My tongue shall all the day proclaim
    My Savior and my God;
His death has brought my foes to shame,
    And saved me by his blood.

7 Awake, awake, my tuneful powers;
    With this delightful song
I'll entertain the darkest hours,
    Nor think the seasons long.

248   C. M.   [BELMONT.

OH, that I had a bosom friend,
    To tell my secrets to;

On whose advice I might depend,
In every thing I do!

2 How do I wander up and down,
And no one pities me!
I seem a stranger quite unknown,
A son of misery.

3 None lends an ear to my complaint,
Nor minds my cries and tears;
None comes to help me though I faint,
Nor my vast burden bears.

4 While others live in mirth and ease,
And feel no want nor woe,
Through this dark, howling wilderness
I full of sorrow go.

5 O faithless soul to reason thus,
And murmur without end!
Did Christ expire upon the cross,
And is he not thy friend?

6 Why dost thou envy carnal men,
And think their state so blest?
How great salvation hast thou seen,
And Jesus is thy rest!

7 What can this lower world afford,
Compared with gospel grace?
Thy happiness is in the Lord,
And thou shalt see his face.

8 Can present griefs be counted great
Compared with future woes?
Will transient pleasures seem so sweet,
Compared with endless joys?

9 How soon will God withdraw the scene,
   And burn the world he made!
   Then woe to carnal, careless men;
   My soul, lift up thine head.

10 Thy Savior is thy real Friend,
   Constant and true and good;
   He will be with thee to the end,
   And bring thee safe to God.

11 What then, my soul, hast thou to fear?
   Or why shouldst thou repine?
   Look up, behold redemption's near,
   Rejoice, for heaven is thine.

12 Why, O my soul, art thou so sad?
   When will thy sighs be o'er?
   Rejoice in Jesus, and be glad,
   Rejoice for evermore.

249   C. M.   [Solon

MY God, the spring of all my joys,
   The life of my delights,
The glories of my brightest days,
   And comfort of my nights.

2 In darkest shades, if he appear,
   My dawning is begun;
He is my soul's bright morning star,
   And he my Rising Sun.

3 The op'ning heavens around me shine
   With beams of sacred bliss;
While Jesus shows his heart is mine,
   And whispers, "I am his."

4 My soul would leave this heavy clay,
   At that transporting word,
Run up, with joy, the shining way,
   T' embrace my dearest Lord.

5 Fearless of hell and ghastly death,
   I'd break through every foe;
The wings of love and arms of faith,
   Should bear me conq'ror through.

259   L. M.   [TREMONT—PORTUGAL.

HOW pleasant, how divinely fair,
   O Lord of hosts, thy dwellings are!
With long desire my spirit faints,
To meet th' assemblies of thy saints.

2 My flesh would rest in thine abode;
My panting heart cries out for God;
My God! my king! why should I be
So far from all my joys and thee?

3 The sparrow chooses where to rest,
And for her young provide her nest;
But will my God to sparrows grant
That pleasure which his children want?

4 Blest are the saints who sit on high,
Around thy throne above the sky;
Thy brightest glories shine above,
And all their work is praise and love.

5 Blest are the souls who find a place
Within the temple of thy grace:
There they behold thy gentler rays,
And seek thy face and learn thy praise.

6 Blest are the men whose hearts are set
   To find the way to Zion's gate;   [road
 God is their strength; and through the
   They lean upon their helper, God.

7 Cheerful they walk with growing strength
   Till all shall meet in heaven at length;
 Till all before thy face appear,
   And join in nobler worship there.

251   C. M.   [Detroit.

FATHER, I long, I faint to see
   The place of thine abode:
 I'd leave these earthly courts, and flee
   Up to thy seat, my God!

2 Here I behold thy distant face.
   And 't is a pleasing sight;
 But to abide in thine embrace,
   Is infinite delight.

3 I'd part with all the joys of sense,
   To gaze upon thy throne;
 Pleasure springs fresh forever thence,
   Unspeakable, unknown.

4 There all the heavenly hosts are seen,
   In shining ranks they move,
 And drink immortal vigor in,
   With wonder and with love.

5 Then, at thy feet, with awful fear,
   Th' adoring armies fall;
 With joy they shrink to nothing there
   Before th' eternal All.

6 There I would vie with all the host,
   In duty and in bliss;
While less than nothing I could boast,
   And vanity confess.
7 The more thy glories strike mine eyes,
   The humbler I shall lie;
Thus, while I sink, my joys shall rise
   Immeasurably high.

252   C. M.   [ATONEMENT.

O LAND of rest, for thee I sigh,
   When will the moment come,
When I shall lay my armor by,
   And dwell in peace at home?

CHORUS.

O this is not my home—
   No, this is not my home;
This world's a wilderness of woe—
   This world is not my home.

2 No tranquil joys on earth I know,
   No peaceful sheltering dome;
This world's a wilderness of woe—
   This world is not my home,
      O, this is not my home, &c.
3 To Jesus Christ I sought for rest,
   He bid me cease to roam,
And fly for refuge to his breast,
   And he'd conduct me home.
      O, this is not my home, &c.
4 I would at once have quit the field,
   Where foes with fury roam,

But O, my passport was not sealed,—
  I could not yet go home.
    O, this is not my home, &c.

5 When by afflictions sharply tried,
  I view the gaping tomb;
Although I dread death's chilling tide,
  Yet still I sigh for home.
    O, this is not my home, &c.

6 Weary of wandering round and round
  This vale of sin and gloom,
I long to quit th' unhallowed ground,
  And dwell with Christ at home.
    O, this is not my home, &c.

253   Metre 36.   [Sweet Home.

'MID scenes of confusion and creature complaints,
How sweet to my soul is communion with saints;
To find at the banquet of mercy there's room,
And feel, in the presence of Jesus, at home,
  Home, home, sweet, sweet home,
Receive me, dear Savior, in glory my home.

2 Sweet bonds that unite all the children of peace,
And thrice, precious Jesus whose love cannot
    cease:
Though oft from thy presence in sadness I roam,
I long to behold thee, in glory at home.
  Home, home, sweet, sweet home,
Receive me, dear Savior, in glory my home.

4 I sigh from this body of sin to be free,
Which hinders my joy and communion with thee:

Though now my temptations like billows may foam,
All, all will be peace, when I'm with thee at home,
   Home, home, sweet, sweet home,
Receive me, dear Savior, in glory, my home.

4 While here in the valley of conflict I stay,
O give me submission and strength as my day;
In all my afflictions to thee would I come,
Rejoicing in hope of my glorious home.
   Home, home, sweet, sweet home,
Receive me, dear Savior, in glory, my home.

5 Whate'er thou deniest, O give me thy grace;
The Spirit's sure witness, and smiles of thy face;
Indulge me with patience to wait till thou come,
And find even now a sweet foretaste of home.
   Home, home, sweet, sweet home,
Receive me, dear Savior, in glory, my home.

6 I long, dearest Lord, in thy beauties to shine,
No more, as an exile, in sorrow to pine,
And in thy fair image, arise from the tomb,
With glorified millions, to praise thee at home,
   Home, home, sweet, sweet home,
Receive me, dear Savior, in glory, my home.

7 The days of my exile are passing away,
The time is approaching when Jesus will say,
Well done, faithful servant, sit down on my throne,
And dwell in my presence forever at home.
   Home, home, sweet, sweet home,
O, there I shall rest with my Savior at home.

254   C. M.   [SALVATION.

HEAR, gracious God, my humble moan,
  To thee I breathe my sighs;
When will the mournful night be gone?
  And when my joys arise?

2 My God—O could I make the claim—
  My Father and my Friend—
And call thee mine by every name,
  On which thy saints depend!

3 By every name of power and love,
  I would thy grace entreat;
Nor should my humble hopes remove,
  Nor leave thy sacred seat.

4 Yet though my soul in darkness mourns,
  Thy word is all my stay;
Here I would rest till light returns,
  Thy presence makes my day.

5 Speak, Lord, and bid celestial peace
  Relieve my aching heart:
O smile and bid my sorrows cease,
  And all the gloom depart.

6 Then shall my drooping spirit rise,
  And bless the healing rays,
And change these deep complaining sighs
  For songs of sacred praise.

255   METRE 13.   [WARNING VOICE.

RISE, my soul, and stretch thy wings,
  Thy better portion trace;

Rise from transitory things,
  Tow'rd heav'n, thy native place!
Sun and moon and stars decay;
  Time shall soon this earth remove;
Rise, my soul, and haste away
  To seats prepared above.

2 Rivers to the ocean run,
  Nor stay in all their course:
Fire ascending seeks the sun;
  Both speed them to their source;
Thus a soul new-born of God,
  Pants to view his glorious face;
Upward tends to his abode,
  To rest in his embrace.

3 Cease, ye pilgrims! cease to mourn;
  Press onward to the prize;
Soon our Savior will return
  Triumphant in the skies;
Yet a season, and you know
  Happy entrance will be given,—
All your sorrows left below,
  And earth exchanged for heaven.

256   Metre 4.   [Charleston.

Hail, my ever blessed Jesus,
  Only thee I wish to sing;
To my soul thy name is precious,
  Thou my Prophet, Priest, and King.

2 Oh, what mercy flows from heaven!
  Oh, what joy and happiness!
Love I much?—I've much forgiven—
  I'm a miracle of grace.

3 Once with Adam's race in ruin,
    Unconcerned in sin I lay,
  Swift destruction still pursuing,
    Till my Savior passed that way.

4 Witness, all ye hosts of heaven,
    My Redeemer's tenderness!
  Love I much?—I've much forgiven—
    I'm a miracle of grace.

5 Shout, ye bright angelic choir;
    Praise the Lamb enthroned above;
  While astonished I admire
    God's free grace and boundless love.

6 That blest moment I received him
    Filled my soul with joy and peace;
  Love I much?—I've much forgiven—
    I'm a miracle of grace.

257　　C. M.　　[MENDOTA—DUBLIN.

HOW sweet the name of Jesus sounds
    In a believer's ear!
  It soothes his sorrows, heals his wounds,
    And drives away his fear.

2 It makes the wounded spirit whole,
    And calms the troubled breast;
  'T is manna to the hungry soul,
    And to the weary rest.

3 Dear Name! the Rock on which I build,
    My shield and hiding place;
  My never failing treasure, filled
    With boundless stores of grace.

4 Jesus! my Shepherd, Husband, Friend,
   My Prophet, Priest and King;
My Lord, my Life, my Way, my End,
   Accept the praise I bring.

5 Weak is the effort of my heart,
   And cold my warmest thought;
But when I see thee as thou art,
   I'll praise thee as I ought.

6 Till then I would thy love proclaim
   With every fleeting breath;
And may the music of thy name
   Refresh my soul in death.

258   L. M.   [Majesty—New.

LORD, I am thine; but thou wilt prove
My faith, my patience, and my love;
When men of spite against me join,
They are the sword—the hand is thine.

2 Their hope and portion lie below;
'T is all the happiness they know,
'T is all they seek; they take their shares,
And leave the rest among their heirs.

3 What sinners value I resign;
Lord, 't is enough that thou art mine;
I shall behold thy blissful face,
And stand complete in righteousness.

4 This life's a dream, an empty show;
But the bright world to which I go,
Hath joys substantial and sincere:
When shall I wake and find me there?

5 O glorious hour! O blest abode!
  I shall be near and like my God;
  And flesh and sin no more control
  The sacred pleasures of the soul.

6 My flesh shall slumber in the ground,
  Till the last trumpet's joyful sound;
  Then burst the chains with sweet surprise
  And in my Savior's image rise.

259   METRE 12.   [GREENFIELDS.

THOU Shepherd of Israel and mine,
  The joy and desire of my heart,
For closer communion I pine,
  I long to reside where thou art:
The pasture I languish to find,
  Where all who their Shepherd obey,
Are fed, on thy bosom reclined,
  And screen'd from the heat of the day.

2 Ah! show me that happiest place,
  The place of thy people's abode:
Where saints in an ecstasy gaze,
  And hang on a crucified God;
Thy love for a sinner declare;
  Thy passion and death on the tree;
My spirit to Calvary bear,
  To suffer and triumph with thee.

3 'T is there with the Lambs of thy flock,
  There only I covet to rest;
To lie at the foot of the rock,
  Or rise to be hid in thy breast;
'T is there I would always abide,
  And never a moment depart;

Concealed in the cleft of thy side,
Eternally held in thy heart.

260   L. M.   [WALLOOMSAC.

O COULD I find some peaceful bower,
Where sin hath neither place nor pow'r;
This traitor vile, I fain would shun,
But cannot from his presence run.

2 When to the throne of grace I flee,
He stands between my God and me;
Where'er I rove, where'er I rest,
I feel him working in my breast.

3 When I attempt to soar above,
To view the heights of Jesus' love,
This monster seems to mount the skies,
And veils his glory from mine eyes.

4 Lord, free me from this deadly foe,
Which keeps my faith and hope so low,
I long to dwell in heaven my home,
Where not one sinful thought can come.

261   C. M.   [JEROME.

RELIGION is the chief concern
Of mortals here below;
May I its great importance learn,
Its sovereign virtue know.

2 More needful this than glittering wealth,
Or aught the world bestows;
Not reputation, food or health,
Can give us such repose.

3 Religion should our thoughts engage
    Amidst our youthful bloom;
'T will fit us for declining age,
    And for the awful tomb.

4 Oh, may my heart, by grace renewed,
    Be my Redeemer's throne.
And be my stubborn will subdued,
    His government to own!

5 Let deep repentance, faith and love,
    Be joined with godly fear;
And all my conversation prove
    My heart to be sincere.

5 Preserve me from the snares of sin.
    Through my remaining days;
And in me let each virtue shine
    To my Redeemer's praise.

7 Let lively hope my soul inspire;
    Let warm affections rise;
And may I wait with strong desire
    To mount above the skies.

262   L. M.   [HEBRON.

UP to the fields where angels lie,
    And living waters gently roll,
Fain would my thoughts leap out and fly,
    But sin hangs heavy on my soul.

2 Thy wondrous blood, dear dying Christ,
    Can make this world of guilt remove;
And thou canst bear me where thou fliest,
    On thy kind wings, celestial Dove.

3 O might I once mount up and see
    The glories of th' eternal skies;
What little things these worlds would be!
    How despicable to mine eyes.

4 Had I a glance of thee, my God,
    Kingdoms and men would vanish soon;
Vanish as though I saw them not,
    As a dim candle dies at noon.

5 Then they might fight and rage and rave,
    I should perceive the noise no more
Than we can hear a shaking leaf,
    When rattling thunders round us roar.

6 Great All in All, eternal king!
    Let me but view thy lovely face;
And all my powers shall bow, and sing
    Thine endless grandeur and thy grace.

263   L. M.   [HEALING BALM.

THOU, whom my soul admires above
    All earthly joy and earthly love;
Tell me, dear Shepherd, let me know,
Where do thy sweetest pastures grow?

2 Where is the shadow of that Rock,
That from the sun defends thy flock?
Fain would I feed among thy sheep,
Among them rest, among them sleep.

3 Why should thy bride appear like one
That turns aside to paths unknown?
My constant feet would never rove,
Would never seek another love.

4 The footsteps of thy flock I see;
  Thy sweetest pastures here they be;
  A wondrous feast thy love prepares,
  Bought with thy wounds and groans and
      tears.
5 His dearest flesh he makes my food,
  And bids me drink his richest blood:
  Here to these hills my soul would come,
  Till my beloved leads me home.

264   L. M.   [ROCKBRIDGE.

OFTEN I seek my Lord by night,
  Jesus, my Love, my soul's delight;
  With warm desire and restless thought
  I seek him oft, but find him not.
2 Then I arise and search the street,
  Till I my Lord, my Savior meet;
  I ask the watchman of the night,
  "Where did you see my soul's delight?"
3 Sometimes I find him in my way.
  Directed by a heavenly ray;
  A leap for joy to see his face,
  And hold him fast in my embrace.
4 I bring him to my mother's home;
  Nor does my Lord refuse to come
  To Zion's sacred chambers, where
  My soul first drew the vital air.
5 He gives me there his bleeding heart,
  Pierced for my sake with deadly smart;
  I give my soul to him, and there
  Our loves their mutual tokens share,

6 I charge you all, ye earthly toys,
  Approach not to disturb my joys;
Nor sin, nor hell, come near my heart,
Nor cause my Savior to depart.

265 C. M. [BROWN.

THERE is a land of pure delight,
  Where saints immortal reign;
Infinite day excludes the night,
  And pleasures banish pain.

2 There everlasting Spring abides,
  And never-with'ring flowers;
Death, like a narrow sea, divides
  This heavenly land from ours.

3 Sweet fields beyond the swelling flood,
  Stand dress'd in living green;
So to the Jews old Canaan stood,
  While Jordan rolled between.

4 But tim'rous mortals start and shrink
  To cross this narrow sea,
And linger, shiv'ring on the brink,
  And fear to launch away.

5 O, could we make our doubts remove,
  Those gloomy doubts that rise,
And see the Canaan that we love,
  With unbeclouded eyes.

6 Could we but climb where Moses stood,
  And view the landscape o'er,   [flood,
Not Jordan's stream, nor death's cold
  Should fright us from the shore.

266   L. M.   [DEVOTION.

DESCEND from heaven immortal Dove,
  Stoop down and take us on thy wings,
And mount and bear us far above
  The reach of these inferior things.

2 Beyond, beyond this lower sky,
  Up where eternal ages roll,
Where solid pleasures never die,
  And fruits immortal feast the soul.

3 O for a sight—a pleasing sight—
  Of our Almighty Father's throne;
There sits our Savior crowned with light,
  Clothed in a body like our own.

4 Adoring saints around him stand,
  And thrones and powers before him fall;
The God shines gracious through the man
  And sheds sweet glories on them all.

5 O what amazing joys they feel,
  While to their golden harps they sing,
And sit on every heavenly hill.
  And spread the triumphs of their King!

6 When shall the day, dear Lord, appear,
  That I shall mount to dwell above.
And stand and bow among them there,
  And view thy face and sing and love?

267   C. M.   [ELIZABETHTOWN.

GOD of my life, look gently down,
  Behold the pains I feel;

But I am dumb before thy throne,
  Nor dare dispute thy will.

2 Diseases are thy servants, Lord,
   They come at thy command;
 I'll not attempt a murmuring word,
   Against thy chast'ning hand.

3 Yet I may plead with humble cries,
   Remove thy sharp rebukes;
 My strength consumes, my spirit dies,
   Through thy repeated strokes.

4 Crushed as moth beneath thy hand,
   We moulder in the dust;
 Our feeble powers can ne'er withstand,
   And all our beauty's lost.

5 I'm but a stranger here below,
   As all my fathers were:
 May I be well prepared to go,
   When I thy summons hear.

6 But if my life be spared awhile,
   Before my last remove,
 Thy praise shall be my business still,
   And I'll declare thy love.

268   L. M.   [PORTUGAL.

AND is the Gospel peace and love!
   Such let our conversation be;
 The serpent blended with the dove,
   Wisdom and meek simplicity.

2 Whene'er the angry passions rise, [strife
   And tempt our thoughts or tongues to

To Jesus let us lift our eyes,
  Bright pattern of the Christian life.

3 Oh, how benevolent and kind!
  How mild! how ready to forgive!
  Be this the temper of our mind
  And these the rules by which we live.

4 To do his heavenly Father's will,
  Was his employment and delight;
  Humility and holy zeal
  Shone through his life divinely bright.

5 Dispensing good where'er he came,
  The labors of his life were love;
  Oh, if we love the Savior's name,
  Let his divine example move.

6 But ah! how blind! how weak we are!
  How frail! how apt to turn aside!
  Lord, we depend upon thy care,
  And ask thy Spirit for our guide.

7 Thy fair example may we trace,
  To teach us what we ought to be;
  Make us by thy transforming grace,
  Dear Savior, daily more like thee.

269   L. M.   [ROCKINGHAM.

THOU art, O God! a Spirit pure,
  Invisible to mortal eyes:
Th' immortal and th' eternal King,
  The Great, the Good, the only Wise.

2 Whilst nature changes, and her works
  Corrupt, decay, dissolve, and die,

Thy essence pure no change shall see,
  Secure of immortality.

3 Thou great Invisible! what hand
    Can draw thine image spotless fair?
  To what in heaven, to what on earth,
    Can men th' immortal King compare?

4 Let stupid heathens frame their gods
    Of gold and silver, wood and stone;
  Ours is the God that made the heavens;
    Jehovah he, and God alone.

5 My soul the purest homage pay,
    In truth and spirit him adore;
  More shall this please than sacrifice—
    Than outward forms delight him more.

270   C. M.   [JEROME.

THERE is a voice of sovereign grace
    Sounds from the sacred word;
  "Ho! ye despairing sinners, come,
    And trust upon the Lord."

2 My soul obeys th' Almighty call,
    And runs to his relief:
  I would believe thy promise, Lord,
    Oh! help my unbelief.

3 To the dear fountain of thy blood,
    Incarnate God, I fly;
  Here let me wash my spotted soul
    From crimes of deepest dye.

4 Stretch out thine arm, victorious King,
    My reigning sin subdue;

Drive the old dragon from his seat,
  With his apostate crew.
5 A guilty, weak, and helpless worm,
  On thy kind arms I fall;
Be thou my strength and righteousness,
  My Jesus and my all.

271   C. M.   [Mear.

O THAT the Lord would guide my ways
  To keep his statutes still!
O that my God would grant me grace
  To know and do his will!
2 O send thy Spirit down, to write
  Thy law upon my heart;
Nor let my tongue indulge deceit,
  Nor act the liar's part!
3 From vanity turn off mine eyes:
  Let no corrupt design,
Nor covetous desire, arise
  Within this soul of mine.
4 Order my footsteps by thy word,
  And make my heart sincere;
Let sin have no dominion, Lord,
  But keep my conscience clear.
5 My soul hath gone too far astray,
  My feet too often slip;
Yet, since I've not forgot thy way,
  Restore thy wand'ring sheep.
6 Make me to walk in thy commands—
  'T is a delightful road;
Nor let my head, nor heart, nor hands
  Offend against my God.

ADORATION AND PRAISE.

272   C. M.   [ARLINGTON.

THE Savior! Oh, what endless charms
   Dwell in the blissful sound?
Its influence every fear disarms,
   And spreads sweet peace around.

2 Here pardon, life, and joys divine,
   In rich effusion flow,
For guilty rebels, lost in sin,
   And doomed to endless woe.

3 Oh, the rich depths of love divine,
   Of bliss, a boundless store!
Dear Savior, let me call thee mine:
   I cannot wish for more.

4 On thee alone my hope relies,
   Beneath thy cross I fall;
My Lord, my Life my Sacrifice,
   My Savior, and my all.

273   C. M.   [SOLON.

ETERNAL Wisdom, thee we praise?
   Thee the creation sings!   [seas,
With thy loved name, rocks, hills, and
   And heaven's high palace rings.

2 Thy hand, how wide it spreads the sky!
   How glorious to behold!
Tinged with the blue of heavenly dye,
   And starred with sparkling gold.

3 Thy glories blaze all nature round,
    And strike the gazing sight,
Through skies and seas and solid ground.
    With terror and delight.

4 Infinite strength and equal skill,
    Shine through the worlds abroad;
Our souls with vast amazement fill,
    And speak the builder, God.

5 But still the wonders of thy grace
    Our softer passions move;
Pity divine in Jesus' face
    We see, adore, and love.

274   C. M.   [BALERMA.

LET Zion and her sons rejoice,
    Behold the proudest hour;
Her God hath heard her mourning voice,
    And comes t' exalt her power.

2 Her dust and ruins that remain,
    Are precious in our eyes:
Those ruins shall be built again,
    And all that dust shall rise,

3 The Lord will raise Jerusalem,
    And stand in glory there;
Nations shall bow before his name,
    And kings attend with fear.

4 He sits a Sovereign on his throne,
    With pity in his eyes:
He hears the dying pris'ners groan,
    And sees their sighs arise.

5 He frees the souls condemned to death,
   And when his saints complain,
  It sha'n't be said "that praying breath
   Was ever spent in vain."

6 This shall be known when we are dead,
   And left on long record;
  That ages yet unborn may read,
   And trust and praise the Lord.

275   C. M.   Philips.

AMID the splendors of thy state,
   My God, thy love appears,
With the soft radiance of the moon,
   Among a thousand stars.

2 Nature, through all her ample round,
   Thy boundless power proclaims,
And in melodious accents, speaks
   The goodness of thy name.

3 Thy justice, holiness, and truth.
   Our solemn awe excite;
But the sweet charms of sovereign grace
   O'erwhelm us with delight.

4 Sinai, in clouds and smoke and fire,
   Thunders thy dreadful name;
But Zion sings in melting notes,
   The honors of the Lamb.

5 In all thy doctrines and commands,
   Thy counsels and designs—
In every work thy hands have framed,
   Thy love supremely shines.

6 Angels and men the news proclaim
　　Through earth and heaven above—
The joyful and transporting news,
　　That God the Lord is love.

276   L. M.   [ROCKBRIDGE.

ETERNAL Power! whose high abode,
　　Becomes the grandeur of a God;
Infinite lengths, beyond the bounds
Where stars revolve their little rounds.

2 The lowest step around thy seat,
　Rises too high for Gabriel's feet:
　In vain the tall archangel tries
　To reach thy height with wond'ring eyes.

3 Lord, what shall earth and ashes do?
　We would adore our maker, too;
　From sin and dust to thee we cry,
　The Great, the Holy, and the high.

4 Earth, from afar, has heard thy fame,
　And worms have learned to lisp thy name;
　But O, the glories of thy mind
　Leave all our soaring thoughts behind.

5 God is in heaven, but man below;
　Be short our tunes; our words be few;
　A sacred reverence checks our songs,
　And praise sits silent on our tongues.

277   C. M.   [MARLOW.

COME, let us join our sacred songs,
　　With angels round the throne;
Ten thousand thousand are their tongues,
　　But all their joys are one.

2 "Worthy the Lamb that died," they cry,
"To be exalted thus;"
"Worthy the Lamb," our lips reply,
"For he was slain for us."

3 Jesus is worthy to receive
Honor and power divine;
And blessings more than we can give,
Be, Lord, forever thine.

4 Let all that dwell above the sky,
And air and earth and seas.
Conspire to raise thy glories high,
And speak thine endless praise.

278 L. M. [PORTUGAL.

PRAISE ye the Lord who reigns above,
Fixed on his throne of truth and love;
Behold the finger of his power,
Contemplate, wonder, and adore.

2 When man, debased and guilty man,
From crime to crime with madness ran:
Well might his arm its thunders launch,
And blast th' ungrateful root and branch.

3 But clemency with justice strove
To save the people of his love;
"Go, my beloved Son!" he cried,
"Be thou their Savior, thou their guide."

4 The eastern star with glory streams;
It comes with healing on its beams;
Dark mists of error flee away,
And Judah hails the rising day.

5 His sacred memory we bless,
  Whose holy gospel we profess!
  And praise that great Almighty Name,
  From whom such light and favor came.

279   L. M.   [Wells.

YE nations round the earth, rejoice
  Before the Lord, your sov'reign King,
Serve him with cheerful heart and voice,
  With all your tongues his glory sing.

2 The Lord is God; 't is he alone
  Doth life and breath and being give;
We are his work, and not our own:
  The sheep that on his pastures live.

3 Enter his gates with songs of joy;
  With praises to his courts repair;
And make it your divine employ,
  To pay your thanks and honors there.

4 The Lord is good, the Lord is kind;
  Great is his grace, his mercy sure;
And the whole race of man shall find
  His truth, from age to age, endure.

280   Metre 10.   [Lyons.

O WHAT shall I do my Savior to praise,
  So faithful and true, so plenteous in grace;
So stong to deliver. so good to redeem,
  The weakest believer that hangs upon him?

2 How happy is the man whose heart is set free!
  The people that can be joyful in thee;

Their joy is to walk in the light of thy face,
And still they are talking of Jesus' grace.

3 Their daily delight shall be in thy name;
They shall as their right thy righteousness claim;
Thy righteousness wearing, and cleansed by thy blood.
Bold shall they appear in the presence of God.

4 For thou art their boast, their glory and power,
And I also trust to see the glad hour;
My soul's new creation, a life from the dead,
The day of salvation that lifts up my head.

5 For Jesus, my Lord, is now my defense,
I trust in his word, none plucks me from thence,
Since I have found favor he all things will do,
My King and my Savior shall make me anew.

6 Yes, Lord, I shall see the bliss of thine own;
Thy secret to me shall soon be made known;
For sorrow and sadness I joy shall receive,
And share in the gladness of all that believe.

281   Metre 16.   [Silver Hall.

GOD of my salvation, hear,
  And help me to believe;
Simply do I now draw near,
  Thy blessing to receive.
Full of guilt, alas! I am,
  But to thy wounds for refuge flee;
Friend of sinners, spotless Lamb,
  Thy blood was shed for me.

2 Standing now as newly slain,
  To thee I lift mine eyes,

Balm of all my grief and pain,
　Thy blood is always nigh,
Now as yesterday the same
　Thou art and wilt forever be;
Friend of sinners, spotless Lamb,
　Thy blood was shed for me.

3 Nothing have I, Lord, to pay,
　Nor can thy grace procure;
Empty send me not away,
　For I, thou knowest, am poor.
Dust and ashes is my name;
　My all is sin and misery;
Friend of sinners, spotless Lamb,
　Thy blood was shed for me.

4 No good word, or work, or thought,
　Bring I to buy thy grace;
Pardon I accept unbought,
　Thy proffer I embrace.
Coming as at first I came,
　To take and not bestow on thee;
Friend of sinners spotless Lamb,
　Thy blood was shed for me.

5 Savior, from thy wounded side
　I never will depart;
Here will I my spirit hide,
　When I am pure in heart,
Till my place above I claim,
　This only shall be all my plea,
Friend of sinners, spotless Lamb,
　Thy blood was shed for me.

RESIGNATION TO GOD.

282   Metre 5.   [Hendon.

1 MINE Ebenezer raise
To my kind Redeemer's praise;
With a grateful heart I own,
Hitherto thy help I've known.

2 What may be my future lot,
Well I know concerns me not;
This should set my heart at rest;
What thy will ordains is best.

3 I my all to thee resign;
Father, let thy will be mine;
May but all thy dealings prove
Fruits of thy paternal love.

4 Guard me, Savior, by thy power;
Guard me in the trying hour;
Let thy unremitting care
Save me from the lurking snare.

5 Let my few remaining days
Be directed to thy praise;
So the last the closing scene,
Shall be tranquil and serene.

6 To thy will I leave the rest,
Grant me but this one request,
Both in life and death to prove
Tokens of thy special love.

283   Metre 8.   [Rakem.

When gathering clouds around I view,
  And days are dark and friends are few,
On Him I lean, who, not in vain,
  Experienced every human pain;
He sees my wants, allays my fears,
  And counts and treasures up my tears.

2 If ought should tempt my soul to stray
  From heavenly virtue's narrow way,
To fly the good I would pursue,
  Or do the sin I would not do,
Still he who felt temptations power
  Shall guard me in that dangerous hour.

3 When vexing thoughts within me rise,
  And sore dismayed my spirit dies,
Yet he who once vouchsafed to bear
  The sickening anguish of despair,
Shall sweetly soothe, shall gently dry,
  The throbbing heart, the streaming eye.

4 When sorrowing o'er some stone I bend,
  Which covers all that was a friend,
And from his voice, his hand, his smile,
  Divides me for a little while,
Thou, Savior, seest the tears I shed,
  For thou didst weep o'er Lazarus dead.

5 And O, when I have safely past,
  Through every conflict but the last,
Still, still unchanging, watch beside
  My painful bed—for thou hast died;
Then point to realms of cloudless day,
  And wipe the latest tear away.

284   L. M.   [ROCKINGHAM.

WHILE I keep silence, and conceal
   My heavy guilt within my heart,
What torments doth my conscience feel!
   What agonies of inward smart!

2 I spread my sins before the Lord,
   And all my secret faults confess;
Thy gospel speaks a pardoning word,
   Thy Holy Spirit seals the grace.

3 For this shall every humble soul
   Make swift addresses to thy seat;
When floods of huge temptation roll,
   There shall they find a blest retreat.

4 How safe beneath thy wings I lie, [pear;
   When days grow dark, and storms ap-
And when I walk, thy watchful eye
   Shall guide me safe from every snare.

285   L. M.   [WELLS.

I SEND the joys of earth away,
   Away, ye tempters of the mind,
False as the smooth, deceitful sea,
   And empty as the whistling wind.

2 Your streams were floating me along
   Down to the gulf of dark despair,
And whilst I listened to your song,
   Your streams had e'en convey'd me there.

3 Lord, I adore thy matchless grace,
   That warned me of that dark abyss;

That drew me from those treach'rous seas,
  And bid me seek superior bliss.

4 Now to the shining realms above
   I stretch my hands and glance mine eyes
  O for the pinions of a dove,
   To bear me to the upper skies!

5 There from the bosom of my God,
   Oceans of endless pleasure roll:
  There would I fix my last abode,
   And drown the sorrows of my soul.

TRUSTING IN GOD.

286 METRE 14. [GALENA.

AH! I shall soon be dying,
   Time swiftly glides away;
  But on my Lord relying,
   I hail the happy day—

2 The day when I must enter
   Upon a world unknown;
  My helpless soul I venture
   On Jesus Christ alone.

3 He once a spotless victim,
   Upon Mount Calv'ry bled;
  Jehovah did afflict him,
   And bruise him in my stead.

4 Hence all my hopes arises,
    Unworthy as I am:
  My soul most surely prizes
    The sin-atoning Lamb.

5 To him by grace united,
    I joy in him alone;
  And now, by faith delighted,
    Behold him on his throne.

6 There he is interceding,
    For all who on him rest;
  The grace from him proceeding
    Shall waft me to his breast.

7 Then, with the saints in glory,
    The grateful songs I'll raise,
  And chant my blissful story
    In high, seraphic lays.

8 Free grace, redeeming merit,
    And sanctifying love,
  Of Father, Son, and Spirit,
    Shall charm the courts above.

287   L. M.   [BACA.

SAY now, ye lovely social band,
Who walk the way to Canaan's land;
Ye who have fled from Sodom's plain,
Say, would you now return again?

2 Have you just ventured to the field,
  Well arm'd with helmet, sword and shield?
  And shall the world with dread alarms,
  Compel you now to ground your arms?

3 Beware of pleasure's siren song;
Alas! it cannot soothe you long;
It cannot quiet Jordan's wave,
Nor cheer the dark and silent grave.

4 O let your thoughts delight to soar,
Where earth and time shall be no more;
Explore by faith the heavenly fields,
And pluck the fruit that Canaan yields.

5 There see the glorious hosts on wing,
And hear the heavenly seraphs sing!
The shining ranks in order stand,
Or move like lightning at command.

6 Jehovah there reigns not alone,
The Savior shares his Father's throne;
While angels circle round his seat,
And worship prostrate at his feet.

7 Behold! I see among the rest,
A host in richer garments dressed:
A host that near his presence stands,
And palms of victory grace their hands.

8 Say, who are these I now behold, [gold?
With blood-washed robes and crowns of
This glorious host is not unknown
To him who sits upon the throne.

9 These are the followers of the Lamb;
From tribulation great they came;
And on the hill of sweet repose,
They bid adieu to all their woes.

10 Soon on the wings of love you'll fly
To join them in that world on high;

O make it now your chiefest care,
The image of your Lord to bear.

288   Metre 9.   [Lenox.

ARISE, my soul, arise,
  Shake off thy guilty fears;
The bleeding Sacrifice
  In my behalf appears:
Before thy throne my Surety stands,
My name is written on his hands.

2 He ever lives above,
  For me to intercede;
His all-redeeming love,
  His precious blood to plead;
His blood atoned for all our race,
And sprinkles now the throne of grace.

3 Five bleeding wounds he bears,
  Received on Calvary;
They pour effectual prayers,
  They strongly speak for me:
Forgive him, O forgive, they cry,
Nor let the ransomed sinner die!

4 The Father hears him pray,
  His dear anointed One;
He cannot turn away
  The presence of his Son:
His spirit answers to the blood,
And tells me I am born of God.

5 My God is reconciled,
  His pard'ning voice I hear;

He owns me for his child,
  I can no longer fear;
With confidence I now draw nigh,
  And Father, Abba Father, cry.

289   S. M.   [IDUMEA.

I LIFT my soul to God,
  My trust is in his name;
Let not my foes, that seek my blood,
  Still triumph in my shame.

2 Sin and the powers of hell
  Persuade me to despair;
Lord, make me know thy cov'nant well,
  That I may 'scape the snare.

3 From gleams of dawning light
  Till evening shades arise,
For thy salvation, Lord, I wait,
  With ever-longing eyes.

4 Remember all thy grace,
  And lead me in thy truth;
Forgive the sins of riper days,
  And follies of my youth.

5 The Lord is just and kind,
  The meek shall learn his ways,
And every humble sinner find
  The method of His grace.

6 For his own goodness' sake
  He saves my soul from shame,
He pardons (though my guilt be great),
  Through my Redeemer's name.

290   S. M.   [Golden Hill.

TO God in whom I trust,
  I lift my heart and voice;
Oh! let me not be put to shame,
  Nor let my foes rejoice.

2 Thy mercies, and thy love,
  O Lord, recall to mind:
And graciously continue still,
  As thou wert ever kind.

3 Let all my youthful crimes
  Be blotted out by thee:
And for thy wondrous goodness' sake,
  In mercy think on me.

4 His mercy and his truth,
  The righteous Lord displays,
In bringing wandering sinners home,
  And teaching them his ways.

WARNING HYMNS.

291   L. M.   [Windham.

BROAD is the road that leads to death,
  And thousands walk together there;
But wisdom shows a narrow path,
  With here and there a traveler.

2 "Deny thyself and take thy cross,"
  Is the Redeemer's great command;

WARNING HYMNS.

Nature must count her gold but dross,
　If she would gain this heavenly land.

3 The fearful soul that tires and faints,
　And walks the ways of God no more,
Is but esteemed almost a saint,
　And makes his own destruction sure.

4 Lord, let not all my hopes be vain,
　Create my heart entirely new;
Which hypocrites could ne'er attain,
　Which false apostates never knew.

292　　　　S. M.　　　　[SANDUSKY.

DESTRUCTION'S dangerous road,
　What multitudes pursue!
While that which leads the soul to God,
　Is known or sought by few.

2 Believers find the way,
　Through Christ the living Gate;
But those who hate this holy way,
　Complain it is too straight.

3 If self must be denied,
　And sin no more caressed,
They rather choose the way that's wide,
　And strive to think it best.

4 Encompassed by a throng,
　On numbers they depend;
They say so many can't be wrong,
　And miss a happy end.

5 But hear the Savior's word,
　"Strive for the heavenly gate,

Many will call upon the Lord,
  And find their cries too late."

6 Obey the gospel call,
  And enter while you may;
The flock of Christ is always small,
  And none are safe but they.

7 Lord, open sinner's eyes
  Their awful state to see:
And make them, ere the storm arise,
  To thee for safety flee.

293   Metre 5.   [Vermont.

SINNER, art thou still secure?
  Wilt thou still refuse to pray?
Can thy heart or hands endure
  In the Lord's avenging day?

2 See! his mighty arm is bared!
  Awful terrors clothe his brow!
For his judgment stands prepared,
  Thou must either break or bow.

3 At his presence nature shakes,
  Earth affrighted hastes to flee;
Solid mountains melt like wax,
  What will then become of thee?

4 Who his advent may abide?
  You that glory in your shame,
Will you find a place to hide,
  When the world is wrapt in flame?

5 Lord, prepare us by thy grace!
  Soon we must resign our breath,

And our souls be called to pass
　　　Through the iron gate of death.

6 Let us now our day improve,
　　　Listen to the gospel voice:
　Seek the things that are above;
　　　Scorn the world's pretended joys.

294　　　　S. M.　　　　[IDUMEA.

　IS this the kind return,
　　　And these the thanks we owe,
　Thus to abuse eternal love,
　　　Whence all our blessings flow?

2 To what a stubborn frame
　　　Hath sin reduced our mind!
　What strange rebellious wretches we,
　　　And God as strangely kind!

3 On us he bids the sun
　　　Shed his reviving rays:
　For us the skies their circles run,
　　　To lengthen out our days.

4 The brutes obey their God,
　　　And bow their necks to men;
　But we, more base, more brutish things,
　　　Reject his easy reign.

5 Turn, turn us, mighty God,
　　　And mould our souls afresh;
　Break, sov'reign grace, these hearts of
　　　And give us hearts of flesh.　　[stone.

6 Let past ingratitude
　　　Provoke our weeping eyes,

WARNING HYMNS. 265

And hourly as new mercies fall,
　Let hourly thanks arise.

295　　　　C. M.　　　　[DUBLIN.

THE time is short!—O sinners, fear,
　Nor trifle time away;
The word of great salvation hear,
　While yet 't is called to-day.

2 The time is short!—O sinners, now
　To Christ, the Lord, submit;
To mercy's golden sceptre bow,
　And fall at Jesus' feet.

3 The time is short!—ye saints, rejoice,
　The Lord will quickly come;
Soon shall you hear the Savior's voice,
　To call you to your home.

4 The time is short!—it swiftly flies—
　The hour is just at hand,
When we shall mount above the skies,
　And reach the wished-for land.

5 The time is short!—the moment near,
　When we shall dwell above;
And be forever happy there,
　With Jesus, whom we love.

296　　　　· C. M.　　　　[MEAR.

THAT awful day will surely come,
　Th' appointed hour makes haste,
When I must stand before my Judge,
　And pass the solemn test.

2 Thou lovely Chief of all my joys,
    Thou Sovereign of my heart,
How could I bear to hear thy voice
    Pronounce the word "Depart!"

3 The thunder of that dismal word
    Would so torment my ear,
'T would tear my soul asunder, Lord,
    With most tormenting fear.

4 What, to be banish'd for my life,
    And yet forbid to die!
To linger in eternal pain,
    Yet death forever fly!

5 O wretched state of deep despair,
    To see my God remove,
And fix my doleful station where
    I must not taste his love!

6 Jesus, I throw my arms around,
    And hang upon thy breast;
Without a gracious smile from thee
    My spirit cannot rest.

7 O tell me that my worthless name
    Is graven on thy hands;
Show me some promise in thy book,
    Where my salvation stands.

8 Give me one kind, assuring word,
    To sink my fears again,
And cheerfully my soul shall wait
    Her threescore years and ten.

297   L. M.   [Ashfield.

Hasten, O sinner, to be wise,
    And stay not for the morrow's sun;
The longer wisdom you despise,
    The harder is she to be won.

2 O hasten mercy to implore,
    And stay not for the morrow's sun;
For fear thy season should be o'er,
    Before this evening's stage be run.

3 O hasten, sinner, to return,
    And stay not for the morrow's sun;
For fear thy lamp should fail to burn,
    Before the needful work is done.

4 O hasten, sinner, to be blest,
    And stay not for the morrow's sun,
For fear the curse should thee arrest,
    Before the morrow is begun.

5 O Lord, do thou the sinner turn!
    Now rouse him from his senseless state!
O let him not thy counsel spurn,
    Nor rue his fatal choice too late.

298   Metre 13.   [Warning Voice.

Stop, poor sinner, stop and think,
    Before you farther go;
Will you sport upon the brink
    Of everlasting woe?
On the verge of ruin stop—
    Now the friendly warning take—
Stay your footsteps, ere you drop
    Into the burning lake.

2 Say, have you an arm like God,
    That you his will oppose?
Fear ye not that iron rod
    With which he breaks his foes?
Can you stand in that dread day,
    Which his justice shall proclaim,
When the earth shall melt away
    Like wax before the flame?

3 Ghastly death will quickly come,
    And drag you to his bar;
Then to hear your awful doom,
    Will fill you with despair!
All your sins will round you crowd;
    You shall mark their crimson dye,
Each for vengeance crying loud,
    And what can you reply?

4 Though your heart were made of steel,
    Your forehead lined with brass;
God at length will make you feel,
    He will not let you pass.
Sinners then in vain will call,
    Those who now despise his grace,
"Rocks and mountains on us fall,
    And hide us from his face."

299   Metre 54.   [Voice of Warning.

All, guilty sinner, ruined by transgression,
    What shall thy doom be, when arrayed in terror,
God shall command thee covered with pollution,
    Up to the judgment!

2 Wilt thou escape from his omniscient notice,
Fly to the caverns, court annihilation?
Vain thy presumption, justice shall still triumph
    In thy destruction.

3 Stop, thoughtless sinner, stop awhile and ponder,
Ere death arrest thee, and the Judge in vengeance
Hurl from his presence thine affrighted spirit,
    Swift to perdition.

4 Oft has he called thee, but thou would'st not hear him,
Mercies and judgment have alike been slighted,
Yet he is gracious, and with arms unfolded,
    Waits to embrace thee.

5 Come then, poor sinner, come away this moment,
Just as you are, come filthy and polluted.
Come to the fountain open for uncleanness:
    Jesus invites you.

6 But if you trifle with his gracious message,
Cleave to the world and love its guilty pleasures
Mercy, grown weary, shall in righteous judgment
    Quit you forever.

7 Where the worm dies not, and the fire eternal
Fills the lost soul with anguish and with terror,
There shall the sinner spend a long forever,
    Dying unpardoned

8 O guilty sinner, hear the voice of warning!
Fly to the savior, and embrace his pardon;
So shall your spirit meet, with joy triumphant,
    Death and the judgment.

PENITENTIAL.

300 L. M. [ROCKINGHAM.

BEHOLD, a stranger at the door!
He gently knocks, has knock'd before;
Hath waited long, is waiting still;
You treat no other friend so ill.

2 O lovely attitude! he stands
With melting heart and loaded hands!
Oh matchless kindness! and he shows
This matchless kindness to his foes!

3 But will he prove a Friend indeed?
He will; the very Friend you need;
The Friend of sinners—yes, 't is He,
With garments dyed on Calvary.

4 Rise, touched with gratitude divine;
Turn out his enemy and thine,
That soul-destroying monster, sin,
And let the heavenly Stranger in.

5 Admit him ere his anger burn,
His feet departed, ne'er return;
Admit him, or the hour's at hand,
You'll at his door rejected stand.

301 C. M. [YOUTHFUL PIETY.

HOW oft, alas! this wretched heart
Has wandered from the Lord!

How oft my roving thoughts depart,
  Forgetful of his word.

2 Yet sovereign mercy calls, "Return;"
  Dear Lord, and may I come?
My vile ingratitude I mourn;
  Oh, take the wanderer home!

3 And canst thou, wilt thou yet forgive,
  And bid my crimes remove?
And shall a pardoned rebel live
  To speak thy wondrous love?

4 Almighty grace! thy healing power,
  How glorious, how divine!
That can to life and bliss restore
  So vile a heart as mine.

5 Thy pard'ning love, so free, so sweet,
  Dear Savior, I adore;
Oh keep me at thy sacred feet,
  And let me rove no more.

302   Metre 8.   [Rakem.

COME, O thou Traveler unknown,
  Whom still I hold, but cannot see;
My company before is gone,
  And I am left alone with thee:
With thee all night I mean to stay,
And wrestle till the break of day.

2 I need not tell thee who I am;
  My misery and sin declare;
Thyself hast called me by my name,
  Look on thy hands and read it there;

PENITENTIAL

 But who, I ask thee, who art thou?
 Tell me thy name, and tell me now.

3 In vain thou strugglest to get free,
 I never will unloose my hold;
Art thou the Man that died for me?
 The secret of thy love unfold;
Wrestling, I will not let thee go,
Till I thy name, thy nature know.

4 Wilt thou not yet to me reveal
 Thy new, unutterable name?
Tell me, I still beseech thee, tell;
 To know it now resolved I am;
Wrestling, I will not let thee go.
Till I thy name, thy nature know.

5 What tho' my shrinking flesh complain,
 And murmur to contend so long;
I rise superior to my pain;
 When I am weak, then I am strong!
And when my all of strength shall fail,
I shall with thee, God-Man, prevail.

303   S. M.   AYLESBURY.

HAVE mercy, Lord, on me,
 As thou wert ever kind;
Let me, oppress'd with loads of guilt,
 The wonted pardon find.

2 Against thee, Lord, alone,
 And only in thy sight,

Have I transgressed; and tho' condemned,
  Must own thy judgments right.

3 Blot out my crying sins,
   Nor me in anger view;
 Create in me a heart that's clean—
   An upright mind renew.

4 Withdraw not thou thy help,
   Nor cast me from thy sight,
 Nor let thy Holy Spirit take
   Its everlasting flight.

5 The joy thy favor gives,
   Let me again obtain;
 And thy free Spirit's firm support
   My fainting soul sustain.

PRODIGAL SON.

304　　　C. M.　　　[Dunlap's Creek.
 BEHOLD the wretch whose lust and
   Have wasted his estate;　　[wine
 He begs a share among the swine
   To taste the husks they eat

2 "I die with hunger here," he cries,
   "I starve in foreign lands;
 My father's house hath large supplies,
   And bounteous are his hands."

3 "I'll go, and with a mournful tongue,
   Fall down before his face;
18

Father, I've done thy justice wrong,
    Nor can deserve thy grace:"

4 He said, and hastened to his home
    To seek his father's love;
The father saw the rebel come,
    And all his bowels move.

5 He ran and fell upon his neck,
    Embraced and kissed his son;
The rebel's heart with sorrow brake
    For follies he had done.

6 "Take off his clothes of shame and sin,"
    (The father gives command),
"Dress him in garments white and clean,
    With rings adorn his hands."

7 " A day of feasting I ordain,
    Let mirth and joy abound;
My son was dead, and lives again,
    Was lost and now is found."

305   C. M.   [SOLON.

AFFLICTIONS, tho' they seem severe,
    In mercy oft are sent;
They stopped the prodigal's career,
    And caused him to repent.

2 Although he no relentings felt,
    Till he had spent his store,
His stubborn heart began to melt,
    When famine pinched him sore.

3 "What have I gained by sin," he said,
   "But hunger, shame, and fear?
   My father's house abounds with bread,
   While I am starving here.

4 "I'll go and tell him all I've done,
   Fall down before his face;
   Unworthy to be called his son,
   I'll seek a servant's place."

5 His father saw him coming back,
   He saw and ran and smiled;
   Then threw his arms around the neck
   Of his rebellious child.

6 "Father, I've sinned, but O forgive,"—
   "Enough," the Father said,
   "Rejoice, my house, my son's alive,
   For whom I mourned as dead.

7 Now let the fatted calf be slain,
   Go, spread the news around,
   My son was dead, but lives again—
   Was lost but now is found."

8 'Tis thus the Lord his love reveals,
   To call poor sinners home;
   More than a father's love he feels,
   And welcomes all that come.

MARRIAGE HYMNS.

306 C. M. [BALERMA.

SINCE Jesus freely did appear
 To grace a marriage feast,
O Lord, we ask thy presence here,
 To make a wedding guest.

2 Upon the bridal pair look down,
 Who now have plighted hands;
Their union with thy favor crown;
 And bless the nuptial bands.

3 In purest love these souls unite,
 That they with Christian care,
May make domestic burdens light,
 By taking mutual share.

4 And when that solemn hour shall come,
 And life's short space be o'er,
May they in triumph reach that home,
 Where they shall part no more.

307 L. M. [HEBRON.

WITH grateful hearts and tuneful lays,
 We bow before th' eternal throne,
And offer up our humble praise,
 To him whose name is God alone.

2 On this auspicious eve draw near,
 And shed thy richest blessings down;
Fill every heart with love sincere,
 And all thy faithful mercies crown.

COMMUNION.

3 Grant now thy presence, gracious Lord,
  And hearken to our fervent prayer;
The nuptial vow in heaven record,
  And bless the newly married pair.

4 O guide them safe this desert through,
  'Mid all the cares of life and love;
At length with joy thy face to view,
  In fairer, better worlds above.

308 L. M. [UXBRIDGE.

WITH cheerful voices rise and sing
  The praises of our God and King;
For He alone can minds unite,
And bless with conjugal delight.

2 O may this pair increasing find,
Substantial pleasures of the mind.
Happy together may they be,
And both united, Lord, to thee.

3 So may they live as truly one;
And when their work on earth is done,
Rise, hand in hand, to heaven, and share
The joys of love forever there.

COMMUNION.

309 L. M. [KEDRON.

YE that pass by, behold the Man!
  The Man of grief condemned for you!

COMMUNION.

 The Lamb of God for sinners slain!
  Weeping, to Calvary pursue.

2 His sacred limbs, they stretch, they tear,
  With nails they fasten to the wood—
 His sacred limbs—exposed and bare,
  Or only covered with his blood.

3 See there! his temples crown'd with thorns
  His bleeding hands extended wide,
 His streaming feet transfixed and torn,
  The fountain gushing from his side.

4 Thou dear, thou suffering Son of God,
  How doth thy heart to sinners move!
 Sprinkle on us thy precious blood,
  And melt us with thy dying love!

5 The earth could to her center quake,
  Convulsed, when her Creator died;
 Oh, may our inmost nature shake,
  And bow with Jesus crucified!

6 At thy last gasp the graves displayed
  Their horrors to the upper skies;
 Oh, that our souls might burst the shades,
  And, quickened by thy death, arise!

7 The rocks could feel thy powerful death,
  And tremble, and asunder part:
 Oh, rend, with thy expiring breath,
  The harder marble of our heart!

310   Metre 7.   [Happy Zion.

HARK! the voice of love and mercy
 Sound aloud from Calvary,

COMMUNION. 279

See, it rends the rocks asunder—
  Shakes the earth and veils the sky!
    "It is finished!"—
  Hear the dying Savior cry.
2 It is finished! Oh, what pleasure
    Do these precious words afford!
  Heavenly blessings without measure,
    Flow to us from Christ the Lord:
      It is finished!—
    Saints the dying words record.
3 Finished—all the types and shadows
    Of the ceremonial law;
  Finished all that God had promised;
    Death and hell no more shall awe:
      It is finished!—
    Saints from hence your comforts draw.
4 Tune your harps anew, ye seraphs—
    Join to sing the pleasing theme;
  All on earth, and all in heaven,
    Join to praise Immanuel's name:
      Hallelujah!
    Glory to the bleeding Lamb.

311   C. M.   [PETERBOROUGH.

LET us adore th' Eternal Word;
  'Tis he our souls hath fed;
Thou art our living stream, O Lord,
  And thou th' immortal bread.
2 The manna came from lower skies,
    But Jesus from above,
  Where the fresh springs of pleasure rise,
    And rivers flow with love.

3 The Jews, the fathers, died at last,
    Who ate that heavenly bread;
But these provisions which we taste
    Can raise us from the dead.

4 Blessed be the Lord, that gives his flesh
    To nourish dying men;
And often spreads his table fresh,
    Lest we should faint again.

5 Our souls shall draw their heav'nly breath
    While Jesus finds supplies;
Nor shall our graces sink to death,
    For Jesus never dies.

6 Daily our mortal flesh decays,
    But Christ our life shall come;
His unresisted power shall raise
    Our bodies from the tomb.

312   C. M.   [SOLON.

LORD, how divine thy comforts are;
    How heavenly is the place,
Where Jesus spreads the sacred feast
    Of his redeeming grace!

2 Our humble faith here takes her rise,
    While sitting round his board;
And back to Calvary she flies,
    To view her groaning Lord.

3 His soul, what agonies it felt,
    When his own God withdrew!
And the large loads of all our guilt,
    Lay heavy on him, too!

4 "Here" (says the kind, redeeming Lord,
    And shows his wounded side),
"See here the springs of all your joys,
    That opened when I died."

5 He smiles and cheers my mournful heart,
    And tells of all his pain;
"All this," says he, "I bore for thee"—
    And then he smiles again.

6 Shout and proclaim the Savior's love,
    Ye saints that taste his wine;
Join with your kindred saints above,
    In loud hosannas join.

7 A thousand glories to the God
    That gives such joy as this:
Hosanna! let it sound abroad,
    And reach where Jesus is.

313   L. M.   [KEDRON.

'TIS midnight—and on Olive's brow,
    The star is dimmed that lately shone;
'Tis midnight—in the garden now
    The suffering Savior prays alone.

2 'Tis midnight—and from all removed,
    Immanuel wrestles 'lone with fears;
E'en the disciple that he loved
    Heeds not his Master's grief and tears.

3 'Tis midnight—and for others' guilt
    The Man of sorrows weeps in blood;
Yet he that hath in anguish knelt,
    Is not forsaken by his God.

4 'T is midnight—and from ether plains,
   Is borne the song that angels know;
  Unheard by mortals are the strains
   That sweetly soothe the Savior's woe.

314   C. M.   [JEROME.

HOW sweet and awful is the place
   With Christ within the doors,
While everlasting love displays
   The choicest of her stores!

2 Here every bowel of our God
   With soft compassion rolls;
Here peace and pardon bought with blood,
   Is food for dying souls.

3 While all our hearts and all our songs
   Join to admire the feast,
Each of us cry with thankful tongues,
   "Lord, why was I a guest?"

4 "Why was I made to hear thy voice,
   And enter while there's room;
When thousands make a wretched choice,
   And rather starve than come?"

5 'T was the same love that spread the feast,
   That sweetly forced us in;
Else we had still refused to taste,
   And perished in our sin.

6 Pity the nations, O our God,
   Constrain the earth to come;
Send thy victorious word abroad,
   And bring the strangers home.

7 We long to see thy churches full,
   That all the chosen race
May with one voice and heart and soul,
   Sing thy redeeming grace.

315   C. M.   [BURFORD.

THAT doleful night before his death,
   The Lamb, for sinners slain,
Did, almost with his latest breath,
   This solemn feast ordain.

2 To keep the feast, Lord, we are met,
   And to remember thee:
Help each poor trembler to repeat,
   "The Savior died for me."

3 Thy sufferings Lord, each sacred sign
   To our remembrance brings;
We eat the bread and drink the wine,
   But think on nobler things.

4 O tune our tongues, and put in frame
   Each heart that pants for thee,
To sing, "Hosanna to the Lamb,
   The Lamb that died for me!"

316   S. M.   [IDUMEA.

JESUS invites his saints
   To meet around his board;
Here pardoned rebels sit and hold
   Communion with their Lord.

2 For food he gives his flesh,
   He bids us drink his blood;

Amazing favor! matchless grace
 Of our descending God!
3 This holy bread and wine
 Maintains our fainting breath,
By union with our living Lord,
 And int'rest in his death.
4 Our heavenly Father calls
 Christ and his members one;
We, the young children of his love,
 And he the first-born Son.
5 We are but several parts,
 Of the same broken bread;
One body hath its several limbs,
 But Jesus is the head.
6 Let all our powers be joined
 His glorious name to raise;
Pleasure and love fill every mind,
 And every voice be praise.

317   S. M.   [BOYLESTON.

LET all our tongues be one,
 To praise our God on high,
Who from his bosom sent his Son,
 To take us strangers nigh.
2 Nor let our voices cease,
 To sing the Savior's name;
Jesus th' Embassador of peace,
 How cheerfully he came!
3 It cost him cries and tears,
 To bring us near to God;
Great was our debt, and he appears
 To make the payment good.

4 Infinite was our guilt,
   But he, our Priest, atones;
On the cold ground his life was spilt,
   And offered with his groans.
5 Look up, my soul, to him
   Whose death was thy desert;
And humbly view the living stream
   Flow from his breaking heart.
6 While the Eternal Three
   Bear their record above,
Here I believe he died for me,
   And seal my Savior's love.

318   C. M.   [RESIGNATION.

JESUS, at whose supreme command,
   We now approach to God,
Before us in thy vesture stand,
   Thy vesture dipped in blood.
Obedient to thy gracious word
   We break the hallowed bread,
Commem'rate thee, our dying Lord
   And trust on thee to feed.
2 Now, Savior, now thyself reveal,
   And make thy nature known,
Affix thy blessed Spirit's seal,
   And stamp us for thine own.
The tokens of thy dying love
   O let us all receive,
And feel the quick'ning Spirit move,
   And sensibly believe!
3 The cup of blessing, blest by thee,
   Let it thy blood impart;

The bread thy mystic body be,
  To cheer each languid heart.
The grace which sure salvation brings,
  Let us herewith receive;
Satiate the hungry with good things,
  That hidden manna give.

4 The living bread sent down from heav'n,
  In us vouchsafe to be;
Thy flesh for all the world is given,
  And all may live by thee.
Now, Lord, on us thy flesh bestow,
  And let us drink thy blood,
Till all our souls are filled below,
  With all the life of God.

319   Metre 16.   [Mendon.

LAMB of God, whose dying love
  We now recall to mind,
Send the answer from above,
  And let us mercy find;
Think on us who think on thee,
  And every struggling soul release!
O, remember Calvary,
  And bid us go in peace.

2 By thine agonizing pain,
  And bloody sweat we pray;
By thy dying love to man,
  Take all our sins away;
Burst our bonds and set us free;
  From all iniquity release;
O, remember Calvary,
  And bid us go in peace!

3 Let thy blood by faith applied,
   The sinner's pardon seal,
Speak us freely justified,
   And all our sickness heal;
By thy passion on the tree,
   Let all our griefs and trouble cease;
O, remember Calvary,
   And bid us go in peace!

4 Never will we hence depart,
   Till thou our wants relieve;
Write forgiveness on our heart,
   And all thy image give.
Still our souls shall cry to thee,
   Till perfected in holiness;
O, remember Calvary,
   And bid us go in peace!

320   Metre 4.   [Bavaria.

COME, thou everlasting Spirit,
   Bring to every thankful mind,
All the Savior's dying merit,
   All his suffering's for mankind;
True recorder of his passion,
   Now the living fire impart,
Now reveal his great salvation,
   Preach his gospel to his heart.

2 Come, thou Witness of his dying,
   Come, Remembrancer divine,
Let us feel thy power applying
   Christ to every soul and mine:
Let us groan thine inward groaning,
   Look on him we pierced and grieved;

All receive the grace atoning,
All the sprinkled blood receive.

FEET-WASHING.

321   C. M.   [Mear.

To show how humble Christians ought
  To one another be.
Christ with his own example taught,
  As plainly we may see.

2 Though he was Lord and Master great,
  Who giveth all commands,
He washed his own disciples' feet,
  With his own blessed hands.

3 When thus their Master with them dealt,
  And proved his love to them,
How must their drooping hearts have felt,
  To meet with such esteem!

4 May they who worldly honor seek,
  Learn what it is to be
Like Jesus, humble, truly meek,
  From self-applauses free.

5 Such facts as these should have effect,
  To bring the haughty low;
The proudest heart should feel a check,
  And deeply humbled, too.

6 Thus Peter's mind was much impressed,
  He thought himself too mean;
But also felt himself distressed,
  To have no part with him.

7 "Till thou art washed, thou hast no part
   With me," the Savior said;
Then Peter cried, "With all my heart!
   Wash thou my hands and head."

322   L. M.   [HEBRON.

THE night in which Christ was be-
   For us a plain example laid, [trayed,
He to a private room retired,
With those he afterward inspired.

2 There the Lord's Supper was prepared,
And Christ the Lord had with them shared
Of which th' apostles did partake:
He thus an ordinance did make.

3 He rose and laid his garments by,
When towel and water were brought nigh;
To prove his love divinely sweet,
Proceeds to wash his servants' feet.

4 So after he had washed their feet,
Resumed his garments. took his seat;
So we should love and kindness show,
To all our brethren here below.

5 Ye call me Master and your Lord,
Which is according to my word;
If I have done this unto you,
Ye ought to serve each other too.

6 Example give I unto you,
As I have done so ye should do;
And if ye then my servants be,
Obey my word and follow me.

7 The Lord who did from heaven descend,
 Bid us his doctrine to defend:
 If we in all things faithful prove,
 We shall obtain redeeming love.

323 L. M. [DEVOTION.

WHEN Jesus Christ was here below,
 He taught his people what to do;
 And if we would his precepts keep,
 We must descend to washing feet.

2 For in that night he was betrayed,
 He for us all a pattern laid;
 So let our works and virtues shine
 To prove his patterns all divine.

3 The Lord who made the earth and sky,
 Arose and laid his garments by,
 And washed their feet to show that we
 Should always kind and humble be.

4 He washed them all to make them clean,
 But Judas still was full of sin;
 May none of us, like Judas, sell
 The Lord for gold, and go to hell.

5 Peter said, "Lord, it shall not be,
 Thou shalt not stoop to washing me;"
 O that no Christian here may say,
 I'm too unworthy to obey

6 You call me Lord, and Master too,
 Then do as I have done to you;
 All my commands and counsels keep,
 And show your love by washing feet.

7 Ye shall be happy if you know,
   And do these things by faith below,
   And I'll protect you till you die,
   And then remove you up on high.

PARTING HYMNS.

324   L. M.   [PARTING HAND.

MY dearest friends, in bonds of love,
   Our hearts in sweetest union prove,
Your friendship's like a drawing band,
Yet we must take the parting hand.
Your presence sweet, your union dear,
Your words delightful to my ear;
And when I see that we must part,
You draw like cords around my heart.

2 How sweet the hours have passed away,
  Since we have met to sing and pray;
  How loth I've been to leave the place
  Where Jesus shows his smiling face!
  O could I stay with friends so kind,
  How would it cheer my struggling mind!
  But duty makes me understand,
  That we must take the parting hand.

3 And since it is God's holy will,
  We must be parted for a while,
  In sweet submission all as one,
  We'll say, our father's will be done.
  Dear fellow youth, in Christian ties,
  Who seek for mansions in the skies:

Fight on you'll win the happy shore,
Where parting hands are known no more.

4 How oft I've seen the flowing tears,
And heard you tell your hopes and fears!
Your hearts with love have seemed to flame,
Which makes me hope we'll meet again.
Ye mourning souls, in sad surprise,
Jesus remembers all your cries:
O taste his grace, in all that land
We'll no more take the parting hand.

325   Metre 11.   [Social Band.

FAREWELL, my dear brethren, the time is at hand,
That we must be parted from this social band;
Our sev'ral engagements now call us away,
Our parting is needful and we must obey.

2 Farewell, my dear brethren, farewell for awhile,
We'll soon meet again, if kind Providence smile;
And while we are parted and scattered abroad,
We'll pray for each other and trust in the Lord.

3 Farewell, faithful soldiers, you'll soon be discharged,
The war will be ended, your bounty enlarged;
With shouting and singing, though Jordan may roar,
We'll enter fair Canaan, and rest on the shore.

4 Farewell, younger brethren, just listed for war;
Sore trials await you, but Jesus is near;
Although you must travel the dark wilderness,
Your Captain's before you, he'll lead you in peace.

5 The World and the devil and sin, all unite,
With bold opposition, your souls to affright;
But Jesus, your leader, is stronger than they,
Let this animate you to march on your way.

6 Farewell, trembling mourner, with sad broken heart,
O hasten to Jesus and choose the good part;
He's full of compassion, and mighty to save,
His arms are extended your soul to receive.

7 Farewell, careless sinners! for you I must grieve
To think of your danger while careless you live;
The judgment approaches—O think of your doom,
And turn to the Savior while yet there is room.

326   C. M.   [SALVATION.

DEAR friends, farewell, I do you tell,
   Since you and I must part;
I go away, and here you stay,
   But still we're joined in heart.
Your love to me has been most free,
   Your conversation sweet;
How can I bear to journey where
   With you I cannot meet?

2 Yet do I find my heart inclined
   To do my work below;
When Christ doth call, I trust I shall
   Be ready then to go.
I leave you all, both great and small,
   In Christ's encircling arms,
Who can you save from the cold grave,
   And shield you from all harm.

3 I trust you'll pray, both night and day,
   And keep your garments white,
For you and me, that we may be
   The children of the light:
If you die first, anon you must,
   The will of God be done;
I hope the Lord will you reward,
   With an immortal crown.

4 If I'm called home whilst I am gone;
   Indulge no tears for me;
I hope to sing and praise my King,
   To all eternity.
Millions of years over the spheres
   Shall pass in sweet repose,
While beauty bright unto my sight,
   Thy sacred sweets disclose.

5 I long to go, then farewell woe,
   My soul will be at rest;
No more shall I complain or sigh,
   But taste the heavenly feast.
O may we meet, and be complete,
   And long together dwell,
And serve the Lord with one accord;
   And so, dear friends, farewell.

327   Metre 8   [Saunders.

FAREWELL, my brethren in the Lord!
   The gospel sounds the Jubilee!
My tongue shall bear the news abroad,
   From land to land, from sea to sea;
And as I preach from place to place,
I'll trust alone in God's free grace.

2 Farewell!—in bonds of union dear,
    Like strings you twine about my heart;
I humbly beg your earnest prayer,
    Till we shall meet no more to part;
Till we shall meet in worlds above,
Encircled in eternal love.

3 Farewell, my earthly friends below!
    Though all so kind and dear to me,
My Jesus calls, and I must go
    To sound the gospel-jubilee;
To bear the joy-inspiring news
To Gentile worlds, and blinded Jews.

4 Farewell, dear people, one and all!
    While God the breath of life shall give,
I hope on him in prayer to call,
    That you, dear souls, in Christ may live;
That you, dear souls, prepared may be,
To reign in bliss eternally.

5 Farewell to all below the sun!
    And as I journey here below,
The path is straight my feet must run,
    And God will keep me as I go;
Will guard me by his powerful hand,
And bring me to the promised land.

6 Farewell! farewell!—I look above;
    Jesus, my Friend, to thee I call;
Be thou my joy, my crown, my love,
    My safeguard, and my heavenly all;
My theme till life shall close, and then
My only hope in death—Amen!

328   L. M.   [HEBRON—DEVOTION.

O HAPPY day when saints shall meet
To part no more, the thought is sweet;
No more to feel the rending smart
Oft felt below, when Christians part.

2 O happy place! I still must say,
Where all but love is done away;
All cause of parting there is past;
There social feast will ever last.

3 Such union here is sought in vain,
As there in every heart will reign,
Their separation can't compel
The saints to bid the sad farewell.

4 On earth when friends together meet,
And find the passing moments sweet,
Time's rapid motions soon compel,
With grief to say—dear friends, farewell.

5 The shepherd feels the smarting shock,
Of parting from his weeping flock;
His feelings for them none can tell,
When forced to say—my friends, farewell.

6 The happy season soon will come, [home;
When saints shall meet in heaven their
Eternally with Christ to dwell.
Nor ever hear the sound, farewell.

329   C. M.   [MEAR.

BLEST be the dear uniting love,
That will not let us part;

Our bodies may far off remove—
  We still are one in heart.

2 Joined in one Spirit to our Head,
  Where he appoints we go;
And still in Jesus' footsteps tread,
  And show his praise below.

3 Partakers of the Savior's grace,
  The same in mind and heart,
Nor joy, nor grief, nor time, nor place,
  Nor life, nor death can part.

4 But let us hasten to the day,
  Which shall our flesh restore;
When death shall all be done away,
  And Christians part no more.

VARIOUS SUBJECTS.

330   Metre 12.   [Greenfields.

HOW tedious and tasteless the hours,
  When Jesus no longer I see!
Sweet prospects, sweet birds, and sweet flowers,
  Have all lost their sweetness to me;
The midsummer sun shines but dim,
  The fields strive in vain to look gay;
But when I am happy in Him,
  December's as pleasant as May.

2 His name yields the richest perfume,
  And sweeter than music his voice;

His presence disperses my gloom,
  And makes all within me rejoice;
I should, were he always thus nigh,
  Have nothing to wish or to fear,
No mortal so happy as I,
  My summer would last all the year.

3 Content with beholding his face,
  My all to his pleasure resigned;
No changes of season or place
  Would make any change in my mind;
While blest with a sense of his love,
  A palace a toy would appear;
And prisons would palaces prove,
  If Jesus would dwell with me there.

4 Dear Lord, if indeed I am thine,
  If thou art my Sun and my Song,
Say, why do I languish and pine?
  And why are my winters so long?
O drive these dark clouds from my sky;
  Thy soul-cheering presence restore;
Or take me to thee up on high,
  Where winter and clouds are no more.

331   Metre 12.   [Greenfields.

When Joseph his brethren beheld,
  Afflicted and trembling with fear,
His heart with compassion was filled,
  From weeping he could not forbear;
A while his behavior was rough,
  To bring their past sin to their mind;
But when they were humbled enough,
  He hastened to show himself kind.

2 How little they thought it was he,
    Whom they had ill-treated and sold!
  How great their confusion must be,
    As soon as his name he had told!
  "I'm Joseph, your brother," he said,
    "And still to my heart you are dear;
  You sold me, and thought I was dead,
    But God, for your sakes sent me here."

3 Though greatly distressed before,
    When charged with purloining the cup;
  They now were confounded much more,
    Not one of them durst to look up;
  "Can Joseph, whom we would have slain,
    Forgive us the evil we did?
  And will he our household maintain?
    O! this is a brother indeed."

4 Thus dragged by my conscience, I came,
    And laden with guilt to the Lord;
  Surrounded with terror and shame,
    Unable to utter a word.
  At first he looked stern and severe,
    What anguish then pierced my heart,
  Expecting each moment to hear
    The sentence, "Thou cursed, depart!"

5 But O! what surprise when he spoke,
    While tenderness beamed in his face,
  My heart then to pieces was broke,
    O'erwhelmed and confounded by grace.
  "Poor sinner, I know thee full well;
    By thee I was sold and was slain;
  But died to redeem thee from hell,
    And raise thee in glory to reign.

6 "I'm Jesus whom thou hast blasphemed,
    And crucified often afresh;
But let me henceforth be esteemed,
    Thy brother, thy bone, and thy flesh;
My pardon I freely bestow,
    Thy wants will I fully supply;
I'll guide thee, and guard thee below,
    And soon will remove thee on high.

7 "Go, publish to sinners around,
    That they may be willing to come,
The mercy which now you have found,
    And tell them that yet there is room."
O sinner! the message obey;
No more vain excuses pretend;
But come without further delay,
    To Jesus, our brother and friend.

332   Metre 7.   [Happy Zion.

SAVIOR, visit thy plantation,
    Grant us, Lord, a gracious rain!
All will come to desolation,
    Unless thou return again.
      CHORUS.
      Lord, revive us!
    All our help must come from thee.

2 Keep no longer at a distance,
    Shine upon us from on high,
Lest for want of thine assistance,
    Every plant should droop and die.
      Lord, revive us, etc.

3 Surely, once thy garden flourished,
    Every plant looked gay and green;

Then thy word our spirit nourished—
  Happy seasons we have seen.
    Lord, revive us, etc.

4 But a drought has since succeeded,
  And a sad decline we see;
Lord, thy help is greatly need,
  Help can only come from thee.
    Lord, revive us, etc.

5 Where are those we counted leaders?
  Filled with zeal and love and truth;
Old professors, tall as cedars,
  Bright examples to our youth.
    Lord, revive us, etc.

6 Some in whom we once delighted,
  We shall meet no more below;
Some, alas! we fear, are blighted,
  Scarce a single leaf they show.
    Lord, revive us, etc.

7 Younger plants—the sight how pleasant!
  Covered thick with blossoms stood;
But they cause us grief at present,
  Frosts have nipped them in the bud.
    Lord, revive us, etc.

8 Dearest Savior, hasten hither;
  Thou canst make them bloom again;
O permit them not to wither,
  Let not all our hopes be vain.
    Lord, revive us, etc.

9 Let our mutual love be fervent,
  Make us prevalent in prayers;

VARIOUS SUBJECTS.

Let each one, esteemed thy servant,
  Shun the world's bewitching snares.
    Lord, revive us, etc.
10 Break the tempter's fatal power,
  Turn the stony heart to flesh;
And begin from this good hour,
  To revive thy work afresh.
    Lord, revive us, etc.

333   Metre 4.   [Moulton.

SAVIOR, I do feel thy merit,
  Sprinkled with redeeming blood;
And my weary, troubled spirit,
  Now finds rest with thee, my God;
I am safe, and I am happy,
  While in thy dear arms I lie,
Sin and Satan cannot hurt me,
  While my Savior is so nigh.

2 Now I'll sing a Savior's merit,
  Tell the world of his dear name;
That if any want his spirit,
  He is still the very same;
He that asketh soon receiveth,
  He that seeks is sure to find;
Whomsoe'er on him believeth,
  He will never cast behind.

3 Now our Advocate is pleading
  With his father and our God;
Now for us is interceding
  As the purchase of his blood:
Now methinks I hear him praying,
  Father, save them, I have died;

And the Father answers, saying,
  They are freely justified.

334   Metre 7.   [Merrick.

OH, thou God of my salvation,
  My Redeemer from all sin;
Moved by thy divine compassion,
  Who has died my heart to win;
    I will praise thee—
Where shall I thy praise begin?

2 While the angel choirs are crying,
  Glory to the great I AM,
I with them would still be vieing,
  Glory, glory to the Lamb!
    O how precious
Is the sound of Jesus' name!

3 Now I see with joy and wonder,
  Whence the healing stream arose;
Angel minds are lost to ponder,
  Dying love's mysterious cause;
    Yet the blessing
Down to all, to me, it flows.

4 Though unseen, I love the Savior—
  He hath brought salvation near;
Manifest his pard'ning favor,
  And when Jesus doth appear,
    Soul and body
Shall his glorious image wear.

5 Angels now are hovering round us,
  Unperceived they mix the throng,

Wondering at the love that crowned us,
  Glad to join the holy song:
    Hallelujah!
Love and praise to Christ belong.

335   Metre 4.   [Bavaria.

DARK and thorny is the desert
  Thro' which pilgrims make their way;
But beyond this vale of sorrows,
  Lie the fields of endless day:
Fiends loud howling through the desert,
  Make them tremble as they go;
And the fiery darts of Satan,
  Often bring their courage low.

2 O, young soldiers, are you weary,
  Of the troubles of the way?
Does your strength begin to fail you,
  And your vigor to decay?
Jesus, Jesus will go with you—
  He will lead you to his throne,
He who dyed his garments for you,
  And the wine press trod alone.

3 He whose thunder shakes creation,
  He who bids the planets roll;
He who rides upon the tempest,
  And whose sceptre sways the whole—
Round him are ten thousand angels,
  Ready to obey command;
They are always hovering round you,
  Till you reach the heavenly land.

4 There on flowery hills of pleasure
  In the fields of endless rest,

Love and joy and peace shall ever
   Reign and triumph in your breast
Who can paint those scenes of glory,
   Where the ransomed dwell on high;
Where the golden harps forever
   Sound redemption through the sky?

5 Millions, there of flaming seraphs,
   Fly across the heavenly plain;
There they sing immortal praises—
   Glory! glory! is their strain
Methinks a sweeter concert
   Makes the heavenly arches ring;
And a song is heard in Zion
   Which the angels cannot sing.

6 See the heavenly host in rapture
   Gaze upon this shining band,
Wond'ring at their costly garment,
   And their laurels in their hand;
There upon the golden pavement,
   See the ransomed march along,
While the splendid courts of glory
   Sweetly echo to their song.

7 O their crowns! how bright they sparkle,
   Such as monarchs never wore!
They have gone to heavenly pastures—
   Jesus is their Shepherd there;
Hail, ye happy, happy spirits!
   Welcome to the blissful plain!
Glory, honor, and salvation!—
   Reign, sweet Shepherd, ever reign!

336   Metre 16.   [Mendon.

VAIN delusive world, adieu!
  With all of creature good,
Only Jesus I pursue,
  Who bought me with his blood!
All thy pleasures I forego,
  I trample on thy wealth and pride;
Only Jesus will I know,
  And Jesus crucified.

2 Other knowledge I disdain,
  'Tis all but vanity;
Christ the Lamb of God was slain,
  He tasted death for me!
Me to save from endless woe,
  The sin-atoning Victim died!
Only Jesus will I know,
  And Jesus crucified!

3 Here will I set up my rest;
  My fluctuating heart,
From the haven of his breast,
  Shall never more depart;
Whither should a sinner go?
  His wounds for me stand open wide;
Only Jesus will I know,
  And Jesus crucified.

4 Him to know is life and peace,
  And pleasure without end;
This is all my happiness,
  On Jesus to depend;
Daily in his grace to grow,
  And ever in his faith abide;

Only Jesus will I know,
  And Jesus crucified.

5 O that I could all invite,
  This saving truth to prove:
Show the length, the breadth, the height,
  And depth of Jesus' love!
Fain I would to sinners show
  The blood by faith alone applied;
Only Jesus will I know,
  And Jesus crucified.

337   Metre 25.   [Redeeming Grace.

COME, all who love my Lord and Master,
  And like old David I will tell,
Though chief of sinners, I've found favor,
  By grace redeemed from death and hell;
Far as the East from West is parted,
  So far my sins by dying love,
From me by faith are separated;
  Blest antepast of joys above.

2 I late estranged from Jesus wandered,
  And thought each dang'rous poison good;
But he in mercy long pursued me,
  With cries of his redeeming blood.
Though, like Bartimeus, I was blinded,
  In nature's darkest night concealed;
But Jesus' love removed my blindness,
  And he his pard'ning grace revealed.

3 Now I will serve him while he spares me,
  And with his people sing aloud;
Though hell oppose, and sinners mock me,
  In rapt'rous songs I'll praise my God:
By faith I view the heavenly concert,
  They sing high strains of Jesus' love;
Oh, with desire my soul is longing,
  And fain would be with Christ above.

4 That blessed day is fast approaching,
   When Christ in glorious clouds will come,
With sounding trumps and shouts of angels,
   To call each faithful spirit home;
There Abra'm, Isaac, holy prophets,
   And all the saints at God's right hand;
There hosts of angels join in concert—
   Shout as they reach the promised land.

338   Metre 4.   [Possession.

JESUS, I my cross have taken,
   All to leave and follow thee;
Naked, poor, despised, forsaken,
   Thou from hence my all shalt be.
Perish, every fond ambition,
   All I've sought, or hoped, or known;
Yet how rich is my condition,
   God and heaven are still my own!

2 Let the world despise and leave me—
   They have left my Savior, too;
Human hearts and looks deceive me—
   Thou art not, like them untrue.
And whilst thou shalt smile upon me,
   God of wisdom, love, and might,
Foes may hate and friends disown me—
   Show thy face and all is bright.

3 Go, then earthly fame and treasure,
   Come, disaster, scorn, and pain;
In thy service pain is pleasure—
   With thy favor loss is gain;
I have called thee Abba, Father,
   I have set my heart on thee;
Storms may howl and clouds may gather,
   All must work for good to me.

4 Man may trouble and distress me,
   'T will but drive me to thy breast;
Life with trials hard may press me,
   Heav'n will give me sweeter rest.
Oh! 't is not in grief to harm me,
   While thy love is left to me;
Oh! 't were not in joy to charm me,
   Were that joy unmixed with thee.

5 Soul, then know thy full salvation—
   Rise o'er sin and fear and care,
Joy to find in every station,
   Something still to do or bear.
Think what Spirit dwells within thee—
   Think what Father's smiles are thine;
Think that Jesus died to win thee—
   Child of heaven, canst thou repine?

6 Haste thee on from grace to glory,
   Armed by faith and winged by prayer;
Heaven's eternal day's before thee—
   God's own hand shall guide thee there.
Soon shall close thy earthly mission,
   Soon shall pass thy pilgrim days;
Hope shall change to glad fruition,
   Faith to sight, and prayer to praise.

339   C. M.   [ARNHEIM.

FATHER, how wide thy glory shines!
   How high thy wonders rise!
Known thro' the earth by thousand signs,
   By thousands through the skies
Those mighty orbs proclaim thy power,
   Their motions speak by skill;

  And on the wings of every hour
   We read thy patience still.
2 Part of thy name divinely stands,
  On all thy creatures writ,
 They show the labor of thy hands,
  Or impress of thy feet;
 But when we view thy strange design
  To save rebellious worms,
 Where vengeance and compassion join
  In their divinest forms—
3 Here the whole Deity is known,
  Nor dares a creature guess
 Which of the glories brightest shone,
  The justice or the grace!
 Now the full glories of the Lamb
  Adorn the heavenly plains;
 Bright seraphs learn Immanuel's name,
  And try their choicest strains.
4 O may I bear some humble part
  In that Immortal song!
 Wonder and joy shall tune my heart,
  And love command my tongue,
 To Father, Son, and Holy Ghost,
  Who sweetly all agree,
 To save a world of sinners lost—
  Eternal glory be.

340   Metre 53.   [Heavenly Treasure.

Religion! 'tis a glorious treasure,
 The purchase of a Savior's blood;
It fills the soul with consolation;
 It lifts the thoughts to things above.

It calms our fears, it soothes our sorrows,
  It smoothes our way o'er life's rough sea;
'T is mixed with goodness, meekness, patience;
  This heavenly portion mine shall be.

2 While journeying here through tribulation,
  In Christian love we'll march along;
And while strife severs the ambition—
  In Jesus Christ we'll all be one.
Religion pure unites together
  In bonds of love and makes us free;
While endless ages are onward rolling,
  This heavenly portion mine shall be.

3 How fleeting—vain—how transitory,
  This world with all its pomp and show!
Its vain delights, and short-lived pleasures,
  I'll gladly leave them all below,
But love and grace shall be my story,
  While I in Christ such beauties see;
While endless ages are onward rolling,
  This heavenly portion mine shall be.

4. This earthly house must be dissolved,
  And mortal life will soon be o'er;
All earthly care and earthly sorrow,
  Shall pain my eyes and heart no more.
Religion pure will stand forever,
  And my glad heart shall strengthened be;
While endless ages are onward rolling,
  This heavenly portion mine shall be.

341   C. M.   [ORTONVILLE.

WHEN languor and disease invade
  This trembling house of clay,
'T is sweet to look beyond my pains,
  And long to fly away.

2 Sweet to look inward, and attend
　The whisper of his love;
Sweet to look upward to the place
　Where Jesus pleads above.

3 Sweet to look back and see my name
　In life's fair book set down;
Sweet to look forward and behold
　Eternal joys my own.

4 Sweet to reflect how grace divine
　My sins on Jesus laid;
Sweet to remember that his blood
　My debt of suffering paid.

5 Sweet in his righteousness to stand,
　Which saves from second death;
Sweet to experience, day by day,
　His Spirit's quick'ning breath.

342   C. M.   Detroit.

COME, let us now forget our mirth,
　And think that we must die;
What are our best delights on earth,
　Compared with those on high?

2 Our pleasures here will soon be past;
　Our brightest joys decay;
But pleasures there forever last,
　And cannot fade away.

3 Here sins and sorrows we deplore,
　With many cares distressed;
But there the mourners weep no more,
　And there the weary rest.

4 Our dearest friends, when death shall call
　At once must hence depart;

But there we hope to meet them all,
  And never, never part.
5 Then let us love and serve the Lord,
  With all our youthful powers,
And we shall gain the great reward,
  The glory shall be ours.

343   Metre 12.   [Deliverance.

How solemn the signal I hear!
  The summons that calls me away,
In regions unknown to appear,
  How shall I the summons obey?
What scenes in that world shall arise,
  When life's latest sigh shall be fled,
And darkness has sealed up mine eyes,
  And deep in the dust I am laid!
2 No longer the world I can view,
  The scenes which so long I have known;
My friends, I must bid you adieu,
  For here I must travel alone.
Yet here my Redeemer has trod,
  His hallowed footsteps I know;
I'll trust for defense to his rod,
  And lean on his staff as I go.
3 Dear Shepherd of Israel, lead on,
  My soul follows hard after thee,
The phantoms of death are all flown,
  When Jesus my Shepherd I see.
Dear brethren and sisters, I go
  To wait your arrival above;
Be faithful and soon you shall know
  The triumphs and joys of his love.

344   C. M.   [BELMONT.

WHAT poor, despised company
   Of travelers are these,
That walk in yonder narrow way,
   Along that rugged maze?

2 Why, they are of a royal line,
   All children of a King:
Heirs of immortal crowns divine,
   And loud for joy they sing.

3 Why do they then appear so mean,
   And why so much despised?
Because of their rich robes unseen,
   The world is not apprized.

4 But some of them seem poor, distressed,
   And lacking daily bread:
Ah! they're of wealth divine possessed—
   With hidden manna fed.

5 Why do they keep that narrow road,
   That rugged, thorny maze?
Because that way their Leader trod—
   They love and keep his ways.

6 Why do they shun the pleasing path,
   That worldings love so well?
Because it is the road to death—
   The open road to hell.

7 What! is there no other road,
   To Canaan's happy ground?
Christ is the only way to God—
   No other can be found.

345   C. M.   [SALVATION.

YE weary, heavy laden souls,
  Who are oppressed sore,
Ye travelers through the wilderness,
  To Canaan's peaceful shore;
Through chilling winds and beating rain,
  The waters deep and cold,
And enemies surrounding you,
  Take courage and be bold.

2 Though storms and hurricanes arise,
  The desert all around,
And fiery serpents oft appear
  Through the enchanted ground;
Dark nights and clouds and gloomy fear,
  And dragons often roar:
But while the gospel trump we hear,
  We'll press for Canaan's shore.

3 We're often like the lonesome dove,
  Who mourns her absent mate,
From hill to hill, from vale to vale,
  Her sorrows to relate;
But Canaan's land is just before,
  Sweet spring is coming on;
A few more beating winds and rains,
  And winter will be gone.

4 Sometimes like mountains to the sky,
  Black Jordan's billows roar,
Which often make the pilgrims fear
  They never will get o'er;
But let us gain Mount Pisgah's top,
  And view the vernal plain,

To fright our souls may Jordan roar,
   And hell may rage in vain.
5 Methinks I now begin to see
   The borders of that land;
The trees of life, with heavenly fruit,
   In beauteous order stand.
The wint'ry time is past and gone,
   Sweet flowers now appear;
The fiftieth year hath now rolled round,
   The great Sabbatic year.
6 O, what a glorious sight appears.
   To my believing eyes;
Methinks I see Jerusalem,
   A city in the skies!
Bright angels whispering me away,
   "O come, my brother, come,"
And I am willing to be gone
   To my eternal home.
7 Farewell my brethren in the Lord,
   Who are to Canaan bound;
And should we never meet again
   Till the last trump shall sound,
I hope that I shall meet you there,
   On that delightful shore;
In oceans of eternal bliss,
   Where parting is no more.

346   Metre 8.   [Saunders.

AND can it be that I should gain
   An int'rest in the Savior's blood?
Died he for me, who caused his pain—
   For me, who him to death pursued?

Amazing love! and can it be,
That thou, my Lord, should'st die for me?
2 'T is myst'ry all, th' Immortal dies!
   Who can explore his strange design?
In vain the first-born seraph tries
   To sound the depths of earth divine!
'T is mercy all! let earth adore;
Let angel minds inquire no more.
3 He left his Father's throne above;
   (So free, so infinite his love!)
Emptied himself of all but love,
   And bled for Adam's helpless race;
'T is mercy all, immense and free,
For, O my God, it found out me!
4 Long my imprisoned spirit lay,
   Fast bound in sin and nature's night;
Thine eye diffused a quick'ning ray;
   I woke: the dungeon flamed with light;
My chains fell off, my heart was free,
I rose, went forth, and followed thee
5 No condemnation now I dread,
   Jesus, and all in him is mine!
Alive in him my living Head;
   And clothed in righteousness divine,
Bold I approach th' eternal throne,
And claim the crown, thro' Christ, my own

347 Metre 6. [PROBATION.

AND am I only born to die?
   And must I suddenly comply
      With nature's stern decree?
What after death for me remains?

Celestial joys or hellish pains,
  To all eternity!
2 How then ought I on earth to live
While God prolongs the kind reprieve,
  And props the house of clay?
My sole concern, my single care,
To watch and tremble, and prepare
  Against that fatal day.
3 No room for mirth or trifling here,
For worldly hope or worldly fear,
  If life so soon is gone;
If now the Judge is at the door,
And all mankind must stand before
  Th' inexorable throne!
4 No matter which my thoughts employ;
A moment's misery or joy;
  But O! when both shall end,
Where shall I find my destined place?
Shall I my everlasting days,
  With fiends or angels spend?
5 Nothing is worth a thought beneath,
But how I may escape the death
  That never, never dies!
How make my own election sure;
And when I fail on earth, secure
  A mansion in the skies.
6 Jesus, vouchsafe a pitying ray,
Be thou my Guide, be thou my Way
  To glorious happiness.
Ah! write the pardon on my heart,
And whenso'er I hence depart,
  Let me depart in peace.

348   S. M.   [AYLESBURY.

AND let our bodies part,
   To different climes repair;
Inseparably joined in heart,
   The friends of Jesus are.

2 Jesus the Corner-Stone,
   Did first our hearts unite;
And still he keeps our spirits one,
   Who walk with him in white.

3 O let us still proceed
   In Jesus' work below;
And foll'wing our triumphant Head,
   To further conquests go.

4 The vineyard of the Lord
   Before his laborers lies;
And lo! we see the vast reward
   Which waits us in the skies.

5 O let our heart and mind
   Continually ascend,
That haven of repose to find,
   Where all our labors end!

6 Where all our toils are o'er,
   Our suff'ring and our pain;
Who meet on that eternal shore,
   Shall never part again.

7 O happy, happy place,
   Where saints and angels meet!
There we shall see each other's face,
   And all our brethren greet.

8 The church of the first born,
    We shall with them be blest,
  And, crowned with endless joy, return
    To our eternal rest.

9 With joy we shall behold,
    In yonder blest abode,
  The patriarchs and prophets old,
    And all the saints of God.

10 Abra'm and Isaac, there,
    And Jacob shall receive
  The followers of their faith and prayer,
    Who now in bodies live.

11 We shall our time beneath,
    Live out in cheerful hope,
  And fearless pass the vale of death,
    And gain the mountain top.

12 To gather home his own,
    God shall his angels send,
  And bid our bliss on earth begun,
    In deathless triumphs end.

349   L. M.   [GALILEE.

THE wond'ring world inquires to know
    Why I should love my Jesus so;
  "What are his charms," say they, "above
    The objects of a mortal love?"

2 Yes, my Beloved, to my sight,
  Shows a sweet mixture, red and white;
  All human beauties, all divine,
  In my beloved meet, and shine.

3 White is his soul from blemish free;
  Red with the blood he shed for me;
  The fairest of ten thousand fairs;
  A Sun among ten thousand stars.

4 His head the finest gold excels;
  There wisdom in perfection dwells;
  And glory, like a crown, adorns
  Those temples once beset with thorns.

5 Compassions in his heart are found,
  Near to the signals of his wound;
  His sacred side no more shall bear
  The cruel scourge, the piercing spear.

6 His hands are fairer to behold
  Than diamonds set in rings of gold;
  Those heavenly hands, that on the tree
  Were nailed and torn, and bled for me.

7 Though once he bowed his feeble knees,
  Loaded with sins and agonies,
  Now on the throne of his command,
  His legs like marble pillars stand.

8 His eyes are majesty and love,
  The eagle tempered with the dove;
  No more shall trickling sorrow roll
  Through those dear windows of his soul.

9 His mouth that pour'd out long complaints
  Now smiles, and cheers his fainting saints;
  His countenance more graceful is
  Than Lebanon with all its trees.

10 All over glorious is my Lord,
   Must be beloved and yet adored!

His worth if all the nations knew,
Sure the whole world would love him too!

350   C. M.   [Woodland.

BEHOLD the glories of the Lamb,
  Amidst his Father's throne;
Prepare new honors for his name,
  And songs before unknown.

2 Let elders worship at his feet,
  The church adore around;
With vials full of odors sweet,
  And harps of sweeter sound.

3 Those are the prayers of all the saints,
  And these the hymns they raise:
Jesus is kind to our complaints;
  He loves to hear our praise.

4 Eternal Father, who shall look
  Into thy secret will?
Who but the Son shall take that Book,
  And open every seal?

5 He shall fulfill thy great decrees,
  The Son deserves it well;
Lo! in his hand, the sovereign keys
  Of heaven and death and hell!

6 Now to the Lamb that once was slain,
  Be endless blessings paid;
Salvation, glory, joy, remain
  Forever on thy head.

7 Thou hast redeemed our souls with blood,
  Hast set the pris'ners free,

Hast made us kings and priests to God,
　And we shall reign with thee.

8 The worlds of nature and of grace
　Are put beneath thy power;
Then shorten these delaying days,
　And bring the promised hour.

351　　　L. M.　　　[WELLS.

LIFE is the time to serve the Lord,
　The time t' insure the great reward,
And while the lamp holds out to burn,
The vilest sinner may return.

2 Life is the hour that God hath given
T' escape from hell and fly to heaven!
The day of grace, and mortals may
Secure the blessings of the day.

3 The living know that they must die,
But all the dead forgotten lie;
Their mem'ry, and their sense is gone,
Alike unknowing and unknown.

4 Their hatred, and their love is lost,
Their envy buried in the dust;
They have no share in all that's done
Beneath the circuit of the sun.

5 Then what my thoughts design to do,
My hands with all their might pursue;
Since no device nor work is found,
Nor faith, nor hope, beneath the ground.

6 There are no acts of pardon passed
In the cold grave to which we haste;

But darkness, death, and long despair,
Reign in eternal silence there,

352   Metre 9.   [Lenox.

BLOW ye the trumpet, blow,
  The gladly solemn sound;
Let all the nations know,
  To earth's remotest bound;
The year of Jubilee is come;
Return, ye ransomed sinners, home.

2 Jesus, our great High Priest,
  Hath full atonement made;
Ye weary spirits, rest,
  Ye mournful souls, be glad;
The year of Jubilee is come;
Return, ye ransomed sinners, home.

3 Extol the Lamb of God,
  The all atoning Lamb;
Redemption in his blood
  Throughout the world proclaim;
The year of Jubilee is come;
Return, ye ransomed sinners, home.

4 Ye slaves of sin and hell,
  Your liberty receive,
And safe in Jesus dwell,
  And blest in Jesus live:
The year of Jubilee is come;
Return, ye ransomed sinners, home.

5 Ye who have sold for naught
  Your heritage above,
Shall have it back unbought,
  The gift of Jesus' love;

The year of Jubilee is come;
Return, ye ransomed sinners, home.

6 The gospel trumpet hear,
   The news of heavenly grace;
And, saved from earth, appear
   Before your Savior's face;
The year of Jubilee is come:
   Return, ye ransomed sinners, home.

353   L. M.   '[GALILEE.

FAR from my thoughts, vain world, be
   Let my religious hours alone; [gone,
Fain would my eyes my Savior see;
I wait a visit, Lord, from thee.

2 My heart grows warm with holy fire,
And kindles with a pure desire;
Come, my dear Jesus, from above,
And feed my soul with heavenly love.

3 The trees of life immortal stand
In fragrant rows at thy right hand,
And in sweet murmurs by their side
Rivers of bliss perpetual glide.

4 Haste then, but with a smiling face,
And spread the table of thy grace;
Bring down a taste of truth divine,
And cheer my heart with sacred wine.

5 Blest Jesus! what delicious fare!
How sweet thy entertainments are!
Never did angels taste above,
Redeeming grace and dying love.

6 Hail, great Immanuel, all divine!
   In thee thy Father's glories shine;
   Thou brightest, sweetest, fairest One,
   That eyes have seen or angels known.

354   L. M.   [WINDHAM.

NOW, in the heat of youthful blood,
   Remember your Creator, God;
Behold the months come hast'ning on,
When you shall say, "My joys are gone."

2 Behold! the aged sinner goes,
   Laden with guilt and heavy woes,
   Down to the regions of the dead,
   With endless curses on his head.

3 The dust returns to dust again;
   The soul in agonies of pain
   Ascends to God; not there to dwell,
   But hears her doom and sinks to hell.

4 Eternal King! I fear thy name;
   Teach me to know how frail I am;
   And when my soul must hence remove,
   Give me a mansion in thy love.

355   L. M.   [ROCKINGHAM.

FIRM was my health, my day was bright,
   And I presumed t'would ne'er be night;
Fondly I said within my heart,
"Pleasure and peace shall ne'er depart."

2 But I forgot thine arm was strong,
   Which made my mountain stand so long;

Soon as thy face began to hide,
My health was gone, my comforts died.

3 I cried aloud to thee, my God,
"What canst thou profit by my blood?
Deep in the dust can I declare
Thy truth, or sing thy goodness there?

4 "Hear me, O God of grace," I said,
"And bring me from among the dead;"
Thy words rebuked the pains I felt,
Thy pard'ning love removed my guilt.

5 My groans and tears and forms of woe,
Are turned to joy and praises now;
I throw my sackcloth on the ground,
And ease and gladness gird me round.

6 My tongue, the glory of my frame,
Shall ne'er be silent of thy name; [heaven,
Thy praise shall sound through earth and
For sickness healed, and sins forgiven.

356   C. M.   [Marlow.

O ALL ye nations, praise the Lord,
  Each with a different tongue!
In every language learn his word,
  And let his name be sung.

2 His mercy reigns through every land;
  Proclaim his grace abroad;
Forever firm his truth shall stand;
  Praise ye the faithful God.

357   S. M.   [St. Thomas.

THE God, Jehovah, reigns,
  Let all the nations fear;
Let sinners tremble at his throne,
  And saints be humble there.

2 Jesus, the Savior, reigns,
  Let earth adore its Lord;
Bright cherubs his attendants stand,
  Swift to fulfill his word.

3 In Zion stands his throne,
  His honors are divine;
His church shall make his wonders known
  For there his glories shine.

4 How holy is his name!
  How terrible his praise!
Justice and truth, and judgment join
  In all his works of grace.

358   Metre 4.   [Charleston.

HAPPY soul, thy days are ended,
  All thy mourning days below;
Go—by angel-guards attended—
  To the sight of Jesus, go!

2 Waiting to receive thy spirit,
  Lo! the Savior stands above;
Shows the glory of his merit,
  Reaches out the crown of love.

3 Struggle through thy latest passion
  To thy dear Redeemer's breast,

  To his uttermost salvation,
   To his everlasting rest.

4 For the joy he sets before thee,
  Bear a momentary pain;
Die, to live the life of glory—
  Suffer, with thy Lord to reign.

359   C. M.   [Detroit.

WHEN rising from the bed of death,
  O'erwhelmed with guilt and fear,
I see my Maker face to face,
  O how shall I appear?

2 If yet, while pardon may be found,
  And mercy may be sought,
My heart with inward horror shrinks,
  And trembles at the thought!

3 When thou, O Lord, shalt stand disclosed,
  In majesty severe,
And sit in judgment on my soul,
  O how shall I appear?

4 But thou hast told the troubled mind,
  Who does her sins lament,
The timely tribute of her tears
  Shall endless woe prevent.

5 Then see the sorrows of my heart,
  Ere yet it be too late;
And hear my Savior's dying groans,
  To give these sorrows weight.

6 For never shall my soul despair
  Her pardon to procure.

Who knows thine only Son has died,
  To make her pardon sure.

360   L. M.   [WESTON.

IN glory bright the Savior reigns,
  And endless grandeur there sustains:
We view his beams, and from afar,
Hail him the bright, the Morning Star.

2 Blest Star! where'er his luster shines,
He all the soul with grace refines;
And makes each happy saint declare,
He is the bright, the Morning Star.

3 Sweet Star! his influence is divine;
Life, peace, and joy attending shine;
Death, hell, and sin before him flee;
The bright, the Morning Star, is he.

4 Great Star, in whom salvation dwells,
His beam the thickest cloud dispels:
The grossest darkness flies afar,
Before this bright, this Morning Star.

5 Eternal Star! our songs shall rise,
When we shall meet thee in the skies;
And, in eternal anthems, there
Praise thee, the bright, the Morning Star.

361   C. M.   [MEAR.

MY drowsy powers, why sleep ye so?
  Awake, my sluggish soul!
Nothing has half thy work to do,
  Yet nothing's half so dull.

2 The little ants, for one poor grain,
    Labor and tug and strive;
  Yet we, who have a heav'n t' obtain,
    How negligent we live!

3 We, for whose sake all nature stands,
    And stars their courses move;
  We, for whose guard the angel bands
    Come flying from above:

4 We, for whom God the Son, came down,
    And labored for our good;
  How careless to secure that crown
    He purchased with his blood.

5 Lord, shall we lie so sluggish still,
    And never act our parts?
  Come, Holy Dove, from th' heavenly hill,
    And sit and warm our hearts.

6 Then shall our active spirits move,
    Upward our souls shall rise;
  With hands of faith, and wings of love.
    We'll fly and take the prize.

362   S. M.   [St. Thomas.

SHALL wisdom cry aloud,
    And not her speech be heard?
The voice of God's eternal Word,
    Deserves it no regard?

2 "I was his chief delight,
    His everlasting Son.
  Before the first of all his works,
    Creation was begun.

3 "Before the flying clouds,
    Before the solid land,
Before the fields, before the floods,
    I dwelt at his right hand.

4 "When he adorned the skies,
    And built them, I was there,
To order when the sun should rise,
    And marshal every star.

5 "When he poured out the sea,
    And spread the flowing deep;
I gave the flood a firm decree,
    In its own bounds to keep.

6 "Upon the empty air
    The earth was balanced well;
With joy I saw the mansion where
    The sons of men should dwell.

7 "My busy thoughts at first
    On their salvation ran,
Ere sin was born, or Adam's dust
    Was fashioned into man.

8 "Then come, receive my grace,
    Ye children, and be wise;
Happy the man that keeps my ways;
    The man that shuns them dies."

363   Metre 5.   [Welton.

WHEN on Sinia's top I see
    God descend in Majesty,
To proclaim his holy law,
All my spirit sinks with awe:

2 When, in ecstacy sublime,
  Tabor's glorious steep I climb,
  At the too transporting light,
  Darkness rushes o'er my sight.

3 When on Calvary I rest,
  God in flesh made manifest,
  Shines in my Redeemer's face,
  Full of beauty, truth, and grace.

4 Here I would forever stay,
  Weep and gaze my soul away;
  Thou art heaven on earth to me,
  Lovely, mournful, Calvary.

364 C. M. [ARLINGTON.

AWAKE, my soul, to sound his praise,
  Awake, my harp, to sing:
Join, all my powers, the song to raise,
  And morning incense bring.

2 Among the people of his care,
    And through the nations round,
  Glad songs of praise will I prepare,
    And there his name resound.

3 Be thou exalted, O my God,
    Above the starry frame;
  Diffuse thy heavenly grace abroad,
    And teach the world thy name.

4 So shall thy chosen sons rejoice,
    And throng thy courts above;
  While sinners hear thy pard'ning voice,
    And taste Redeeming love.

365 C. M. [SOLON.

Dear Refuge of my weary soul,
  On thee, when sorrows rise,
On thee, when waves of trouble roll,
  My fainting hope relies.

2 To thee I tell each rising grief,
  For thou alone canst heal;
Thy word can bring a sweet relief,
  For every pain I feel.

3 Hast thou not bid me seek thy face?
  And shall I seek in vain?
And can the ear of sovereign grace
  Be deaf when I complain?

4 No; still the ear of sovereign grace
  Attends the mourner's prayer;
Oh, may I ever find access
  To breathe my sorrows there!

5 Thy mercy-seat is open still:
  Here let my soul retreat;
With humble hope attend thy will,
  And wait beneath thy feet.

366 Metre 26. [New Haven.

Glory to God on high!
  Let heaven and earth reply,
    "Praise ye his name!"
Angels, his love adore,
Who all our sorrows bore,
Saints, sing for evermore,
  "Worthy the Lamb!"

2 Ye, who surround the throne,
  Cheerfully join in one,
    Praising his name;
Ye, who have felt his blood
Sealing your peace with God,
Sound through the earth abroad,
  "Worthy the Lamb!"

3 Join all the ransomed race,
  Our Lord and God to bless:
    Praise ye his name;
In him we will rejoice,
Making a cheerful noise,
Shouting with heart and voice,
  "Worthy the Lamb!"

4 Soon must we change our place,
  Yet we will never cease
    Praising his name;
Still we will tribute bring,
Hail him our gracious King;
And through all ages sing,
  "Worthy the Lamb!"

367   C. M.   [Azmon.

VAIN man, thy fond pursuits forbear;
  Repent!—thy end is nigh;
Death at the farthest can't be far;
  O think before thou die!

2 Reflect, thou hast a soul to save:
  Thy sins, how high they mount!
What are thy hopes beyond the grave?
  How stands that dread account?

3 Death enters—and there's no defense—
    His time there's none can tell;
He'll in a moment call thee hence,
    To heaven—or to hell.

4 Thy flesh, perhaps thy chiefest care,
    Shall crawling worms consume;
But ah! destruction stops not there—
    Sin kills beyond the tomb.

5 To-day the gospel calls—to-day,
    Sinners, it speaks to you;
Let every one forsake his way,
    And mercy will ensue.

368   C. M.   [PETERBOROUGH.

BLESS'D is the man who shuns the place
    Where sinners love to meet;
Who fears to tread their wicked ways,
    And hates the scoffer's seat:

2 But in the statutes of the Lord,
    Has placed his chief delight;
By day he reads or hears the word,
    And meditates by night.

3 (He, like a plant of generous kind,
    By living water set,
Safe from the storms and blasting wind,
    Enjoys a peaceful state)

4 Green as the leaf, and ever fair
    Shall his profession shine;
While fruits of holiness appear
    Like clusters on the vine.

5 Not so the impious and unjust;
    What vain designs they form!
  Their hopes are blown away like dust,
    Or chaff before the storm.

6 Sinners in judgment shall not stand
    Among the sons of grace;
  When Christ, the Judge, at his right hand
    Appoints his saints a place.

7 His eye beholds the path they tread,
    His heart approves it well;
  But crooked ways of sinners lead
    Down to the gates of hell.

369   L. M.   [Portugal.

HOW lovely, how divinely sweet,
    O Lord, thy sacred courts appear!
  Fain would my longing passions meet
    The glories of thy presence there.

2 O blest the man; blest their employ,
    Whom thy indulgent favors raise
  To dwell in those abodes of joy,
    And sing thy never-ceasing praise.

3 Happy the men whom strength divine
    With ardent love and zeal inspires:
  Whose steps to thy blest way incline,
    With willing hearts and warm desires.

4 One day within thy sacred gate
    Affords more real joy to me,
  Than thousands in the tents of state:
    The meanest place is bliss with thee.

5 God is a Sun—our brightest day
   From his reviving presence flows:
 God is a shield through all the way,
   To guard us from surrounding foes.

6 He pours his kindest blessings down,
   Profusely down on souls sincere;
 And grace shall guide, and glory crown
   The happy fav'rites of his care.

7 O Lord of hosts, thou God of grace,
   How blest, divinely blest, is he
 Who trusts thy love, and seeks thy face,
   And fixes all thy hope on thee!

370   Metre 5.   [Hendon.

COME, my soul, thy suit prepare,
  Jesus loves to answer prayer:
He himself has bid thee pray;
Rise and ask without delay.

2 With my burden I begin;
 Lord, remove this load of sin:
 Let thy blood for sinners spilt,
 Set my conscience free from guilt.

3 Lord! I come to thee for rest,
 Take possession of my breast;
 There thy sovereign right maintain,
 And without a rival reign.

4 While I am a pilgrim here,
 Let thy love my spirit cheer;
 Be my Guide, my Guard, my Friend;
 Lead me to my journey's end.

5 Show me what I have to do,
　Every hour my strength renew;
　Let me live a life of faith,
　Let me die thy people's death.

371　　　C. M.　　[Walsel—Evan.

LORD, I approach thy mercy-seat,
　Where thou dost answer prayer;
There humbly fall before thy feet,
　For none can perish there.

2 Thy promise is my only plea;
　　With this I venture nigh;
　Thou callest burdened souls to thee,
　　And such, O Lord, am I.

3 Bowed down beneath a load of sin,
　　By Satan sorely pressed,
　By war without and fear within,
　　I come to thee for rest.

4 Be thou my Shield and Hiding-place;
　　That, sheltered near thy side,
　I may my fierce accuser face,
　　And tell him thou hast died.

5 Oh, wondrous love! to bleed and die,
　　To bear the cross and shame,
　That guilty sinners, such as I,
　　Might plead thy gracious name.

372　　　Metre 4.　　Greenville.

SWEET the moment, rich in blessing,
　Which before the cross I spend;

Life and health and peace possessing
　From the sinner's dying Friend;
Here I'll sit forever viewing,
　Mercy's streams in streams of blood;
Precious drops my soul bedewing,
　Plead and claim my peace with God.

2 Truly blessed is this station,
　　Low before his cross to lie;
　While I see divine compassion,
　　Floating in his languid eye;
　Here it is I find my heaven,
　　While upon the Lamb I gaze;
　Love I much—I've much forgiven—
　　I'm a miracle of grace.

3 Love and grief my heart dividing,
　　With my tears his feet I'll bathe;
　Constant still in faith abiding,
　　Life deriving from his death:
　May I still enjoy this feeling,
　　In all need to Jesus go;
　Prove his wounds each day more healing,
　　And himself more deeply know.

373　　Metre 24.　[Gospel Trumpet.

HARK! how the gospel trumpet sounds!
　Thro' all the earth the echo bounds;
And Jesus by redeeming blood,
Is bringing sinners back to God,
And guides them safely by his word,
　To endless day.

2 Hail! all-victorious, conquering Lord!
Be thou by all thy works adored,

Who undertook for sinful man,
And brought salvation through thy name,
That we with thee may ever reign
　　In endless day.

3 Fight on, ye conquering souls, fight on,
And when the conquest you have won,
Then palms of victory you shall bear,
And in his kingdom have a share,
And crowns of glory ever wear
　　In endless day.

4 There we shall in full chorus join,
With saints and angels all combine,
To sing of his redeeming love,
When rolling years shall cease to move,
And this shall be our theme above
　　In endless day.

374　　　C. M.　　　[Mendota.

O HOW I love thy holy law!
　'T is daily my delight:
And thence my meditations draw
　Divine advice by night.

2 My waking eyes prevent the day
　To meditate thy word;
My soul with longing melts away
　To hear thy gospel, Lord.

3 How doth thy word my heart engage!
　How well employ my tongue!
And in my tiresome pilgrimage,
　Yields me a heavenly song!

4 Am I a stranger, or at home,
   'T is my perpetual feast:
Not honey dropping from the comb,
   So much allures my taste.

5 No treasures so enrich the mind;
   Nor shall thy word be sold
For loads of silver well refined,
   Or heaps of choicest gold.

6 When nature sinks and spirits droop,
   Thy promises of grace
Are pillars to support my hope—
   And there I write thy praise.

375   Metre 5.   [Hendon.

TO thy pastures, fair and large,
   Heavenly Shepherd, lead thy charge,
And my couch with tenderest care,
Midst the springing grass prepare.

2 When I faint with summer's heat,
Thou shalt guide my weary feet
To the streams that, still and slow,
Through the verdant meadows flow.

3 Safe the dreary vale I tread,
By the shades of death o'erspread;
With my rod and staff supplied,
This my guard—and that my guide.

4 Constant to my latest end,
Thou my footsteps shall attend;
And shalt bid thy hallowed dome
Yield me an eternal home.

VARIOUS SUBJECTS.

376   Metre 5.   Pleyel.

SEEK, my soul, the narrow gate,
Enter ere it be too late;
Many ask to enter there,
When too late to offer prayer.

2 God from mercy's seat shall rise,
And forever bar the skies;
Then, though sinners cry without,
He will say, "I know you not."

3 Mournfully will they exclaim,
"Lord we have professed thy name;
We have ate with thee, and heard
Heavenly teachings in thy word."

4 Vain, alas! will be their plea,
Workers of iniquity;
Sad their everlasting lot—
Christ will say, "I know you not."

377   L. M.   [Portugal.

BLESSED Redeemer, how divine—
How righteous is this rule of thine,
"Never to deal with others worse
Than we would have them deal with us."

2 This golden lesson, short and plain,
Gives not the mind nor memory pain;
And every conscience must approve
This universal law of love.

3 'T is written in each mortal, breast,
Where all our tend'rest wishes rest;

We draw it from our inmost veins,
Where love to self resides and reigns.

4 Is reason ever at a loss?
Call in self-love to judge the cause;
Let our own fondest passions show
How we should treat our neighbor, too.

5 How bless'd would every nation prove,
Thus ruled by equity and love!
All would be friends without a foe,
And form a paradise below.

378   C. M.   [BALERMA.

YE mourning saints, whose streaming
   Flow o'er your children dead, [tears
Say not in transports of despair,
   That all your hopes are fled.

2 While cleaving to that darling dust,
   In fond distress ye lie,
Rise, and with joy and rev'rence view
   A Heavenly Parent nigh.

3 Though your young branches torn away,
   Like withered trunks ye stand;
With fairer verdure shall ye bloom,
   Touched by th' Almighty's hand.

4 "I'll give the mourner," saith the Lord,
   "In my own house a place:
No names of daughters and of sons
   Could yield so high a grace.

5 "Transient and vain is every hope
   A rising race can give;

    In endless honor and delight,
      My children all shall live."
6 We welcome, Lord, those rising tears,
      Through which thy face we see,
  And bless those wounds, which thro' our
      Prepare a way for thee.   [hearts,

379   Metre 41.   [Evening Thought.

ERE I sleep for every favor,
    This day shown
      By my God,
I do bless my Savior.

2 Leave me not, but ever love me;
    Let thy peace
      Be my bliss,
Till thou hence remove me.

3 Thou my Rock, my Guard, my Tower,
    Safely keep
      While I sleep,
Me with all thy power.

4 And whene'er in death I slumber,
    Let me rise
      With the wise,
Counted in their number.

380   C. M.   [Balerma.

IN evil long I took delight,
    Unawed by shame or fear,
Till a new object struck my sight,
    And stopped my wild career.

2 I saw one hanging on a tree,
   In agonies and blood;
He fixed his languid eyes on me,
   As near his cross I stood.

3 O! never, till my latest breath,
   Shall I forget that look;
It seemed to charge me with his death,
   Though not a word he spoke.

4 My conscience felt and owned the guilt,
   It plunged me in despair;
I saw my sins his blood had spilt,
   And helped to nail him there.

5 A second look he gave, which said,
   I freely all forgive;
This blood is for thy ransom paid;
   I die that thou may'st live.

6 Thus while his death my sin displays,
   In all its darkest hue,
Such is the mystery of grace,
   It seals my pardon, too.

381   C. M.   [ORTONVILLE.

MAJESTIC sweetness sits enthroned,
   Upon the Savior's brow;
His head with radiant glories crowned,
   His lips with grace o'erflow.

2 No mortal can with him compare,
   Among the sons of men;
Fairer is he than all the fair
   Who fill the heavenly train.

3 He saw me plunged in deep distress,
    And flew to my relief;
For me he bore the shameful cross,
    And carried all my grief.

4 To him I owe my life and breath,
    And all the joys I have;
He makes me triumph over death,
    And saves me from the grave.

5 To heaven the place of his abode,
    He brings my weary feet;
Shows me the glories of my God,
    And makes my joys complete.

6 Since from his bounty I receive
    Such proofs of love divine;
Had I a thousand hearts to give,
    Lord, they should all be thine.

382   L. M.   [UXBRIDGE.

THE heavens declare thy glory, Lord,
    In every star thy wisdom shines;
But when our eyes behold thy word,
    We read thy name in fairer lines.

2 The rolling sun, the changing light,
    And nights and days thy power confess;
But that blest volume thou hast writ,
    Reveals thy justice and thy grace.

3 Sun, moon, and stars convey thy praise,
    Around the earth, and never stand;
So, when thy truth began its race,
    It touched and glanced on every land.

4 Nor shall thy spreading gospel rest
    Till through the world thy truth has run,
Till Christ has all the nations blest,
    That see the light or feel the sun.

5 Great sun of righteousness arise;
    O, bless the world with heavenly light;
Thy gospel makes the simple wise;
    Thy laws are pure, thy judgments right.

6 Thy noblest wonders here we view,
    In souls renewed, and sins forgiven;
Lord, cleanse my sins, my soul renew,
    And make thy word my guide to heav'n.

383   Metre 5.   [Martyn.

MARY to the Savior's tomb,
    Hasted at the early dawn;
Spice she brought, and sweet perfume,
    But the Lord she loved had gone;
For a while she ling'ring stood,
    Filled with sorrow and surprise;
Trembling while a crystal flood
    Issued from her weeping eyes.

2 But her sorrows quickly fled,
    When she heard his welcome voice;
Christ had risen from the dead;
    Now he bids her heart rejoice.
What a change his word can make,
    Turning darkness into day!
Ye who weep for Jesus' sake.
    He will wipe your tears away.

384   Metre 14.   [Webb.

Go when the morning shineth,
  Go when the noon is bright,
Go when the eve declineth,
  Go in the hush of night;
Go with pure mind and feeling,
  Fling earthly thought away,
And in thy closet kneeling,
  Do thou in secret pray.

2 Remember all who love thee,
  All who are loved by thee;
Pray too, for those who hate thee,
  If any such there be;
Then for thyself in meekness,
  A blessing humbly claim;
And blend with each petition,
  Thy great Redeemer's name.

3 Or if 't is e'er denied thee
  In solitude to pray,
Should holy thoughts come o'er thee,
  When friends are round thy way,
E'en then the silent breathing,
  Thy spirit raised above,
Will reach his throne of glory,
  Where dwells eternal love.

4 O, not a joy or blessing,
  With this can we compare—
The grace our Father gave us,
  To pour our souls in prayer;
Whene'er thou pin'st in sadness,
  Before his footstool fall;

Remember in thy gladness,
  His love who gave thee all.

385   L. M.   [ROCKINGHAM.

LO! round the throne at God's right hand,
The saints in countless myriads stand,
Of every tongue redeemed to God,
Arrayed in garments washed in blood.

2 Through tribulation great they came:
They bore the cross, despised the shame:
From all their labors now they rest,
In God's eternal glory blest.

3 Hunger and thirst they feel no more;
Nor sin, nor pain, nor death deplore;
The tears are wiped from every eye,
And sorrow yields to endless joy.

4 They see their Savior face to face,
And sing the triumphs of his grace:
Him day and night they ceaseless praise;
To him their loud hosannas raise.

5 Worthy the Lamb, for sinners slain,
Through endless years to live and reign;
Thou hast redeemed us by thy blood,
And made us kings and priests to God.

386   C. M.   [DUBLIN—WALSEL.

HAVE mercy, gracious Lord, forgive;
  Are not thy mercies free?
May not a dying sinner live;
  Who truly turns to thee?

2 My sins are great, I must confess,
　　Far more than I can know;
　But O, thy love and pardoning grace
　　Are great and boundless, too!

3 O, cleanse me from my sin and guilt,
　　And make my conscience clean;
　My heart with godly sorrow melt,
　　To mourn for every sin.

4 Great God! I must confess with shame,
　　I can't deny, but own,
　Corrupted, vile, and base I am,
　　As I to thee am known.

5 Yet, save my soul from deep despair,
　　According to thy word;
　To thee I make my feeble prayer—
　　To thee, my gracious Lord.

387   Metre 5.   [Tremont.

WHO is this that comes from far,
　　Clad in garments dipped in blood?
Strong, triumphant traveler,
　　Is he man or is he God?
I that speak in righteousness,
　　Son of God and Man I am;
Mighty to redeem your race,
　　Jesus is your Savior's name.

2 Wherefore are thy garments red,
　　Dyed as in a crimson sea?
　They that in the wine vat tread,
　　Are not stained so much as thee!

"I, the Father's favorite Son,
  Have the dreadful wine-press trod;
Borne the vengeful wrath alone—
  All the fiercest wrath of God."

3 Kind thou art and full of love,
  Savior, God, to suffer thus;
Rich the grace thy people prove,
  Thou hast shed thy blood for us;
May thy love's constraining power
  Tune our hearts and tongues to sing—
May we in this favored hour
  To the cross our trophies bring.

388   Metre 9.   [Zebulon.

WELCOME, delightful morn,
  Thou day of sacred rest!
I hail thy kind return;
  Lord, make these moments blest;
From the low train of mortal toys,
I soar to reach immortal joys.

2 Now may the King descend,
  And fill his throne of grace;
Thy sceptre, Lord, extend,
  While saints address thy face;
Let sinners feel thy quick'ning word,
And learn to know and fear the Lord.

3 Descend, celestial Dove,
  With all thy quick'ning powers;
Disclose a Savior's love,
  And bless the sacred hours;
Then shall my soul new life obtain,
Nor Sabbaths be bestowed in vain.

389   L. M.   [UXBRIDGE.

FROM every stormy wind that blows,
  From every swelling tide of woes,
There is a calm, a sure retreat;
'T is found before the mercy-seat

2 There is a place where Jesus sheds
  The oil of gladness on our heads—
A place of all on earth most sweet;
It is the blood-bought mercy-seat.

3 There is a scene where spirits blend,
  Where friend holds fellowship with friend;
Though sundered far, by faith they meet,
Around one common mercy-seat.

4 There, there, on eagles' wings we soar,
And sin and sense molest no more;
And heaven comes down our souls to greet,
And glory crowns the mercy-seat.

390   METRE 13.   [PILGRIM.

SINNER, hear the Savior's call,
  He now is passing by;
He has seen thy grievous thrall,
  And heard thy mournful cry;
He has pardons to impart,
  Grace to save thee from thy fears,
See the love that fills his heart,
  And wipes away thy tears.

2 Why art thou afraid to come,
  And tell him all thy case?

He will not pronounce thy doom,
  Nor frown thee from his face;
Wilt thou fear Immanuel?
  Wilt thou dread the Lamb of God,
Who to save thy soul from hell,
  Has shed his precious blood?

3 Think how on the cross he hung,
  Pierced with a thousand wounds!
Hark from each, as with a tongue,
  The voice of pardon sounds!
See from all his bursting veins,
  Blood of wondrous virtue flow!
Shed to wash away thy stains,
  And ransom thee from woe.

4 Though his majesty be great,
  His mercy is no less;
Though he thy transgressions hate,
  He feels for thy distress;
By himself the Lord has sworn,
  He delights not in thy death;
But invites thee to return,
  That thou mayest live by faith.

5 Raise thy downcast eyes, and see
  What throngs his throne surround!
These, though sinners once like thee,
  Have full salvation found.
Yield not then to unbelief,
  While he says, "There yet is room;"
Though of sinners thou art chief,
  Since Jesus calls thee, "Come."

391   S. M.   [Heavenly Portion.

Blest are the sons of peace,
  Whose hearts and hopes are one:
Whose kind designs to serve and please
  Through all their actions run.

2 Blest is the pious house
  Where zeal and friendship meet,
Their songs of praise, their mingled vows,
  Make their communion sweet.

3 Thus when on Aaron's head
  They poured the rich perfume,
The oil through all his raiment spread,
  And pleasure filled the room.

4 Thus on the heavenly hills,
  The saints are blest above,
Where joy, like morning dew, distils,
  And all the air is love.

392   Metre 4.   [Possession.

Mighty God, while angels bless thee,
  May a mortal lisp thy name?
Lord of men as well as angels,
  Thou art every creature's theme;
Lord of every land and nation,
  Ancient of eternal days,
Sounded through the wide creation
  Be thy just and lawful praise.

2 For the grandeur of thy nature—
  Grand beyond a seraph's thought,

For the wonders of Creation,
  Works with skill and kindness wrought
For thy providence that governs
  Through thine empire's wide domain,
Wings an angel, guides a sparrow—
  Blessed be thy gentle reign.

3 For thy rich, thy free redemption—
  Bright though veiled in darkness long,
Thought is poor, and poor expression;
  Who can sing that wondrous song?
Brightness of the Father's glory;
  Shall thy praise unuttered lie?
Break, my tongue, such guilty silence!
  Sing the Lord who came to die!

4 From the highest throne of glory,
  To the cross of deepest woe,
Came to ransom guilty captives;—
  Flow my praise, forever flow;
Re-ascend, immortal Savior;
  Leave thy footstool, take thy throne;
Thence return and reign forever;
  Be the kingdom all thine own.

393   Metre 5.   [Tremont.

WHILE with ceaseless course the sun
  Hasted through the former year,
Many souls their race have run,
  Never more to meet us here:
Fixed in an eternal state,
  They have done with all below;
We a little longer wait;
  But how little—none can know.

2 Spared to see another year,
   Let thy blessing meet us here;
Come, thy dying work revive,
   Bid thy drooping garden thrive;
Sun of righteousness, arise!
   Warm our hearts and bless our eyes;
Let our prayer thy pity move;
   Make this year a time of love.

3 Thanks for mercies past receive,
   Pardon of our sins renew;
Teach us henceforth how to live
   With eternity in view;
Bless thy word to old and young,
   Fill us with a Savior's love,
When our life's short race is run,
   May we dwell with thee above.

394   C. M.   [Balerma.

SHEPHERD divine, our wants relieve,
   In this our evil day;
To all thy tempted followers give
   The power to watch and pray.

2 Long as our fiery trials last,
   Long as the cross we bear;
O let our souls on thee be cast
   In never-ceasing prayer!

3 The spirit of redeeming grace,
   Give us in faith to claim;
To wrestle till we see thy face,
   And know thy hidden name.

4 Till thou thy perfect love impart,
   Till thou thyself bestow;
Be this the cry of every heart,
   "I will not let thee go."

5 Then let me on the mountain top,
   Behold thy open face;
Where faith in sight is swallowed up,
   And prayer in endless praise.

395   C. M.   [ARLINGTON.

DAUGHTER of Zion, from the dust
   Exalt thy fallen head;
Again in thy Redeemer trust;
   He calls thee from the dead.

2 Awake—awake! put on thy strength,
   Thy beautiful array;
The day of freedom dawns at length,
   The Lord's appointed day.

3 Rebuild thy walls—thy bounds enlarge,
   And send thy heralds forth;
Say to the south—"Give up thy charge
   And keep not back, O North!"

4 They come! they come! thine exile bands,
   Where'er they rest or roam,
Have heard thy voice in distant lands,
   And hasten to their home.

5 Thus, though the world at last shall burn
   And God his works destroy,
With songs thy ransomed shall return,
   And everlasting joy.

396   L. M.   [Weston.

ANOTHER day has passed along,
  And we are nearer to the tomb;
Nearer to join the heavenly song,
  Or hear the last eternal doom.

2 Sweet is the light of Sabbath eve,
  And soft the sunbeams lingering there;
For these blest hours the world I leave,
  Wafted on wings of faith and prayer.

3 The time, how lovely and how still!
  Peace shines and smiles on all below,
The plain, the stream, the wood, the hill,
  All fair with evening's setting glow.

4 Season of rest! the tranquil soul
  Feels the sweet calm, and melts to love;
And while these sacred moments roll,
  Faith sees a smiling heaven above.

5 Nor will our days of toil be long,
  Our pilgrimage will soon be trod;
And we shall join the ceaseless song—
  The endless Sabbath of our God.

397   L. M.   [Rockingham.

O HAPPY day that fixed my choice
  On thee, my Savior and my God!
Well may this glowing heart rejoice,
  And tell its raptures all abroad.

2 O happy bond, that seals my vows,
  To him who merits all my love;

Let cheerful anthems fill his house,
    While to that sacred shrine I move.

3 'Tis done—the great transaction's done;
    I am my Lord's, and he is mine;
He drew me, and I followed on,
    Charmed to confess the voice divine.

4 Now rest, my long divided heart,
    Fixed on this blissful center rest;
With ashes who would grudge to part,
    When called on angel's bread to feast.

398   S. M.   [AYLESBURY.

OH! where shall rest be found,
    Rest for the weary soul?
'T were vain the ocean depths to sound,
    Or pierce to either pole.

2 The world can never give
    The bliss for which we sigh;
'Tis not the whole of life to live,
    Nor all of death to die.

3 Beyond this vale of tears
    There is a life above,
Unmeasured by the flight of years;
    And all that life is love.

4 There is a death whose pang
    Outlasts the fleeting breath;
Oh! what eternal horrors hang
    Around the second death!

5 Lord God of truth and grace!
    Teach us that death to shun;

Lest we be banished from thy face,
  And evermore undone.

399   Metre 9.   [Lenox.

YES, the Redeemer rose;
  The Savior left the dead;
And o'er our hellish foes
  High raised his conquering head;
In wild dismay
  The guards around,
  Fall to the ground,
And sink away.

2 Lo! the angelic bands,
  In full assembly meet,
To wait his high commands,
  And worship at his feet;
Joyful they come,
  And wing their way,
  From realms of day,
To Jesus' tomb.

3 Then back to heaven they fly,
  The joyful news to bear;
Hark! as they soar on high,
  What music fills the air!
Their anthems say,
  "Jesus who bled,
  Hath left the dead;
He rose to-day."

4 Ye mortals! catch the sound,—
  Redeemed by him from hell;
And send the echo round
  The globe on which you dwell;

Transported cry,—
"Jesus who bled,
Hath left the dead,
No more to die."

5 All hail! triumphant Lord!
Who saved us with thy blood;
Wide be thy name adored,
Thou rising, reigning God!
With thee we rise,
With thee we reign,
And empires gain,
Beyond the skies.

400 Metre 14. [Webb.

THE morning light is breaking,
The darkness disappears;
The sons of earth are waking
To penitential tears;
Each breeze that sweeps the ocean
Brings tidings from afar,
Of nations in commotion,
Prepared for Zion's war.

2 Rich dews of grace come o'er us
In many a gentle shower,
And brighter scenes before us
Are opening every hour;
Each cry to heaven going,
Abundant answers brings,
And heavenly gales are blowing,
With peace upon their wings.

3 See heathen nations bending
Before the God we love,

And thousand hearts ascending
   In gratitude above;
While sinners now confessing,
   The gospel call obey,
And seek the Savior's blessing—
   A nation in a day.

4 Blest river of salvation,
   Pursue thy onward way;
Flow thou to every nation,
   Nor in thy richness stay;
Stay not till all the lowly
   Triumphant reach their home;
Stay not till all the holy
   Proclaim, "The Lord is come."

401   Metre 11.   [Expostulation.

O ZION, afflicted with wave upon wave,
   Whom no man can comfort, whom no man can save;
With darkness surrounded, by terror dismayed,
In toiling and rowing thy strength is decayed.

2 Loud roaring the billows now nigh overwhelm,
But skillful's the Pilot that sits at the helm,
His wisdom conduct's thee, his pow'r thee defends;
In safety and quiet, the warfare he ends.

3 "O fearful! O faithless!" in mercy he cries,
"My promise, my truth, are they light in thine eyes?
Still, still I am with thee, my promise shall stand;
Thro' tempest and tossing I'll bring thee to land.

4 "Then trust me, and fear not: thy life is secure;
　My wisdom is perfect, supreme is my power;
　In love I correct thee, thy soul to refine,
　To make thee at length in my likeness to shine."

402   C. M.   [BALERMA.

BY cool Siloam's shady rill
　　How fair the lily grows!
How sweet the breath, beneath the hill,
　　Of Sharon's dewy rose!

2 Lo! such the child whose early feet
　　The path of peace have trod,
Whose secret heart with influence sweet,
　　Is upward drawn to God.

3 By cool Siloam's shady rill,
　　The lily must decay;
The rose that bloom's beneath the hill,
　　Must shortly fade away.

4 And soon, too soon, the wint'ry hour,
　　Of man's maturer age,
Will shake the soul with sorrow's power,
　　And stormy passion's rage.

5 O Thou who givest life and breath,
　　We seek thy grace alone;
In childhood, manhood, age, and death,
　　To keep us still thine own.

CONTENTS.

PUBLIC Worship.......From page 1 to 53
Nativity of Christ........................ 54— 63
New Year............ .... 64— 68
Crucifixion............................... 69— 83
Resurrection .... 84— 86
The Word of God........................ 87— 91
Faith and Repentance.................. 91— 93
Baptism................................... 94—101
Prayer and Supplication..............101—130
Invitation................................131—150
Comfort in Tribulation................150—153
Infinite Mercy..........................154—158
The Love of God.......................159—164
Morning Hymns........................165—171
Evening Hymns........................172—177
Frailty of Man..........................178—180
Funeral.................................. 181—194
Judgment ....194—200
Vanity of Earthly Things............200—202
Heavenly Joy..........................202—215
Breathing after God and Holiness 216—244
Adoration and Praise.................245—252
Resignation to God...................253—255
Trusting in God.......................256—261
Warning Hymns......................261—269
Penitential............................270—272
Prodigal Son..........................273—275
Marriage Hymns.....................276—277
Communion...........................277—287
Feet-Washing.........................288—291
Parting Hymns.......................291—297
Various Subjects.....................297—364

METRICAL INDEX.

This index shows which hymns will be sung to the same Metre. The first three—Long, Common, and Short—are here omitted. These Metres correspond with the Metrical Index of the Music Book entitled, "Philharmonia."

METRE 4.
8's and 7's.

	Page.
Come, thou everlasting Spirit	287
Come, thou Fount of every blessing	219
Dark and thorny is the desert	304
God is love, his mercy brightens	163
Great High Priest, we view thee stooping	82
Hail, my ever-blessed Jesus	231
Hail, thou once despised Jesus	72
Happy soul, thy days are ended	328
Hark! what mean those holy voices	62
Jesus, I my cross have taken	308
Mighty God, while angels bless thee	355
Prince of Peace, be ever near us	52
Savior, I do feel thy merit	302
Sinners, take the friendly warning	195

METRE 5.
4 lines 7's and 8 lines 7's.

	Page.
Angels, roll the rock away	86
Depth of mercy! can there be	154
Hark! my soul, it is the Lord	19
Hark! the Herald angels sing	61
Holy Jesus, lovely Lamb	122
I mine Ebenezer raise	253
Jesus! lover of my soul	113
Jesus' precious name excels	131
Lord, I cannot let thee go	112
Lord, we come before thee now	116
Mary to the Savior's tomb	348
Now the shades of night are gone	169
Seek, my soul, the narrow gate	343
Sinner, art thou still secure?	263
Sinners, turn, why will ye die?	14
Softly now the light of day	177
To thy pastures fair and large	342
Tell me, Savior, from above	221
When on Sinai's top I see	332
Who is this that comes from far?	351

METRE 6.
8,8,6,8,8,6.

And am I only born to die	317
My God, thy boundless love we praise	157

METRE 7.
8,7,8,7,4,7.

Angels from the realms of glory	63

	Page.
Come, ye sinners, come to Jesus............	38
Come, ye sinners, poor and needy........	148
Day of Judgment! day of wonders......	196
Hark! the voice of love and mercy......	278
Lo! he comes with clouds descending...	198
Lo! he cometh countless trumpets.......	199
Lord, dismiss us with thy blessing.......	50
O thou God of my Salvation.................	303
On the mountain's top appearing.........	42
Savior, visit thy plantation....................	300
See, from Zion's sacred mountain.........	213

METRE 8.

6 lines 8's.

And can it be that I should gain..........	316
Farewell, my brethren in the Lord......	294
Go watch and pray, thou canst not tell.	115
Jesus, thy boundless love to me...........	110
My Savior, thou thy love to me............	111
When gathering clouds around I view..	254
Would Jesus have the sinner die?........	152

METRE 9.

6,6,6,6,8,8.

Arise, my soul, arise.............................	259
Blow ye the trumpet, blow....................	324
Come, every pious heart.......................	140
The Lord of earth and sky....................	66
Welcome, delightful morn.....................	352
Yes, the Redeemer rose........................	361

METRE 10.
10,10,11,11.

Page.
Begone, unbelief, my Savior is near.....162
Come, Lord, from above, the mountain..126
O all that pass by, to Jesus draw near...135
O tell me no more of this world's vain..161
O what shall I do my Savior to praise...250
Ye thirsty for God, to Jesus give ear.....137

METRE 11.
4 lines 11's.

Come, children of Zion, and help us to.. 29
Farewell, my dear brethren, the time...292
How firm a foundation ye saints..........155
I would not live alway; I ask not to....212
O Zion, afflicted with wave upon wave..363
Thy mercy, my God, is the theme of....164
Why sleep ye my brethren, come...... ..136

METRE 12.
8 lines 8's.

Away with our sorrow and fear............211
How blest is our brother bereft............188
How solemn the signal I hear...............313
How shall a lost sinner in pain.............123
How tedious and tasteless the hours.....297
Inspirer and hearer of prayer................176
Thou Shepherd of Israel and mine......234
When sinners awake and perceive......100
When Joseph his brethren beheld........298

METRE 13.
7,6,7,6,7,7,7,6.

                                                              Page.
Help thy servant, gracious Lord............ 39
Rise, my soul, and stretch thy wings....230
Sinner, hear the Savior's call.................353
Stop, poor sinners, stop and think.........267

METRE 14.
7,6,7,6.

Ah, I shall soon be dying........................256
Go when the morning shineth................349
The morning light is breaking...............362

METRE 15.
11,8,11,8.

O thou, in whose presence my soul......216

METRE 16.
7,6,7,6,7,8,7,6.

God of my salvation, hear......................251
Lamb of God, for sinners slain..............122
Lamb of God, whose dying love............286
Vain, delusive world, adieu....................306

METRE 17.
6 lines 7's.

Hearts of stone, relent, relent................ 74
Safely through another week................. 49

METRE 19.
8,7,8,7,8,7,8,7. PEC.

Ye nations all, on you I call.................... 56

METRE 20.
6,6,9,6,6,9.

Page.
Oh! how happy are they..................209

METRE 21.
12,11,12,11,12,12,12,11.

How sweet to reflect on those joys that 163

METRE 24.
8,8,8,8,4.

Hark! how the gospel trumpet sounds..340

METRE 26.
6,6,4,6,6,6,4.

Glory to God on high..........................334

METRE 29.
8,8,7,8,8,7.

See the Lord of glory dying................. 75

METRE 32.
5,5,5,11.

Come, let us anew our journey pursue...64

METRE 33.
11,10,11,10.

Hail the blest morn when the great..... 59
Restless thy spirit poor wand'ring........138

METRE 36.
11,11,11,11,5,11.

'Mid scenes of confusion and creature...228

METRE 40.
7,6,7,6,7,6,7,6.

Page.
Drooping souls, no longer grieve............145

METRE 41.
8,3,3,6.

Ere I sleep for every favor...................345

METRE 52.
9,8,9,8,9,8,9,8.

Come, all who love my Lord and..........307

METRE 53.
9,8,9,8,9,8,10,8.

Religion! 't is a glorious treasure..........310

METRE 54.
11,11,11,5.

Ah! guilty sinner, ruined by transgress'n 268

METRE 55.
10,10,10,10.

Again the day returns of holy rest........167

METRE 56.
8,8,8,8,8,8,3.

Hear the royal proclamation................147

METRE 60.
7,7,7,7,6,6,7,7.

See the fountain opened wide................134

INDEX OF FIRST LINES.

	Page.
Afflictions, though they seem severe	274
Again the day returns of holy rest	167
Again our earthly cares we leave	33
Ah! guilty sinner! ruined by transgression	268
Ah! I shall soon be dying	256
Alas! and did my Savior bleed	70
All hail the power of Jesus' name	23
All praise to him who dwells in bliss	175
Almighty Father bless the word	53
Almighty Maker, God	218
Amazing sight, the Savior stands	132
Am I a soldier of the cross	28
Amid the splendors of thy state	247
And am I only born to die	317
And can it be that I should gain	316
And is the gospel peace and love	241
And let our bodies part	319
And let this feeble body fail	187
And must this body die	181
And must I be to judgment brought	196
And now, my soul, another year	68
Angels! from the realms of glory	63
Angels! roll the rock away	86
Angels in shining order stand	77
Another day has passed along	359
Approach, my soul, the mercy-seat	118
Arise, my soul, arise	259
Arise, my tenderest thoughts, arise	220
As on the cross the Savior hung	73
As the apostles sat at meat	101
Assist thy servant, Lord	35

INDEX OF FIRST LINES.

                                                          Page.

Attend, young friends, while I relate 185
Awake, awake, the sacred song.................   5
Awake, my soul, in joyful lays................ 16
Awake, my soul, to sound his praise........... 333
Awake my heart, arise my tongue............... 24
Away with our sorrow and fear................. 211

Before Jehovah's awful throne................. 25
Begone unbelief! my Savior is near............ 162
Behold a stranger at the door................. 270
Behold the lofty sky.......................... 20
Behold, the glories of the Lamb............... 322
Behold, the Savior of mankind................. 83
Behold the wretch whose lust and wine......... 273
Blest are the sons of peace................... 355
Bless'd is the man who shuns the place........ 336
Blessed Redeemer, how divine.................. 343
Bless, O my soul, the living God.............. 17
Blest are the humble souls that see........... 91
Blest be the dear uniting love................ 296
Bestow, dear Lord, upon our youth............. 108
Blow ye the trumpet, blow..................... 324
Broad is the road that leads to death......... 261
By cool Siloam's shady rill................... 364

Come, all who love my Lord and Master......... 307
Come, children, learn to fear the Lord........ 15
Come, children of Zion, and help us to sing... 29
Come, every pious heart....................... 140
Come, gracious Spirit, heavenly Dove.......... 130
Come, Holy Spirit, heavenly Dove.............. 101
Come, happy souls, approach your God.......... 10
Come hither, all ye weary souls............... 146
Come, humble sinner, in whose breast.......... 107
Come in, ye blessed of the Lord............... 95
Come, Lord from above, the mountains.......... 126
Come let us all unite to praise...............   8

INDEX OF FIRST LINES.

Page.

Come, let us now forget our mirth............312
Come, let us join our cheerful songs 248
Come, let us anew our journey pursue......... 64
Come, let your voices join to raise.............44
Come, my soul, thy suit prepare................338
Come, O thou traveler unknown................271
Come, sound his praise abroad................. 7
Come, thou desire of all thy saints............ 32
Come, thou fount of every blessing............ 219
Come, thou everlasting Spirit..................287
Come, we that love the Lord 203
Come, weary souls with sins distressed......... 48
Come, ye that love the Savior's name.......... 47
Come, ye sinners, come to Jesus 38
Come, ye sinners, poor and needy............. 148
Comfort ye ministers of grace................. 43

Day of Judgment! day of wonders.............196
Daughter of Zion from the dust................358
Dark and thorny is the desert................. 304
Dear friends, farewell, I do you tell...........293
Dear refuge of my weary soul..................334
Death, 'tis a melancholy day...................186
Depth of mercy, can there be..................154
Descend from heaven, Immortal Dove......... 240
Dismiss us with thy blessing, Lord 50
Destruction's dangerous road..................262
Dread Sovereign, let my evening song.........174
Drooping souls, no longer grieve,..............145

Earth has engrossed my love too long......... 205
Ere I sleep for every favor....................345
Eternal power whose high abode...............248
Eternal wisdom, thee we praise................245

Farewell, my brethren in the Lord.............294
Farewell, my dear brethren, the time is at....292

	Page.
Far from my thoughts, vain world, be gone	325
Father, how wide thy glories shine	309
Father, I long, I faint to see	226
Father, I stretch my hands to thee	103
Father of mercies, in thy word	87
Firm was my health, my day was bright	326
From all that dwell below the skies	31
From every stormy wind that blows	353
From thee, my God, my joys shall rise	207
Glory to thee, my God, this night	172
Glory to God on high	334
Go watch and pray, thou canst not tell	115
Go when the morning shineth	349
God is love, his mercy brightens	163
God of my life, look gently down	240
God of my life, my morning song	171
God of my salvation, hear	251
Great God, indulge my humble claim	109
Great God, preserved by thine arm	170
Great High Priest, we view thee stooping	82
Hail, my ever blessed Jesus	231
Hail! thou once despised Jesus	72
Hail the blest morn when the great Mediator	59
Hark! from on high those blissful strains	60
Hark! from the tombs a doleful sound	182
Hark! how the gospel trumpet sounds	340
Hark! my soul, it is the Lord	19
Hark! the herald angels sing	61
Hark! the glad sound, the Savior comes	55
Hark! the Redeemer from on high	138
Hark! the voice of love and mercy	278
Hark! what mean those holy voices	62
Happy soul, thy days are ended	328
Hasten, O sinner, to be wise	267
Have mercy, Lord, on me	272

INDEX OF FIRST LINES.

Page.
Have mercy, gracious Lord, forgive..........350
He dies, the Friend of sinners, dies............ 69
Hear, gracious God, my humble moan........230
Hear the royal proclamation....................147
Hearts of stone, relent, relent... 74
Help thy servant, gracious Lord............... 39
High on his everlasting throne................. 45
Holy Jesus, lovely Lamb......................122
Hosanna to the Prince of Light............... 84
How beauteous are their feet.................. 22
How blest is our brother, bereft..............188
How condescending and how kind........... 155
How did my heart rejoice to hear............. 9
How firm a foundation ye saints of the Lord...155
How long, O Lord, shall I complain..........118
How lovely, how divinely sweet... 337
How oft, alas! this wretched heart............270
How pleasant, how divinely fair..............225
How shall the young secure their hearts...... 88
How shall a lost sinner in pain............... 123
How shall we praise th' Eternal God........... 6
How solemn the signal I hear................. .313
How sweet and awful is the place.......... 282
How sweet the name of Jesus sounds.........232
How tedious and tasteless the hours..........297
How sweet to reflect on those joys that.........163
How vain are all things here below............201

I'm not ashamed to own my Lord.... 37
If glorious angels do rejoice..................... 94
If Paul in Cæsar's court must stand............150
I mine Ebenezer raise.......... 253
Indulgent Father, by whose care.... 175
In evil long I took delight..... 345
In glory bright the Savior reigns...............330
Inspirer and Hearer of prayer..................176

INDEX OF FIRST LINES.

                                                    Page.
I lift my soul to God.....................260
I'll bless the Lord from day to day........106
I love to steal awhile away................177
I send the joys of earth away..............255
Is this the kind return....................264
I would not live alway, I ask not to stay..212

Jesus! and shall it ever be................ 30
Jesus, at whose supreme command............285
Jesus, grant us all a blessing............. 53
Jesus, I my cross have taken...............308
Jesus invites his saints...................283
Jesus, lover of my soul....................113
Jesus, my Savior, Brother, Friend..........129
Jesus, my Savior, let me be................114
Jesus, thy boundless love to me............110
Jesus' precious name excels................131
Jesus, thou art the sinner's Friend........125
Jesus, the spring of joys divine...........129
Jesus, thy blessings are not few........... 37
Jerusalem, my happy home...................210

Lamb of God, for sinners slain.............122
Lamb of God, whose dying love..............286
Let all our tongues be one.................284
Let every mortal ear attend................ 18
Let me but hear my Savior say.............. 36
Let sinners take their course.............. 89
Let the whole race of creatures lie........ 90
Let us adore th' Eternal Word..............279
Let Zion and her sons rejoice..............246
Life is the time to serve the Lord.........323
Lo! he comes in clouds descending..........198
Lo he cometh! countless trumpets...........199
Lo! round the throne at God's right hand...350
Lo! what a glorious sight appears..........215
Lord, at thy temple we appear.............. 28

INDEX OF FIRST LINES. 379

                                            Page.
Lord, if thine eyes survey our faults........... 183
Lord, I approach thy mercy-seat.............. 339
Lord, in the morning thou shalt hear........... 168
Lord, I cannot let thee go 112
Lord, I am thine, but thou wilt prove.......... 233
Lord, dismiss us with thy blessing............. 50
Lord, at thy sacred feet..................... 40
Lord, how divine thy comforts are............. 280
Lord, thou wilt hear me when I pray........... 173
Lord, must I die, O let me die................ 192
Lord, teach thy servant how to pray........... 125
Lord, what a feeble piece.................... 180
Lord, we come before thee now............... 116
Lord, what is man, poor feeble man........... 178

Majestic sweetness sits enthroned 346
Mary to the Savior's tomb.................... 348
Mighty God. while angels bless thee........ 355
'Mid scenes of confusion and creature comp... 228
My dearest friends, in bonds of love........... 291
My drowsy powers, why sleep ye so........... 330
My God, the spring of all my joys............. 224
My God, thy boundless love we praise 157
My God, consider my distress................. 127
My hope, my all, my Savior thou.............. 31
My lovely Jesus while on earth................ 169
My Savior and my King....................... 10
My Savior, thou thy love to me................ 111
My Savior, my Almighty Friend............... 221
My soul, be on thy guard 117
My soul, with joy attend..................... 158

Now, gracious Lord, thine arm reveal......... 65
Now in the heat of youthful blood............. 326
Now is th' accepted time..................... 25
Now is the time, th' accepted hour 39
Now the shades of night are gone............. 169

INDEX OF FIRST LINES.

                                                                    Page.

O all ye nations, praise the Lord.........327
Oh, all that pass by, to Jesus draw near.......135
O could I find some peaceful bower............235
Of all the joys we mortals know................159
Often I seek my Lord by night.................238
Oh for a sweet inspiring ray....................208
Oh for a closer walk with God............ 104
Oh how happy are they..........................209
Oh happy day when saints shall meet..........296
O happy is the man who hears.................. 36
O happy day that fixed my choice...... 359
Oh how I love thy holy law................. ...341
O if my soul was formed for woe................ 92
O land of rest for thee I sigh...................227
On Jordan's stormy banks I stand.............204
On the mountain top appearing................. 42
On Judah's plains as shepherds sat. 54
Once more we come before our God............ 12
Once more, my soul, the rising day............166
Once more before we part....................... 51
Oppress'd with fear, oppress'd with grief 152
O tell me no more of this world's vain.........161
O thou to whose all-searching sight............102
O thou in whose presence my soul takes.......216
O that I had a bosom friend... 222
O that the Lord would guide my ways.. 244
O, thou God of my salvation 303
O thou that hearest when sinners pray......... 93
Our life is ever on the wing............ 67
Our God, our help in ages past.................178
Oh what amazing words of grace.... 141
O what shall I do my Savior to praise..........250
O where shall rest be found...................360
O Zion afflicted with wave upon wave.........363

INDEX OF FIRST LINES.

Page.
Prayer is the soul's sincere desire..............120
Praise ye the Lord who reigns above..........249
Prince of Peace, be ever near us............... 52

Religion, 't is a glorious treasure............ 310
Religion is the chief concern..................235
Rejoice in Jesus' birth........................ 56
Remember, Lord, our mortal state.............191
Restless thy spirit, poor wandering sinner.....138
Rise, my soul, and stretch thy wings..........230

Safely through another week................... 49
Salvation! O the joyful sound.................. 50
Savior, visit thy plantation...................300
Savior, I do feel thy merit....................302
Saw ye my Savior, saw ye my Savior........... 76
Say now, ye lovely social band.................257
See the Lord of glory dying................... 75
See from Zion's sacred mountain...............213
See the fountain open'd wide...................134
Seek, my soul, the narrow gate.................343
Shall wisdom cry aloud.........................331
Shepherd divine, our wants relieve.............357
Show pity, Lord, O Lord forgive................105
Sing to the Lord, ye heavenly hosts............194
Sing to the great Jehovah's praise............ 65
Since Jesus freely did appear..................276
Sinner, art thou still secure..................263
Sinner, hear the Savior's call.................353
Sinners, take the friendly warning.............195
Sinners turn, why will you die................. 14
Sinners, the voice of God regard...............143
So let our lives and lips express..............159
Softly now the light of day....................177
Stop, poor sinner, stop and think..............267

INDEX OF FIRST LINES.

                                                                                             Page.

Sweet is the work, my God, my King..........165
Sweet the moment, rich in blessing...........339

Teach me the measure of my days..............179
Tell me, Savior, from above. ... .221
That awful day will surely come..... 265
That doleful night before his death.......... 283
Thee we adore, Eternal Name...................190
The day is past and gone......................172
The God, Jehovah, reigns....... 328
To thy pastures fair and large..... 342
The heavens declare thy glory, Lord...........347
The Lord of earth and sky...................... 66
The Lord's disciples when they spread......... 99
The morning light is breaking.................362
The name of the Lord is a fountain of life...... 97
The night on which Christ was betrayed......289
The Savior calls, let every ear. ... .141
The Savior, O what endless charms............245
The Son of Man they did betray................ 79
The swift declining day...................... 52
The time is short, O sinners fear.............265
The wondering world inquires to know........320
The voice of my beloved sounds................144
There is a house not made with hands.........202
There is a voice of sovereign grace............243
There is a land of pure delight................239
These glorious minds how bright they shine..214
This is the day the Lord hath made............ 84
Thou art, O God a Spirit, pure.................242
Thou Shepherd of Israel and mine.............234
Thou whom my soul admires above.............237
'T is midnight—and on Olive's brow 281
To-day, if you will hear his voice.... ... .133

INDEX OF FIRST LINES. 383

                                      Page.

To God, the great, the ever blessed........ 13
To God, in whom I trust......................261
To show how humble Christians ought..... ...288
To thy pastures fair and large.................342
Through every age, eternal God................191
'T was on that dark, that doleful night......... 71
'T was the commission of our Lord.......... ... 96
Thy life I read, my dearest Lord............184
Thy mercy, my God, is the theme of my song..164
Thy presence, gracious God, afford........ 35

Up to the fields where angels lie.. 236

Vain, delusive world, adieu......... 306
Vain man, thy fond pursuits forbear........ 335

Welcome, delightful morn......................352
We sing the glories of thy love. 42
We've no abiding city here.. 41
Welcome, sweet day of rest..................... 34
What glory gilds the sacred page. 91
What poor, despised company.................314
What various hindrances we meet...... 121
When blooming youth is snatched away...... 193
When gathering clouds around I view........254
When I survey the wondrous cross............. 69
When I can read my title clear................219
When Jesus Christ was here below............290
When Jesus Christ, the Virgin's Son.......... 98
When Jesus did from heaven descend.......... 46
When Joseph his brethren beheld.......... ...298
When languor and disease invade............311
When on Sinai's top I see.................... 332
When rising from the bed of death............329
When sinners awake and perceive............100

INDEX OF FIRST LINES.

Page.

When we with welcome slumber pressed......170
Where two or three with sweet accord.........21
While with ceaseless course the sun..........356
While I keep silence and conceal..............255
While life prolongs its precious light..........142
While shepherds watch'd their flocks by.....59
Whilst thee I seek, Protecting Power.........112
Who is this fair one in distress?..............160
Who is this that comes from far?...............351
With grateful hearts and tuneful lays.........276
With cheerful voices rise and sing............277
With humble heart and tongue.................119
With my whole heart I've sought thy face.....128
With rev'rence let thy saints appear...........12
With sacred joy we lift our eyes 33
Would Jesus have the sinner die................152
Why do we mourn departing friends.........184
Why doth the man of riches grow..............200
Why should we start and fear to die............189
Why sleep ye, my brethren, come, let us.......136

Ye humble souls that seek the Lord............85
Ye nations all, on you I call....................56
Ye nations round the earth rejoice..............250
Ye mourning saints, whose streaming tears...344
Ye sinners fear the Lord........................150
Ye that pass by, behold the man................277
Ye thirsty for God, to Jesus give ear..........137
Ye weary, heavy laden souls. 315
Ye wretched, hungry, starving poor............149
Yes, the Redeemer rose..........................361
Young people all, attention give...............26

APPENDIX

1   C. M.   [Cleansing Fountain.

THERE is a fountain filled with blood,
  Drawn from Immanuel's veins;
And sinners plunged beneath that flood,
  Lose all their guilty stains.

2 The dying thief rejoiced to see
  That fountain in his day:
And there may I, though vile as he,
  Wash all my sins away.

3 Thou dying Lamb! thy precious blood
  Shall never lose its power,
Till all the ransomed Church of God
  Are saved to sin no more.

4 E'er since, by faith, I saw the stream
  Thy flowing wounds supply,
Redeeming love has been my theme,
  And shall be till I die.

5 Then in a nobler, sweeter song,
  I'll sing thy power to save,   [tongue
When this poor, lisping, stamm'ring
  Lies silent in the grave.

2   Metre 17.   [Rock of Ages.

Rock of ages, cleft for me,
  Let me hide myself in thee;
Let the water and the blood,
From thy wounded side that flowed,
Be of sin the perfect cure:
Save me, Lord, and make me pure.

2 Should my tears forever flow,
Should my zeal no languor know,
These for sin could ne'er atone;
Thou must save, and thou alone.
In my hand no price I bring
Simply to thy cross I cling.

3 While I draw this fleeting breath,
When my eyes shall close in death,
When I rise to worlds unknown,
And behold thee on thy throne,
Rock of Ages, cleft for me,
Let me hide myself in thee.

3   Metre 27.   [Nearer to Thee.

Nearer, my God, to thee,
  Nearer to thee,
E'en though it be a cross
  That raiseth me;
Still all my song shall be,
Nearer, my God, to thee,
  Nearer to thee.

2 Though like a wanderer—
  Weary and lone,

Darkness comes over me,
　　　　My rest a stone;
　　Yet in my dreams I'd be,
　　Nearer, my God to thee,
　　　　Nearer to thee.

3 There let my way appear,
　　　Steps unto heaven;
　All that thou sendest me,
　　　In mercy giv'n;
　Angels to beckon me
　Nearer, my God, to thee,
　　　Nearer to thee.

4 Then with my waking thoughts,
　　　Bright with thy praise,
　Out of my stony griefs
　　　Altars I'll raise;
　So by my woes to be,
　Nearer, my God, to thee,
　　　Nearer to thee!

5 Or if on joyful wings,
　　　Cleaving the sky,
　Sun, moon, and stars forgot,
　　　Upward I fly;
　Still all my song shall be,
　Nearer, my God, to thee!
　　　Nearer to thee!

4　　L. M.　　[SWEET HOUR OF PRAYER.

SWEET hour of prayer! sweet hour of prayer!
　　That calls me from a world of care,
And bids me at my Father's throne,
Make all my wants and wishes known:

APPENDIX.

In seasons of distress and grief,
My soul has often found relief;
And oft escaped the tempter's snare,
By thy return, sweet hour of prayer.

2 Sweet hour of prayer! sweet hour of prayer!
Thy wings shall my petition bear,
To Him whose truth and faithfulness,
Engage my waiting soul to bless;
And since He bids me seek his face,
Believe his word and trust his grace,
I'll cast on Him my every care,
And wait for thee, sweet hour of prayer.

3 Sweet hour of prayer! sweet hour of prayer!
May I thy consolation share;
Till from Mount Pisgah's lofty height,
I view my home and take my flight;
This robe of flesh I'll drop, and rise
To seize the everlasting prize;
And shout, while passing through the air,
Farewell, farewell, sweet hour of prayer!

5   METRE 4.   [SHIELDS.

WHAT a friend we have in Jesus,
 All our sins and griefs to bear;
What a privilege to carry
 Everything to God in prayer.
Oh, what peace we often forfeit,
 Oh, what needless pain we bear—
All because we do not carry
 Everything to God in prayer.

2 Have we trials and temptations?
 Is there trouble anywhere?
We should never be discouraged,
 Take it to the Lord in prayer.

Can we find a friend so faithful,
 Who will all our sorrows share?
Jesus knows our every weakness,
 Take it to the Lord in prayer.

3 Are we weak and heavy laden,
 Cumbered with a load of care?
Precious Savior, still our refuge—
 Take it to the Lord in prayer;
Do thy friends despise, forsake thee?
 Take it to the Lord in prayer;
In his arms he'll take and shield thee,
 Thou wilt find a solace there.

6   L. M.   [GALILEE.

HE leadeth me! O blessed thought!
 O, words with heav'nly comfort fraught!
Whate'er I do, where'er I be,
 Still 't is God's hand that leadeth me!

CHO.—He leadeth me! he leadeth me!
 By his own hand he leadeth me;
His faithful follower I would be,
 For by his hand he leadeth me.

2 Sometimes 'mid scenes of deepest gloom,
Sometimes where Eden's bowers bloom,
By waters still, o'er troubled sea—
 Still 't is God's hand that leadeth me.

3 Lord, I would clasp thy hand in mine,
Nor ever murmur nor repine—
Content, whatever lot I see,
 Since 't is my God that leadeth me!

4 And when my task on earth is done,
 When, by thy grace, the victory's won,
 E'en death's cold wave I will not flee;
 Since God through Jordan leadeth me!

7   Pec. Metre.   [Elliott.

JUST as I am, without one plea,
 But that thy blood was shed for me,
 And that thou bidst me come to thee,
  O Lamb of God, I come!

2 Just as I am, and waiting not,
 To rid my soul of one dark blot,   [spot,
 To thee whose blood can cleanse each
  O Lamb of God, I come!

3 Just as I am, though tossed about
 With many a conflict, many a doubt,
 Fightings within, and fears without,
  O Lamb of God, I come!

4 Just as I am—poor, wretched, blind:
 Sighs, riches, healing of the mind,
 Yea, all I need, in thee to find,
  O Lamb of God, I come!

5 Just as I am—thou wilt receive,
 Wilt welcome, pardon, cleanse, relieve—
 Because thy promise I believe,
  O Lamb of God, I come!

6 Just as I am—thy love unknown
 Hath broken every barrier down:
 Now, to be thine, yea, thine alone.
  O Lamb of God, I come!

8   Metre 7.   [Happy Zion.

Savior, like a shepherd, lead us,
  Much we need thy tender care;
In thy pleasant pastures feed us,
  For our use thy folds prepare:
    Blessed Jesus!
Thou hast bought us, thine we are.

2 Thou hast promised to receive us,
  Poor and sinful though we be;
Thou hast mercy to relieve us,
  Grace to cleanse and power to free:
    Blessed Jesus!
Let us early turn to thee.

3 Early, let us seek thy favor,
  Early let us learn thy will;
Do thou, Lord, our only Savior,
  With thy love our bosoms fill:
    Blessed Jesus!
Thou hast loved us—love us still!

9   L. M.   [Rest.

Asleep in Jesus! blessed sleep,
From which none ever wake to weep
A calm and undisturbed repose,
Unbroken by the last of foes.

2 Asleep in Jesus! O, how sweet
To be for such a slumber meet!
With holy confidence to sing
That death hath lost his venomed sting.

3 Asleep in Jesus! peaceful rest,
  Whose waking is supremely blest;
  No fear, no woe, shall dim that hour,
  That manifests the Savior's power.

4 Asleep in Jesus! O, for me
  May such a blissful refuge be:
  Securely shall my ashes lie,
  And wait the summons from on high.

10   Pec. Metre.

O THINK of the home over there,
  By the side of the river of light,
Where the saints all immortal and fair,
  Are robed in their garments of white.
    Over there, over there,
O, think of the home over there.

2 O, think of the friends over there,
  Who before us the journey have trod,
Of the songs that they breathe on the air,
  In their home in the palace of God.
    Over there, over there,
O, think of the friends over there.

3 My Savior is now over there,   [rest;
  There my kindred and friends are at
Then away from my sorrow and care,
  Let me fly to the land of the blest.
    Over there, over there,
My Savior is now over there.

4 I'll soon be at home over there,
  For the end of my journey I see;

Many dear to my heart over there,
　Are watching and waiting for me.
　　Over there, over there,
I'll soon be at home over there.

11　　　　C. M.　　　　[TRIBULATION.

FOND parents, calm the heaving breast,
　The Savior called him home;
Grieve not, your darling is at rest
　Beyond this vale of gloom.

2 Let hope's bright beams dispel the gloom,
　That fills your throbbing breast;
'T was Jesus kindly bade him come,
　And called him to his rest

3 He's gone to join the cherub band,
　His prattling tongue to raise,
And swell along God's holy land
　Glad notes of joy and praise.

4 That cherub band had need of one
　To join their song of love—
Then weep not for your darling son;
　He sweetly sings above.

5 Go, cease your silent, flowing tears,
　Bid meek submission reign;
A few short days, or months, or years,
　And you shall meet again.

12　　　　METRE 4.　　　　[WELTON.

LITTLE children gather'st thou,
　Faithful Shepherd, to thy rest;

Far from sorrow, far from woe,
  They with thee are ever blest.
2 Free from sickness, free from pain,
  Free from every sinful snare;
Free from Satan's bonds and chain,
  Keep them, Savior, in thy care.
3 Cheered by faith we follow thee;
  Gazing on thy pallid face;
Thou with Jesus now shalt be
  Crowned with heavenly love and grace.
4 Thee we loved, our darling dear,
  Loved thee more than words can tell;
Little thinking death so near,
  When with angels thou shouldst dwell.
5 But the Lord has called thee home,
  Thou to us wilt ne'er return;
Therefore we will go to thee,
  And no longer weep or mourn.
6 Bless the Lord, O bless his name!
  For the treasure which he gave;
Only for his own he came,
  Them to take and them to save.

13   L. M.   [SUPPLICATION.

WEEP not for me, my parents dear;
  Since I must go and leave you here;
With Jesus I shall happy be,
O parents, do not weep for me.
2 My brothers, do not mourn for me,
  In heav'n I hope you all to see,

Where parting words are heard no more,
But dwell fore'er on Canaan's shore.

3 Dear sisters, do not grieve for me,
While I am in eternity;
But be content and trust in God,
And you'll receive a great reward.

4 Weep not for me, since 't is in vain;
In heav'n I hope we'll meet again,
Where we can then together be,
Forever in eternity.

14   Metre 11.   [Social Band.

DEAR mother*, don't think of me as in the tomb,
For I shall not fear its dark shadows and gloom
And I shall not fear though the rivers be wide,
For Jesus will carry me over the tide.

2 You'll know where to find me, dear mother, in heaven,
Though every fond tie you have cherished be riven,
You'll follow me home to the land of the blest,
Where sighs are not heard, and the weary ones rest.

3 I'm going to live with the angels so fair,
I'll look for you, mother, and wait for you there;
Where tears do not fl w, and where death cannot come,
Together we'll dwell in that beautiful home.

15   S. M.   [Idumea.

O FOR the death of those,
   Who slumber in the Lord!
O be like theirs my last repose,
   Like theirs my last reward.

2 Their bodies in the ground,
   In silent hope may lie,

---
* Father, brother, or sister may be substituted.

Till the last trumpet's joyful sound
   Shall call them to the sky.

3 Their ransomed spirits soar,
   On wings of faith and love,
To meet the Savior they adore,
   And reign with him above.

4 O for the death of those
   Who slumber in the Lord!
O be like theirs my last repose,
   Like theirs my last reward.

16   L. M.   [REST

Dear is the spot where Christians sleep,
   And sweet the strains the spirits pour;
Oh, why should we in anguish weep!
   They are not lost, but gone before.

2 Secure from every mortal care,
   By sin and sorrow vexed no more;
Eternal happiness they share
   Who are not lost, but gone before.

3 To Zion's peaceful courts above,
   In faith triumphant may we soar,
Embracing in the arms of love,
   The friends not lost, but gone before.

4 To Jordan's banks whene'er we come,
   And hear the swelling waters roar;
Jesus, convey us safely home,
   To friends not lost, but gone before.

17   L. M.   [RELIANCE

How blest the righteous when he dies!
   When sinks a weary soul to rest:

How mildly beam the closing eyes,
  How gently heaves th' expiring breast!
2 So fades a summer cloud away;
  So sinks the gale when storms are o'er,
  So gently shuts the eye of day;
  So dies the wave along the shore.
3 A holy quiet reigns around,
  A calm which life nor death destroys;
  Nothing disturbs that peace profound
  Which his unfettered soul enjoys.
4 Farewell, conflicting hopes and fears,
  Where lights and shades alternate dwell!
  How bright th' unchanging morn appears;
  Farewell, inconstant world, farewell!
5 Life's duties done, as sinks the clay,
  Light from its load the spirit flies,
  While heaven and earth combine to say,
  "How blest the righteous when he dies!"

18   Metre 4.   [Charleston.

CEASE here longer to detain me,
  Fondest mother, drowned in woe;
Now thy kind caresses pain me,
  Morn advances—let me go.

2 Lately launched, a trembling stranger,
  On the world's wide, boist'rous flood,
  Pierced with sorrows, toss'd with danger,
  Gladly I return to God.

3 Now my cries shall cease to grieve thee,
  Now my trembling heart finds rest;
  Kinder arms than thine receive me,
  Softer pillows than thy breast.

4 Weep not o'er these eyes that languish,
   Upward turning tow'rd their home:
Raptured, they'll forget all anguish,
   While they wait to see thee come.

5 Yet to leave thee sorrowing rends me
   Though again His voice I hear:
"Rise, my every grace attend thee;"
   Rise! and seek to meet me there.

19   Metre 4.   [Talmar.

JESUS, while our hearts are bleeding
   O'er the spoils that death has won,
We would, at this solemn meeting,
   Calmly say,—Thy will be done.

2 Tho' cast down, we're not forsaken;
   Though afflicted, not alone;
Thou didst give, and thou hast taken;
   Blessed Lord—Thy will be done.

3 By thy hands the boon was given;
   Thou hast taken but thine own;
Lord of earth, and God of heaven,
   Evermore,—Thy will be done.

20   C. M.   [Brown.

HOW happy are these little ones
   Which Jesus Christ has blest;
Come let us praise with all our hearts
   The God who gives them rest.

2 With his own blood he made them free
   From every sin and stain;

For them he suffered on the tree,
  For them was Jesus slain.

3 He takes them home where pain and woe
    Will ne'er disturb them more;
Oh, let us all prepare to go
  And with them Christ adore!

4 We'll watch and pray from day to day
    Till Jesus calls us home;
With our dear children there to stay—
  'Midst joys divine to roam.

21   L. M.   [HEBRON.

THE hand which gives us joys of earth
  May pluck the fairest at its birth;
'T is *His* who strews our path to-day,
To take our pleasures all away.

2 May God be kind in this sad hour,
  And give his grace with healing pow'r;
His will be done, O may you say,
Who took our precious charge away?

3 Think, that tho' hid from mortal eyes,
  Your darling lives above the skies,
And, be the great Redeemer set
Into his precious coronet.

4 And while you sorrow o'er the tomb
  Which holds her in its silent gloom,
O hear her accents from above,
I'm with your God, the God you love.

22   C. M.   [Mear.

WHY should our tears in sorrow flow,
    When God recalls his own,
And bids them leave a world of woe
    For an immortal crown?

2 Is not e'en death a gain to those
    Whose life to God was given?
Gladly to earth their eyes they close,
    To open them in heaven.

3 Their toils are past, their work is done,
    And they are fully blest;
They fought the fight, the vict'ry won,
    And entered into rest.

4 Then let our sorrows cease to flow,
    God has recalled his own;
But let our hearts in every woe,
    Still say—Thy will be done.

23   L. M.   [Reliance.

THE morning flow'rs display their sweets,
    And light their silken leaves unfold,
As careless of the noon-tide heats,
    As fearless of the evening cold.

2 Nipp'd by the wind's untimely blast,
    Parched by the sun's directer ray,
The momentary glories waste,
    The short lived beauties die away.

3 So blooms the human face divine,
    When youth its pride of beauty shows;

  Fairer than spring the colors shine,
   And sweeter than the virgin rose.
4 Or worn by slowly rolling years,
   Or broke by sickness in a day,
  The fading glory disappears,
   The short-lived beauties die away.
5 Yet these, new rising from the tomb,
   With luster brighter far shall shine,
  Revive with ever-during bloom,
   Safe from diseases and decline.
6 Let sickness blast, let death devour,
   If heav'n must recompense our pains;
  Perish the grass, and fade the flower,
   If firm the word of God remains.

24   Metre 4.   [Mount Vernon.

SISTER, thou wast mild and lovely,
   Gentle as the summer breeze:
  Pleasant as the air of evening,
   When it floats among the trees.
2 Peaceful be thy silent slumber.
   Peaceful in the grave so low;
  Thou no more wilt join our number:
   Thou no more our songs shalt know.
3 Dearest sister! thou hast left us,
   Here thy loss we deeply feel;
  But 't is God that hath bereft us,
   He can all our sorrows heal.
4 Yet again we hope to meet thee,
   When the day of life is fled,
  Then in heav'n with joy to greet thee,
   Where no farewell tear is shed.

25   C. M.   [BALERMA

TO thee, O God, when creatures fail,
   Thy flock deserted flies;
And on th' eternal Shepherd's care,
   Our steadfast hope relies.

2 When o'er thy faithful servant's dust,
   Thy saints assembled mourn,
In speedy tokens of thy grace,
   O Zion's God return!

3 The pow'rs of nature all are thine,
   And thine the aids of grace;
Thine arm hath borne the churches up
   Through each succeeding race.

4 Exert thy sacred influence here,
   And here thy suppliants bless;
And change to strains of cheerful praise
   Our accents of distress.

26   C. M.   [CONDESCENSION.

NOW let our drooping hearts revive,
   And all our tears be dry;   [grief,
Why should those eyes be drowned in
   That view a Savior nigh?

2 Tho' earthly shepherds dwell in dust—
   The aged and the young;
The watchful eye in darkness closed,
   And mute th' instructive tongue.

3 Th' eternal Shepherd still survives,
   New comforts to impart;
His eye still guides us, and his voice
   Still animates our heart.

APPENDIX. 19

4 "Lo! I am with you," saith the Lord,
  My church shall safe abide;"
The Lord will ne'er forsake his own,
  Who in his love confide.
5 Through every scene of life and death
  His promise is our trust;
And this shall be our children's song,
  When we are cold in dust.

27   L. M.   [MARCH.

THE hour of my departure's come;
  I hear the voice that calls me home;
Now, O my God, let trouble cease,
And let thy servant die in peace.
2 The race appointed I have run;
The combat's o'er, the prize is won;
And now my witness is on high,
And now my record's in the sky.
3 Not in mine innocence I trust,
I bow before thee in the dust;
And through my Savior's blood alone
I look for mercy at thy throne.
4 I come, I come, at thy command,
I give my spirit to thy hand;
Stretch forth thine everlasting arms,
And shield me in the last alarms.

28   METRE 26.   [HARVEST.

THE God of harvest praise:
  In loud thanksgiving raise,
    Hand, heart, and voice;

The valleys smile and sing,
Forests and mountains ring,
The plains their tribute bring,
　　The streams rejoice.

2 The God of harvest praise;
Hearts, hands, and voices raise,
　　With sweet accord;
From field to garner throng,
Bearing your sheaves along,
And in your harvest song,
　　Praise ye the Lord.

29 　　　C. M.　　[ORTONVILLE.

'TIS by thy strength the mountains
　God of eternal power!　　[stand,
The sea grows calm at thy command,
　The tempests cease to roar.

2 Thy morning light and evening shade
　　Successive comforts bring;
Thy plenteous fruits make harvest glad,
　　Thy flowers adorn the spring.

3 Seasons and times, and moons and hours,
　　Heav'n, earth, and air are thine;
When clouds distil in fruitful showers,
　　The author is divine.

4 Thy show'rs the thirsty furrows fill,
　　And ranks of corn appear;
Thy ways abound with blessings still—
　　Thy goodness crowns the year.

30   C. M.   [BALERMA.

FOUNTAIN of mercy, God of love,
  How rich thy bounties are!
The rolling seasons, as they move,
  Proclaim thy constant care.

2 When in the bosom of the earth
   The sower hid the grain,
Thy goodness marked its secret birth,
   And sent the early rain.

3 The spring's sweet influence, Lord, was
   The plants in beauty grew;   [thine,
Thou mad'st refulgent suns to shine,
   And gav'st refreshing dew.

4 These various mercies from above
   Matured the swelling grain;
A kindly harvest crowns thy love,
   And plenty fills the plain.

5 We own and bless thy gracious sway;
   Thy hand all nature hails:
Seed time nor harvest, night nor day,
   Summer nor winter, fails.

31   L. M.   [WESTON.

JESUS, my all, to heav'n is gone,
  He whom I fix my hopes upon;
His track I see, and I'll pursue
The narrow way, till him I view.

2 This is the way I long have sought,
  And mourned because I found it not;

Till late I heard my Savior say,
"Come hither, soul! I am the way."

3 Lo! glad I come, and thou, blest Lamb,
Shalt take me to thee as I am;
My sinful self to thee I give—
Nothing but love shall I receive.

4 Now will I tell to sinners round,
What a dear Savior I have found;
I'll point to his redeeming blood,
And say, "Behold the way to God!"

32   S. M.   [SANDUSKY.

A CHARGE to keep I have,
  A God to glorify;
A never-dying soul to save,
  And fit it for the sky.

2 To serve the present age,
  My calling to fulfill;
O may it all my powers engage,
  To do my Master's will.

3 Arm me with jealous care,
  As in thy sight to live;
And O, thy servant, Lord, prepare,
  A strict account to give!

4 Help me to watch and pray,
  And on thyself rely,
Assured if I my trust betray,
  I shall forever die.

33   Metre 5.   [Grace.

CHILDREN of the heavn'ly King,
As ye journey, sweetly sing;
Sing your Savior's worthy praise,
Glorious in his works and ways.

2 Ye are trav'ling home to God,
In the way the fathers trod;
They are happy now, and ye
Soon their happiness shall see.

3 Fear not, brethren, joyful stand
On the borders of your land;
Jesus Christ your Father's Son,
Bids you undismayed, go on.

4 Lord, submissive make us go,
Gladly leaving all below:
Only thou our leader be,
And we still will follow thee.

34   Metre 5.   [Brian.

JESUS, lover of mankind,
All my peace in thee I find;
Thou the price for me hast paid,
Thou hast full atonement made.

2 Though I wandered far from thee,
Thou in love didst pity me;
Broughtst me back from error's ways,
Now I sing my Savior's praise.

3 Help me, Savior, day by day,
Still to walk in wisdom's way;

    Publish it to all around,
    What a Savior I have found.

4 When from earth I take my flight
    To the heavenly mansions bright,
    There, in nobler strains adore
    Thee, my Savior, evermore.

35   S. M.   [STAMFORD.

THE Lord my Shepherd is;
    I shall be well supplied;
Since he is mine and I am his,
    What can I want beside?

2 He leads me to the place
    Where heav'nly pasture grows;
  Where living waters gently pass,
    And full salvation flows.

3 If e'er I go astray,
    He doth my soul reclaim,
  And guides me, in his own right way
    For his most holy name.

4 While he affords his aid,
    I cannot yield to fear;
  Tho' I should walk thro' death's dark shade
    My Shepherd's with me there.

5 In sight of all my foes,
    Thou dost my table spread;
  My cup with blessings overflows,
    And joy exalts my head.

6 The bounties of thy love
    Shall crown my future days;

Nor from thy house will I remove,
  Nor cease to speak thy praise.

36   L. M.   [BACA.

THOU only sov'reign of my heart,
  My refuge, my almighty Friend,
And can my soul from thee depart,
  On whom alone my hopes depend?

2 Whither, ah! whither shall I go,
  A wretched wand'rer from my Lord?
Can this dark world of sin and woe
  One glimpse of happiness afford?

3 Eternal life thy words impart;
  On these my fainting spirit lives;
Here sweeter comforts cheer my heart
  Than all the round of nature gives.

4 Let earth's alluring joys combine;
  While thou art near, in vain they call;
One smile, one blissful smile of thine,
  My gracious Lord, outweighs them all.

5 Low at thy feet my soul would lie;
  Here safety dwells, and peace divine;
Still let me live beneath thine eye,
  For life, eternal life, is thine.

37   METRE 5.   [MOULTON.

ONE there is above all others,
  Well deserves the name of Friend;
His is love beyond a brother's,
  Costly, free and knows no end.

2 Which of all our friends, to save us,
   Could or would have shed his blood?
But this Savior died to have us
   Reconciled in him to God.

3 When he lived on earth abased,
   Friend of sinners was his name;
Now above all glory raised,
   He rejoices in the same.

4 Oh, for grace our hearts to soften!
   Teach us, Lord, at length to love;
We, alas! forget too often,
   What a Friend we have above.

38   L. M.   [RELIANCE.

O WHEN I reflect, and see
   How oft the Savior followed me,
As from his presence still I fled,
The crooked paths of sin to tread—

2 I feel oppress'd for what I've done,
O, where can now relief be found?
There's none can help but Israel's King,
To him I'll come—no price I'll bring.

3 Lord, give me grace my sins to mourn,
And like the prodigal, return;
I come, O, cast me not away,
But pardon all my sins I pray.

4 I come, O Lord, and here would show
That only thee as Lord I'd know;
Help me to die to self and sin,
That grace may make me pure within.

5 And now, baptized in thy name,
 Keep me, O Lord, from sin and shame;
Grant me thy Spirit, truth, and love,
To guide me to thy courts above.

39   L. M.   [DEVOTION.

JESUS, thou Shepherd of the sheep,
 Thy "little flock" in safety keep;
These lambs within thine arms now take,
And let them ne'er thy fold forsake.

2 Secure them from the scorching beam,
And lead them to the living stream;
In verdant pastures let them lie,
And watch them with a Shepherd's eye.

3 Oh, teach them to discern thy voice,
And in its sacred sound rejoice;
From strangers may they ever flee,
And know no other guide but thee.

4 Lord, bring thy sheep that wander yet,
And let their number be complete;
Then let the flock from earth remove,
And reach the heavenly fold above.

40   METRE 14.   [NEWARK.

O WHEN shall I see Jesus,
 And dwell with him above?
To drink the flowing fountains
 Of everlasting love?
When shall I be delivered
 From this vain world of sin.

And with my blessed Jesus
　　　Drink endless pleasures in?
2 But now I am a soldier,
　　My Captain's gone before;
　He's given me my orders,
　　And tells me not to fear.
　And if I hold out faithful,
　　A crown of life he'll give,
　And all his valiant soldiers
　　Eternal life shall have.
3 Through grace I am determined
　　To conquer though I die;
　And then away to Jesus
　　On wings of love I'll fly.
　Farewell to sin and sorrow,
　　I bid them both adieu:
　And you, my friends prove faithful,
　　And on your way pursue.
4 And if you meet with troubles
　　And trials on the way,
　Then cast your care on Jesus,
　　And don't forget to pray.
　Gird on the heav'nly armor
　　Of faith and hope and love;
　And when your warfare's ended,
　　You'll reign with him above.

41　　　　C. M.　　　　[BROWN.

AWAKE, my soul! stretch every nerve,
　　And press with vigor on:
A heav'nly race demands thy zeal,
　　A bright immortal crown.

2 A cloud of witnesses around
   Hold thee in full survey;
Forget the steps already trod,
   And onward urge thy way.

3 'T is God's all-animating voice,
   That calls thee from on high;
'T is his own hand presents the prize
   To thine aspiring eye.

4 That prize with peerless glories bright,
   Which shall new lustre boast, [gems,
When victors' wreaths and monarchs'
   Shall blend in common dust.

5 Blest Savior, introduced by thee,
   Have I my race begun;
And, crowned with vict'ry, at thy feet
   I'll lay my honors down.

42   Metre 30.   [Owen.

SAVIOR, blessed Savior,
   Listen while we sing,
Hearts and voices raising
   Praises to our King.
All we have we offer;
   All we hope to be,
Body, soul, and spirit,
   All we yield to thee.

2 Nearer, ever nearer,
   Christ, we draw to thee,
Deep in adoration
   Bending low the knee:

Thou for our redemption
 Cam'st on earth to die;
Thou, that we might follow,
 Hast gone up on high.

3 Great and ever greater
 Are thy mercies here,
True and everlasting
 Are thy glories there,
Where no pain or sorrow,
 Toil or care is known,
Where the angel-legions
 Circle round thy throne.

4 Bliss, all bliss excelling,
 When the ransomed soul
Earthly toils forgetting
 Finds its promised goal;
Where in joys unheard of
 Saints with angels sing,
Never weary raising
 Praises to their King.

43   Metre 14.   [Precious Jesus.

I NEED thee, precious Jesus,
 For I am very poor;
A stranger and a pilgrim,
 I have no earthly store;
I need the love of Jesus
 To cheer me on my way,
To guide my doubting footsteps,
 To be my strength and stay.

2 I need thee, precious Jesus,
 I need a friend like thee,

APPENDIX. 31

 A friend to soothe and pity,
  A friend to care for me:
 I need the heart of Jesus
  To feel each anxious care,
 To tell my every trial,
  And all my sorrows share.

3 I need thee, precious Jesus,
  I need thee day by day,
 To fill me with thy fullness,
  To lead me on my way:
 I need thy Holy Spirit
  To teach me what I am,
 To show me more of Jesus,
  And point me to the Lamb.

4 I need thee, precious Jesus,
  And hope to see thee soon,
 Encircled in the rainbow,
  And seated on thy throne;
 There, with thy blood-bought children
  My joy shall ever be
 To sing thy praises, Jesus,
  And gaze, my Lord, on thee.

44   Metre 5.   [Eltham.

WHO are these in bright array,
  This innumerable throng,
Round the altar night and day,
  Hymning one triumphant song?—
"Worthy is the Lamb once slain,
  Blessing, honor, glory, power,
Wisdom, riches to obtain,
  New dominion every hour."

2 These through fiery trials trod;
   These from great affliction came;
Now before the throne of God,
   Sealed with his almighty name.
Clad in raiment pure and white,
   Victor-palms in every hand,
Through their dear Redeemer's might,
   More than conquerors they stand.

3 Hunger, thirst, disease unknown,
   On immortal fruits they feed:
Them the Lamb amid the throne
   Shall to living fountains lead:
Joy and gladness banish sighs;
   Perfect love dispels all fear;
And forever from their eyes
   God shall wipe away the tear.

45   L. M.   [HEBRON.

AWAKE, my soul! lift up thine eyes;
   See where thy foes against thee rise,
In long array, a num'rous host;
Awake, my soul, or thou art lost!

2 Thou tread'st upon enchanted ground;
Perils and snares beset thee round;
Beware of all; guard every part;
But most, the traitor in the heart.

3 Come then, my soul! now learn to wield
The weight of thine immortal shield;
Put on the armor from above,
Of heav'nly truth, and heav'nly love.

4 The terror and the charm repel,
And pow'rs of earth, and pow'rs of hell;

The Man of Calv'ry triumphed here;
Why should his faithful foll'wers fear?

46   L. M.   [REST.

YE Christian heralds! go proclaim
  Salvation through Immanuel's name;
To distant climes the tidings bear.
And plant the rose of Sharon there.

2 He'll shield you with a wall of fire,
With flaming zeal your breasts inspire,
Bid raging winds their fury cease,
And hush the tempest into peace.

3 And when our labors are all o'er,
Then we shall meet to part no more—
Meet with the blood-bought throng, to fall
And crown our Jesus—Lord of all.

47   L. M.   [ROCKINGHAM.

POUR out thy Spirit from on high;
  Lord, thine assembled servants bless;
Graces and gifts to each supply,
  And clothe thy priests with righteousness.

2 Within thy temple, where we stand
  To teach the truth as taught by thee,
May we like stars in thy right hand,
  The angels of the churches be.

3 Wisdom and zeal and faith impart,
  Firmness with meekness from above,
To bear thy people on our heart.
  And love the souls whom thou dost love.

4 To watch and pray, and never faint;
  By day and night strict guard to keep,
To warn the sinner, cheer the saint,
  Nourish thy lambs, and feed thy sheep.

5 Then, when our work is finished here,
   In humble hope our charge resign:
When the chief Shepherd shall appear,
   O God, may they and we be thine!

48   S. M.   [AUGUSTA.

LORD of the harvest, hear
   Thy needy servants' cry;
Answer our faith's effectual pray'r,
   And all our wants supply.

2 On thee we humbly wait—
   Our wants are in thy view;
The harvest, truly, Lord, is great,
   The laborers are few.

3 Convert and send forth more
   Into thy church abroad,
And let them speak thy word of power
   As workers with their God.

4 O let them spread thy name—
   Their missions fully prove;
Thy universal grace proclaim—
   Thine all-redeeming love.

49   L. M.   [HEBRON.

THUS spake the Savior, when he sent
   His ministers to preach his word;
They through the word obedient went,
   And spread the gospel of their Lord:

2 "Go forth, ye heralds, in my name;
   Bid the whole earth my grace receive;
The gospel jubilee proclaim,
   And call them to repent and live.

3 "The joyful news to all impart,
    And teach them where salvation lies;
Bind up the broken, bleeding heart,
    And wipe the tear from weeping eyes.

4 " Be wise as serpents, where you go,
    But harmless as the peaceful dove;
And let your heav'n-taught conduct show
    That you're commissioned from above.

5 " Freely from me ye have received;
    Freely in love to others give;
Thus shall your doctrines be believed,
    And by your labors sinners live."

6 Happy those servants of the Lord,
    Who thus their Master's will obey!
How rich, how full is their reward,
    Reserved until the final day!

50   L. M.   [DESIRE.

THE Lord hath called thee—in his name
    Go forth—the blessed Gospel preach,
From Zion's walls his word proclaim,
    And all who hear thee, boldly teach.

2 Go as a *shepherd*, guard and keep,
    His church from hell, and earth and sin;
Nourish the lambs and feed the sheep;
    The wounded heal, the lost bring in.

3 Go as a *watchman*; take thy stand
    Upon the tow'r of Zion high,
And when the sword comes on the land,
    Call us to fight, or warn to fly.

4 Go as an *angel*, hence to guide
  A band of pilgrims on their way,
That, safely walking at thy side,
  They faint not, fail not, turn, nor stray.

5 Go as a *teacher*, sent from God,
  Charged his whole counsel to declare;
Lift o'er the church the prophet's rod,
  While they uphold thy hands with pray'r

6 Go as a *messenger* of peace,
  Filled with the Spirit, fired with love;
Live to behold a large increase,
  And die to meet us all above.

51   L. M.   [ORIEL.

THY Father's house, thy own bright home,
  And thou hast there a place for me!
Though yet an exile here I roam,
  That distant home by faith I see.

2 I see its domes resplendent glow,
  Where beams of God's own glory fall;
And trees of life immortal grow,
  Whose fruits o'erhang the sapphire wall.

3 I know that Thou, who on the tree
  Didst deign our mortal guilt to bear,
Wilt bring thine own to dwell with thee,
  And waitest to receive me there!

4 Thy love will there array my soul
  In thine own robe of spotless hue,
And I shall gaze, while ages roll,
  On thee, with rapture ever new.

5 Oh, welcome, day! when thou my feet
  Shalt bring the shining threshold o'er;
  A Father's warm embrace to meet,
  And dwell at home for evermore!

52   L. M.   [BACA.

WE have no outward righteousness,
  No merit or good works to plead;
We only can be saved by grace;
  Thy grace, O Lord, is free indeed.

2 Save us by grace, through faith alone—
  A faith thou must thyself impart;
A faith that would by works be shown,
  A faith that purifies the heart.

3 A faith that doth the mountains move,
  A faith that shows our sins forgiven,
A faith that sweetly works by love,
  And ascertains our claim to heaven.

53   L. M.   [WINDHAM.

NOW let my soul, eternal King!
  To thee its grateful tribute bring;
My knee with humble homage bow,
My tongue perform its solemn vow.

2 All nature sings thy boundless love,
In worlds below, and worlds above;
But in thy blessed word I trace
Diviner wonders of thy grace.

3 There, what delightful truths I read!
There I behold the Savior bleed:

His name salutes my list'ning ear,
Revives my heart and checks my fear.

4 There Jesus bids my sorrows cease,
And gives my lab'ring conscience peace;
Raises my grateful passions high,
And points to mansions in the sky.

5 For love like this, Oh! let my song,
Thro' endless years, thy praise prolong;
Let distant climes thy name adore,
Till time and nature are no more.

54   Metre 5.   [Roland.

PRAISE to God!—Immortal praise,
For the love that crowns our days:
Bounteous source of every joy!
Let thy praise our tongues employ.

2 All that spring with bounteous hand,
Scatters o'er the smiling land:
All that lib'ral autumn pours
From her rich o'erflowing stores:

3 These to that dear source we owe,
Whence our sweetest comforts flow;
These, through all my happy days,
Claim my cheerful songs of praise.

4 Lord! to thee my soul should raise
Grateful never ending praise:
And, when every blessing's flown,
Love thee for thyself alone.

55   L. M.   [KEDRON.

'Tis finished!—so the Savior cried,
And meekly bowed his head and died;
'Tis finished!—yes, the race is run,
The battle fought, the vict'ry won.

2 'Tis finished!—this, his dying groan,
Shall sin of every kind atone:
Millions shall be redeemed from death,
By this his last expiring breath.

3 'Tis finished!—heav'n is reconciled,
And all the pow'rs of darkness spoiled:
Peace, love, and happiness, again
Return and dwell with sinful men.

4 'Tis finished!—let the joyful sound
Be heard through all the nations round:
'Tis finished!—let the echo fly,
Thro' heaven and hell, thro' earth and sky.

56   L. M.   [DESIRE.

STRETCHED on the cross, the Savior dies!
Hark! his expiring groans arise;
See—from his hands, his feet, his side,
Fast flows the sacred crimson tide!

2 But life attends the deathful sound,
And flows from every bleeding wound:
The vital stream—how free it flows,
To save and cleanse his rebel foes!

3 Can I survey this scene of woe,
Where mingling grief and wonder flow,
And yet my heart unmoved remain,
Insensible to love or pain?

4 Come, dearest Lord, thy grace impart,
To warm this cold, this stupid heart;
Till all its pow'rs and passions move,
In melting grief and ardent love.

57   Metre 26.   [New Haven.

MY faith looks up to thee,
  Thou Lamb of Calvary,
    Savior divine!
Now hear me while I pray,
Take all my guilt away,
O let me from this day
    Be wholly thine.

2 May thy rich grace impart
  Strength to my fainting heart;
    My zeal inspire:
As thou hast died for me,
O may my love to thee,
Pure, warm, and changeless be,
    A living fire.

3 While life's dark maze I tread,
  And griefs around me spread,
    Be thou my guide:
Bid darkness turn to day,
Wipe sorrow's tears away,
Nor let me ever stray
    From thee aside.

4 When ends life's transient dream,
  When death's cold, sullen stream
    Shall o'er me roll,
  Blest Savior, then in love,
  Fear and distrust remove,
  And bear me safe above,
    A ransomed soul!

58   7s.   [Ennius.

PEOPLE of the living God,
  I have sought the world around,
Paths of sin and sorrow trod,
  Peace and comfort nowhere found.
Now to you my spirit turns,—
  Turns a fugitive unblest:
Brethren, where your altar burns,
  O receive me into rest.

2 Lonely I no longer roam,
    Like the cloud, the wind, the wave:
  Where you dwell shall be my home,
    Where you die shall be my grave.
  Mine the God whom you adore;
    Your Redeemer shall be mine;
  Earth can fill my soul no more:
    Every idol I resign.

59   L. M.   [Portugal.

ALMIGHTY Sov'reign of the skies,
To thee let songs of gladness rise,
Each grateful heart its tribute bring,
And every voice thy goodness sing.

2 From thee our choicest blessings flow,
  Life, health and strength thy hands bestow;
  The daily good thy creatures share,
  Springs from thy providential care.

3 The rich profusion nature yields,
  The harvest waving o'er the fields,
  The cheering light, refreshing show'r,
  Are gifts from thy exhaustless store.

4 At thy command the vernal bloom
  Revives the world from winter's gloom;
  The summer's heat the fruit matures,
  And autumn all her treasures pours.

5 From thee proceed, domestic ties,
  Connubial bliss, paternal joys;
  On thy support the nations stand,
  Obedient to thy high command.

6 Let every power of heart and tongue,
  Unite to swell the grateful song;
  While age and youth in chorus join,
  And praise the Majesty divine.

60   C. M. [SUFFERING SAVIOR.

ALAS! what hourly dangers rise!
  What snares beset my way!
To heaven, O let me lift mine eyes,
  And hourly watch and pray.

2 How oft my mournful thoughts complain,
  And melt in flowing tears!
My weak resistance, O how vain!
  How strong my foes and fears!

3 O gracious God, in whom I live,
   My feeble efforts aid:
Help me to watch and pray and strive,
   Though trembling and afraid.

4 Increase my faith, increase my hope,
   When foes and fears prevail;
O bear my fainting spirit up,
   Or soon my strength will fail.

5 Whene'er temptations lure my heart,
   Or draw my feet aside,
My God, thy pow'rful aid impart,
   My Guardian and my Guide.

6 O keep me in thy heav'nly way,
   And bid the tempter flee;
And let me never, never stray
   From happiness and thee.

61   L. M.   [MARCH.

COME in, thou blessed of the Lord!
   O come with humble praise and pray'r;
We welcome thee with one accord,
   O come, and heav'nly blessings share.

2 Those joys which earth cannot afford,
   We'll seek in fellowship to prove,
Joined in one spirit to our Lord,
   Together bound by mutual love.

3 And while we pass this vale of tears,
   We'll make our joys and sorrows known;
We'll share each other's hopes and fears,
   And count a brother's care our own.

4 Once more our welcome we repeat,
   And give assurance of our love,
Until we all together meet,
   Around the throne of God above.

62   S. M.   [SANDUSKY.

WHEN on the brink of death
   My trembling soul shall stand,
Waiting to pass that awful flood,
   Great God, at thy command!—

2 When every scene of life
   Stands ready to depart,
And the last sigh that shakes the frame
   Shall rend this bursting heart.

3 Thou Source of joy supreme,
   Whose arm alone can save—
Dispel the darkness that surrounds
   The entrance to the grave.

4 Lay thy supporting hand
   Beneath my sinking head;
And with a ray of love divine
   Illume my dying bed.

5 Leaning on Jesus' breast,
   May I resign my breath;
And in his kind embraces lose
   The bitterness of death.

63   Metre 6.   [Pembroke.

THY mercy heard my infant prayer,
  Thy love, with kind, paternal care,
    Sustained my childish days;   [youth
Thy goodness watched my ripening
And formed my heart to love thy truth,
    And filled my lips with praise.

2 And now, in age and grief, thy Name
Doth still my languid heart inflame,
    And bow my falt'ring knee:
O, yet this bosom feels the fire;
This trembling hand and drooping lyre
    Have yet a strain for thee.

3 Yes: broken, tuneless, still, O Lord,
This voice, transported, shall record
    Thy goodness, tried so long;
Till, sinking slow, with calm decay,
Its feeble murmurs melt away,
    Into a seraph's song.

64   C. M.   [Memphis.

YE men and angels! witness now,
  Before the Lord we speak;
To him we make our solemn vow,
  A vow we dare not break.

2 That long as life itself shall last,
  Ourselves to Christ we yield;
Nor from his cause will we depart,
  Nor ever quit the field.

3 We trust not in our native strength,
   But on his grace rely;
May he, with our returning wants,
   A needful aid supply.

4 Oh! guide our doubtful feet aright,
   And keep us in thy ways;
And, while we turn our vows to pray'rs,
   Turn thou our prayers to praise.

65   Metre 55.   [Holy Rest.

Abide with me! fast falls the eventide,
The darkness deepens, Lord, with me abide;
When other helpers fail, and comforts flee,
Help of the helpless, O, abide with me!

2 Swift to its close ebbs out life's little day;
Earth's joys grow dim, its glories pass away,
Change and decay on all around I see;
O Thou, who changest not, abide with me!

3 I need thy presence every passing hour;
What but thy grace can foil the tempter's power!
Who like thyself, my guide and stay can be?
Through cloud and sunshine, Lord, abide with me!

4 I fear no foe, with thee at hand to bless;
Ills have no weight, and fears no bitterness.
Where is death's sting? where, grave, thy victory?
I triumph still, if thou abide with me.

5 Hold thou the cross before my closing eyes;
Shine through the gloom, and point me to the skies;
Heaven's morning breaks, and earth's vain shad-
      ows flee,
In life in death, O Lord, abide with me!

INDEX TO APPENDIX.

	Page.
Abide with me! fast falls the eventide	46
A charge to keep I have	22
Alas! what hourly dangers rise	42
Almighty Sov'reign of the skies	41
Asleep in Jesus! blessed sleep	7
Awake my soul! lift up thine eyes	32
Awake, my soul! stretch every nerve	28
Cease here longer to detain me	13
Children of the heavenly King	23
Come in, thou blessed of the Lord	43
Dear is the spot where Christians sleep	12
Dear mother, don't think of me as in	11
Fond parents, calm the heaving breast	9
Fountain of mercy, God of love	21
He leadeth me! O, blessed thought	5
How blest the righteous when he dies	12
How happy are these little ones	14
I need thee, precious Jesus	30
Jesus, lover of mankind	23
Jesus my all to heaven is gone	21
Jesus, thou Shepherd of the sheep	27
Jesus, while our hearts are bleeding	14
Just as I am, without one plea	6
Little children gatherest thou	9
Lord of the harvest, hear	34
My faith looks up to Thee	40
Nearer, my God, to thee	2
Now let my soul, eternal King	37
Now let our drooping hearts revive	18
O for the death of those	11
O think of the home over there	8
O when I now reflect and see	26
O when shall I see Jesus	27

INDEX TO APPENDIX.

	Page.
One there is above all others	25
People of the living God	41
Pour out thy Spirit from on high	33
Praise God,—immortal praise.	38
Rock of ages, cleft for me.	2
Savior, blessed Savior	29
Savior, like a shepherd, lead us.	7
Sister, thou wast mild and lovely	17
Stretched on the cross, the Savior dies	39
Sweet hour of pray'r, sweet hour of pray'r	3
The God of harvest praise	19
The hand which gives us joys of earth	15
The hour of my departure's come	19
The morning flowers display their sweets	16
The Lord has called thee,—in his name	35
The Lord my Shepherd is	24
There is a fountain filled with blood	1
Thou only Sov'reign of my heart	25
Thus spake the Savior, when he sent	34
Thy Father's house! thine own bright	36
Thy mercy heard my infant prayer	45
'T is by thy strength the mountains	20
'T is finished—so the Savior cried	39
To thee, O God, when creatures fail	18
We have no outward righteousness	37
Weep not for me, my parents dear	10
What a Friend we have in Jesus	4
When on the brink of death	44
Who are these in bright array	31
Why should our tears in sorrow flow	16
Ye Christian heralds! go proclaim	33
Ye men and angels, witness now	45

www.ingramcontent.com/pod-product-compliance
Lightning Source LLC
Chambersburg PA
CBHW051735300426
44115CB00007B/577